Developing
a Comprehensive Faculty
Evaluation System

Developing a Comprehensive Faculty Evaluation System

A Handbook for College Faculty and Administrators on Designing and Operating a Comprehensive Faculty Evaluation System

Http://members.aol.com/cedarnet/coda.html

Raoul A. Arreola

With Special Contributions by
Lawrence M. Aleamoni

Anker Publishing Company, Inc.
Bolton, MA

DEVELOPING A COMPREHENSIVE FACULTY EVALUATION SYSTEM

A Handbook for College Faculty and Administrators on Designing and Operating a Comprehensive Faculty Evaluation System

ISBN 1–882982–03–7

Composition by Deerfoot Studios.
Cover design by Deerfoot Studios.

Anker Publishing Company, Inc.
176 Ballville Road
P.O. Box 249
Bolton, MA 01740–0249

Dedicated to

Russell P. Kropp

About the Author

Raoul A. Arreola received his Ph.D. in Educational Psychology from Arizona State University in 1969, specializing in educational research and measurement. He has taught in the areas of statistics, educational psychology, and personnel evaluation, and has held a number of administrative positions involved in designing, developing, and operating large-scale faculty evaluation and instructional development programs. These include: Director of the Office of Evaluation Services and Associate Director of the Learning Systems Institute at Florida State University; Director of the Center for Instructional Services and Research at the University of Memphis; and Chair of the Department of Education and Assistant Dean for Assessment and Planning at the University of Tennessee-Memphis, where he currently holds an appointment as Professor of Health Informatics and Director of Educational Technology.

Dr. Arreola has worked and published in the field of faculty evaluation and development for more than 20 years, and has served as a consultant nationally and internationally to over 100 colleges and universities in designing and operating faculty evaluation and development programs. He has also served as a consultant to the U.S. Department of Labor and the Florida House of Representatives on designing and evaluating professional and occupational licensing examination procedures. He is president of his own consulting firm, the Center for Educational Development and Assessment (CEDA), which annually conducts national workshops on faculty evaluation, academic leadership, and assessing student learning. These workshops have been attended by faculty and administrators from more than 350 colleges and universities. His model for developing a comprehensive faculty evaluation system has been used by community colleges, small liberal arts colleges, technical institutes, and research universities to produce faculty evaluation systems that respond to, and reflect, the unique needs, characteristics, and values of each institution. Raoul A. Arreola is married to Dr. Mona J. Arreola, Associate Director of the Cancer Center at the University of Tennessee-Memphis, and has four grown children.

Contents

Reporting Student Rating Results
    Directionality of Numerical Scale
    Distributing Rating Results—Voluntary Systems
    Distributing Results—Mandatory Systems
    Publishing Rating Results
Format of the Student Rating Form Computerized Analysis Output
Interpreting and Using Student Rating Results
Faculty Evaluation and Faculty Development
Chapter References

STUDENT RATING FORM SELECTION AND DEVELOPMENT KIT

G. Clarity of Presentation
H. Instructor Characteristics
I. Interest of Presentation
J. Expectations and Objectives
K. Behavioral Indications of Student Attitude Toward Course
L. General Student Attitude Toward Instructor
M. Speed and Depth of Coverage
N. Instructor Availability Outside of Class
O. Examinations
P. Visual Aids
Q. Grading
R. Assignments (homework, reading, written, textbook, laboratory, etc.)
S. Laboratory and Discussion
T. Clinical
U. Student-Instructor Interaction
V. Seminars
W. Team Teaching
X. Field Trips

TABLES

Acknowledgements

I want to acknowledge the special contributions made to this work by my good friend and colleague Lawrence M. Aleamoni. In 1988, in response to numerous requests by colleges and universities for practical, yet research-based, guidelines for developing and operating large-scale faculty evaluation systems, Larry and I teamed up to offer a series of workshops on faculty evaluation. These workshops have now been attended by faculty and administrators from more than 350 colleges and universities. Over the years the workshops have grown and the materials assembled for it have become the basis for this handbook. I am indebted to Larry for allowing me to use material from the Aleamoni Course/Instructor Evaluation Questionnaire (CIEQ), the CIEQ Optional Item Catalog, and several of his articles relating to peer evaluation and the development and use of student rating forms. I am especially grateful, however, for the many, many hours Larry has spent reviewing my work, helping me flesh out ideas, and providing a research-based perspective for the administratively-based experiences I wished to translate into an operational set of guidelines for developing and operating a faculty evaluation system. The result is this handbook.

Raoul A. Arreola, 1994

1

Introduction

Every year academic administrators must evaluate faculty performance for the purpose of making retention, promotion, tenure, and merit pay decisions. Inevitably, questions of fairness, validity, objectivity, and reliability of the evaluation system arise during the making of these decisions. The purpose of this handbook is to provide a practical, proven model for developing and using a comprehensive faculty evaluation system that responds to these issues. Following the steps in this handbook will result in developing a customized faculty evaluation system which responds to the specific needs, concerns, and characteristics of the faculty and administration of an individual academic unit. The evaluation system developed using the steps outlined in this handbook will have the greatest probability of acceptance and successful use by faculty and administrators, because both constituencies will have had ample input to its design and construction.

THE VALUE IN EVALUATION

Any evaluation system rests upon a base of an implicitly assumed set of values. Observations are made of the performance of interest and a judgment made as to whether that performance conforms to the set of values held by those making the observations. If there is a good match between observed performance and values held, such performance is generally given a positive or good evaluation. If there is a poor match or a discrepancy between what is observed and what is held to be of value, such performance is generally given a negative or poor evaluation. Clearly, before any evaluation system can be built, the values of those who intend to use it must be determined. In order to develop a faculty evaluation system which correctly reflects the values of the institution, we must not only determine those values and have them clearly in mind, but we must also express them in such a way that enables us to apply them consistently in our evaluation process. The model described in this handbook permits us to do just that.

SYSTEMATIC FACULTY INVOLVEMENT

The model for developing a faculty evaluation system described in this handbook assumes that there is no one best faculty evaluation system that could be successfully applied to any and all faculty groups. It is assumed that a necessary part of the process of developing a successful faculty evaluation system is the planned and systematic inclusion of the faculty's values—the values which form the base of our evaluation system. Experience has shown that the best approach to developing a faculty evaluation system is to appoint a committee, composed primarily of faculty, a few key administrators, and, perhaps, even a student or two, which is responsible for gathering the information and following the steps outlined in this handbook. Thus, various steps in the process will refer to the faculty evaluation committee as the operational entity carrying out the process. Of course, the procedure may be used primarily by administrative groups. However, an essential component of the process described involves systematic faculty input. It is important that the faculty see their input being used as an integral part of the design and construction of the system.

EVALUATION AND NUMBERS

A second assumption is that evaluation necessarily includes some element of measurement or systematic observation of performance. Whether we recognize it or not, every campus has some form of faculty evaluation system that includes the formal or informal observation of faculty performance and that then assigns a label (Outstanding, Satisfactory, Unsatisfactory; top 10%, top 25%, etc.) to that performance. The model used here assumes that the labels assigned will be expressed numerically. That is, the evaluations developed will result in a measurement expressed as an overall numerical rating.

Because even faculty evaluation systems which ostensibly use only qualitative labels eventually arrive at some form of numerical transformation of the evaluations (i.e., Outstanding = 1, Satisfactory = 2, etc., or Outstanding = 10% raise, Satisfactory = 5% raise, etc.), the procedure described here deals with the numerical transformations from the beginning. An essential part of the model is the careful reflection of labels by appropriate numerical transformations. However, variations of this model can be used to aid in developing a system that uses only qualitative labels or categories as well.

CONTROLLED SUBJECTIVITY

A third assumption relates to the issue of objectivity of the faculty evaluation system. Often, when embarking upon developing a faculty evaluation system, the goal of the institution's administration or faculty evaluation committee is to devise an objective system. *True objectivity in a faculty evaluation system is a myth.* It is virtually impossible to achieve any great measure of objectivity in a system which, of necessity, relies on the *subjective judgment* of peers, administrators, students, and others for its data. Rather, because subjectivity in our system is unavoidable, the goal should be to *control its impact.* The underlying premise of the model used in this handbook is that the impact of the subjective information derived from various sources should be controlled and, even more importantly, specified to coincide or agree with the values of the faculty and of the institution as a whole.

EVALUATION FOR SELF-IMPROVEMENT AND PERSONNEL DECISIONS

A final assumption made in this handbook is that the results of any faculty evaluation system will serve two, seemingly contradictory, purposes—namely, (1) providing feedback information for faculty growth and development and (2) providing evaluative information on which to base personnel decisions. These two diverse purposes *can* be well served by one system. The key to constructing a system that serves these differing purposes is in the policies determining the distribution of the information gathered. The general principle to be followed is that detailed information from questionnaires or other forms should be given exclusively to the faculty member for use in professional growth. However, aggregate data which summarize and reflect the overall *pattern of performance over time* of an individual can and should be used for such personnel decisions as promotion, tenure, continuation, and merit raise determination.

USING THIS HANDBOOK

Many decision points in this handbook can lead to significantly different evaluation systems. However, any system developed by the method described here will result in a faculty evaluation system which should have the maximum probability of being successfully implemented.

The following suggested schedule of key events is effective in using the model described in this handbook for successfully developing a comprehensive faculty evaluation system. The events described generally take 18–24 months to complete.

Event 1: A faculty evaluation committee or task force is appointed to coordinate the development of the faculty evaluation system. The committee should include faculty members representing the various faculty constituencies, union representatives (if any), and one or two senior administrators. Student representatives may also be appointed to the committee, depending upon the culture and tradition of the institution.

Event 2: The committee becomes familiar with the steps in the process for developing a comprehensive faculty evaluation system described in this handbook.

Event 3: A presentation is made to the administration concerning the approach to be taken. Administration becomes acquainted with the steps of the process.

Event 4: A presentation is made to the general faculty concerning the process to be followed in developing the faculty evaluation system. *This event is critical.* The faculty should be given the opportunity to become acquainted with the steps to be followed by the committee in developing the faculty evaluation system.

Event 5: The committee begins the process of gathering the information and data specified by the various steps in the process.

Event 6: A preliminary trial of the new faculty evaluation system is implemented.

Event 7: Any problems detected during the preliminary trial are corrected.

Event 8: The full system is implemented.

At the end of Chapter 10 is a more specific calender for the steps in developing a comprehensive faculty evaluation system which constitute the model described in this handbook. This model has been successfully used by many colleges and universities to create a system that works best for that individual institution. No two institutions using this model may necessarily come up with the same system, although similarities will exist, of course, at least to the extent that the assumptions implicit in the model are accepted.

2

Preliminary Issues in Planning for the Development of a Comprehensive Faculty Evaluation System

FACULTY EVALUATION AND DEVELOPMENT— TWO SIDES OF THE SAME COIN

Before proceeding with a discussion about developing any faculty evaluation system, it should be noted that faculty evaluation and faculty development are really two sides of the same coin. Ideally, faculty evaluation programs and faculty development programs should work hand-in-hand. The operational rule of thumb assumed here is *if some aspect of faculty performance is to be evaluated, then there should exist resources or opportunities which enable faculty to develop that performance.*

Faculty evaluation systems, no matter how well designed, which are implemented without reference to faculty development programs are inevitably viewed by faculty as being primarily punitive in intent. Such faculty evaluation systems tend to be interpreted as sending the message, "We're going to find out what you're doing wrong and get you for it!"

On the other hand, faculty development programs which are implemented without clear reference to information generated by faculty evaluation systems tend to be disappointing in their effect, no matter how well designed and funded. The reason for this is simple, if not always obvious. Without reference to a faculty evaluation system, faculty development programs tend to attract primarily those faculty who are *already* motivated to seek out resources and opportunities to improve their performance. In short, the good seek out ways to get better—that's what tends to make them good in the first place. However, those individuals who are not thus motivated, and who, accordingly, are probably in greatest need of self-improvement opportunities, generally tend to be the last who seek them out. Only when the elements of a faculty evaluation program are carefully integrated into a faculty development program

does the institution obtain the greatest benefit from both. Thus, if an instructor's skill in assessing student learning is going to be evaluated, somewhere there should be resources and training opportunities to become proficient in that skill. If a faculty member's ability to deliver a well-organized and exciting lecture is going to be evaluated, somewhere in the institution there should be resources available to learn and become proficient in that area. It should never be forgotten that most college and university faculty have had little or no formal training in the complex and highly technical skills involved in designing, delivering, and evaluating instruction. Most faculty tend to teach in the same way they were taught. If we are going to evaluate faculty performance, especially in teaching, we should do our best to help develop it.

In this section we will examine the general issues involved in planning for the development of a comprehensive faculty evaluation system. In doing so, we must have a clear vision about what constitutes both a successful faculty evaluation system and a successful faculty development program. This vision will help us avoid all-to-common pitfalls in the development of faculty evaluation systems.

DEFINING SUCCESS

A successful faculty evaluation program can be defined as one that *provides information which faculty, administrators, and, where appropriate, students consider important and useful.* Note that by this definition, no particular set of elements, forms, questionnaires, workshops, or procedures is being suggested. There is purposely no reference to the word "valid." The issue of the validity of faculty evaluation systems and programs will be discussed later. However, one thing is clear. If the faculty evaluation system or program that is devised is considered by the faculty to be fair and useful, it is functionally valid, regardless of its validity in some statistical or psychometric sense.

Taking this same orientation to faculty development programs, *a successful faculty development program is one perceived by the faculty as being a valuable resource or tool in assisting them to solve problems or achieve goals that both they and the administration consider to be important.* From this perspective, the problem of establishing successful faculty evaluation and development programs does not lie so much in not knowing what procedures to follow in evaluating faculty or not knowing how to develop new skills or enhance old ones. The problem lies in getting faculty and administrators to change their behavior in important and fundamental ways.

OBSTACLES TO ESTABLISHING SUCCESSFUL PROGRAMS

If we examine the problem of how to establish faculty evaluation and development programs as not so much a technical one of developing the right questionnaires or procedures and look at it for what it really is, a problem in getting large numbers of intelligent, highly educated, and independent people to change their behavior, then we have a much greater chance of establishing a successful program. Faculty evaluation and development programs fail for two major reasons: (1) the administration is not interested in whether it succeeds, and (2) the faculty are against it. The first reason will be referred to as *administrator apathy* and the second as *faculty resistance*. A close look at these two obstacles to establishing successful faculty evaluation and development programs can provide us with insights as to how to overcome them.

Administrator Apathy
Of the two threats to success—administrator apathy and faculty resistance—administrator apathy is the more deadly. If the administration is apathetic toward, or actively against, the whole program, *it will not succeed.* Anyone who has encountered a successful faculty evaluation and development program can point to one or two top administrators with a strong commitment to establishing and maintaining the program. Having a top administrator strongly committed to the program is a necessary but insufficient condition for success. The reasons for this will become obvious as we examine the issue.

One of the more common situations found in colleges and universities is one where a second-level administrator, say a vice president or academic dean, is strongly committed to establishing a faculty evaluation and development program. The top-level administrator of the institution may be in favor of the program, apathetic toward it, or resistant to it. In the case of apathy, it is necessary to demonstrate to the top administrator the potential benefits of the program in terms of improved instruction, improved learning, better faculty production, and better personnel decisions and management.

Resistance by the top-level administrator creates a different and more difficult problem. Resistance to faculty evaluation programs revolves around two issues: cost of the program and fear of loss of control in the personnel decision-making process. Faculty evaluation and development programs can vary widely in their cost, and institutions need not spend great amounts of money to have moderately successful and effective programs.

The fear of loss of control or threat to authority is a much more difficult problem to address, but several approaches have been helpful. Establishing the program on purely an experimental basis for a period of two years enables administrators to use the results of the program as they see fit. A consultant from another institution where a successful faculty evaluation and development program is already in place can present a more objective view to the administration as to how such a program can benefit the institution as a whole. Another good strategy is to entice the resistant top administrator to attend one of several professionally recognized conferences on faculty evaluation and development that are held annually. In any case, it is helpful for administrators to see that their fears and concerns do not have to be realized.

A less common situation is one where a faculty evaluation and development program is initiated by the faculty. This generally means that they are unhappy with the present formal or informal program being operated by the administration. This situation can easily lead to administrative apathy toward a revised program and perhaps to outright resistance for the reasons noted above. The key is to gain the support of at least a second-level administrator so that some resources can be allocated for an experimental trial of some part of the proposed program.

Administrator apathy diminishes the chances of implementing a successful faculty evaluation and development program. Outright resistance drops the chances of implementing a successful program practically to zero.

Faculty Resistance
Administrative commitment is a necessary but insufficient condition for establishing a successful faculty evaluation and development program. Faculty acceptance is also necessary. Faculty resistance to establishing faculty evaluation and development programs stems from numerous sources. Most of the resistance, however, reflects two or three major concerns.

In examining these concerns, let's begin, once again, by stating the obvious: No one enjoys being evaluated. Few people enjoy being told that they need to improve, or, worse, need to be developed—especially people who have spent six to eight years in college being evaluated and developed to the point where they have been awarded advanced degrees. The overall phenomenon of faculty resistance is composed of two reactions: *resistance to being evaluated* and *apathy toward being developed*. Resistance to being evaluated appears to grow out of three basic concerns: (1) resentment of the implied assumption that faculty may be incompetent in their subject area, (2) suspicion that they will be evaluated by unqualified people, and (3) an anxiety that they will be held accountable for performance in an area in which they have little or no training or interest. This last anxiety is not unusual or unexpected, even though most faculty may attribute most of their concern to the second factor. Milton and Shoben (1968, p. xvii) point out the basis for this anxiety when they state that "college teaching is probably the only profession in the world for which no specific training is required. The profession of scholarship is rich in prerequisites for entry, but not that of instruction."

This statement holds the key to faculty resistance to establishing faculty evaluation and development programs. Faculty understandably resent being tacitly questioned on their competence in an area "rich in prerequisites" for which they have been well trained. They are, not surprisingly, apathetic toward the idea of receiving further training, although, ironically, professional seminars in one's content area are generally held in high esteem. Faculty also view with some concern and trepidation the prospect of being evaluated in an area in which they may have little or no training or interest—namely, the design, development, and delivery of instruction.

Several publications have addressed the issue of overcoming faculty resistance to evaluation programs (Grasha, 1977; O'Connell & Smartt, 1979; Seldin, 1980; Arreola, 1979). The underlying premise for developing a comprehensive faculty evaluation system described in this handbook is the careful and deliberate preclusion or elimination of faculty resistance. It is useful, therefore, to examine some of the major dimensions of faculty resistance that may not be immediately apparent.

COMMON ERRORS

Several common errors are made when establishing faculty evaluation and development programs. The first and most common error is committed when a faculty evaluation program is implemented without reference or clear relation to a faculty development program. As noted earlier, when this is done, the message the faculty are likely to receive is, "We're going to find out what you're doing wrong and get you for it." By developing an integrated faculty evaluation and development program, the message we try to send is, "We're going to help you determine your strengths and weaknesses and provide you with the resources you need to both enhance your strengths and overcome your weaknesses."

Unfortunately, most often only a faculty evaluation program is implemented. Even then the form of its implementation almost guarantees faculty resistance. Generally, a faculty evaluation program begins by constructing or adopting a questionnaire that is administered to students. These questionnaires usually contain questions that faculty perceive as boiling down to, "Was this instructor entertaining?" "Does this instructor know his or her stuff?" and "What grade would you give this instructor—A, B, C, D, or F?" The questionnaires are usually analyzed by computer and the results sent to the department head, college dean, or, in some instances, directly to the president. This action triggers all the concerns and anxieties that result in full-blown faculty resistance. Couple this, as occasionally happens, with a student publication that lists the best and worst teachers—perceived as job-threatening by the untenured—and hostile and negative reactions from the faculty are guaranteed.

On the other side of the coin, when faculty development programs are installed without reference to an evaluation system, apathy tends to run rampant among the faculty. This is not to say that the programs may not be innovative, creative, and effective for those who do participate. But what commonly occurs in the absence of a tie to an evaluation system is that only those faculty who are already committed to the concept of self-improvement, who are already wedded to the idea of becoming as effective and efficient as possible both as teachers and researchers, will be the ones who seek out the program. Thus, the faculty who need developing the least will be the ones who tend to use the program the most. Those faculty who don't have that commitment and who genuinely need assistance tend to avoid it. If a faculty development program is mandatory, based on the referral of the dean or department head, it is very easy for the program to take on the aura of being for losers only—a place where faculty are sentenced to several weeks of development when they are caught with a poor syllabus, bad student ratings, or declining enrollments.

How do we overcome these not inconsiderable obstacles? There is no easy answer to this question. However, the following suggestions, cautions, and strategies gleaned from the experiences of those trying to establish faculty evaluation and development programs may prove useful.

GUIDELINES FOR OVERCOMING OBSTACLES AND AVOIDING ERRORS

Seek administrative assistance. Identify and enlist the aid of a higher level administrator committed to establishing an integrated faculty evaluation and development program. The administrator must be prepared to overcome a year to eighteen months of faculty resistance, some of which can become quite vocal.

Expect faculty to resist. Experience has shown that faculty resistance undergoes five predictable stages.

Stage 1: Disdainful Denial. During this stage, faculty generally take the attitude that "It'll never work" or, in the case of old-timers, "We tried something like that 10 years ago. It didn't work then, and it's not going to work this time either."

Stage 2: Hostile Resistance. During this stage, faculty begin to realize that the administration is going ahead with developing and implementing what they consider an overly complex and unwanted faculty evaluation system. Faculty senate meetings are hot and heavy. Special subcommittees are appointed. Complaints flow into the various levels of administration.

Stage 3: Apparent Acquiescence. Faculty seem to resign themselves to the fact that an arbitrary and overly complex system is going to be implemented despite objections. Most faculty hope that, if they ignore it, the evaluation system will go away. A few voices of support are heard at this stage, however.

Stage 4: Attempt to Scuttle. At this stage, certain elements of the faculty and perhaps some department heads or deans greatly exaggerate the impact of the problems caused by the faculty evaluation system. Some isolated incidents of outright misuse may be perpetrated in an effort to get the system to collapse. Pressure on the sponsoring administrator to resign is intensified.

Stage 5: Grudging Acceptance. After 18 months to two years of operation, faculty find that the system can actually be of some value once in a while. When all faculty are equally, but minimally, unhappy with the system, the faculty resistance barrier will have been successfully overcome.

It should be apparent at this point why administrator commitment is so critical to the success of any faculty evaluation and development program. Only that commitment can get the institution through the first few stages of faculty resistance. If the administrator responsible for implementing the program is a second-level administrator and has to fight apathy or resistance from the top-level administrator, the probability of success is smaller and the probability of that administrator's looking for another job is greater.

Be prepared to respond to common faculty concerns. Some of those concerns, and the responses that have been found helpful include:

> *"Students aren't competent to evaluate me!"* It needs to be made clear that most evaluation systems do not ask students to actually evaluate faculty in the sense that students make decisions about the faculty in any definitive way. Opinions, perceptions, and reactions are solicited from students. This information is considered along with other information from other sources when the evaluation is carried out by the appropriate person or committee.

> *"Teaching is too complex an activity to be evaluated validly!"* The best response to this concern is to point out that faculty are being evaluated in their teaching all the time by their colleagues and administrators. A formal system can make that evaluation fairer and more reliable and valid.

> *"You can't reduce something as complex as an evaluation of my performance to a number—some things just can't be measured!"* Remember, in responding to this and similar concerns, that an infallible, absolutely valid and accurate method of evaluating the totality of faculty performance has not been developed. The best response to this concern is to point out that faculty are already being evaluated and their evaluation translated into a number every time a list of applicants for promotion or tenure is placed in some priority order or a decision is made about merit raises, assuming merit raises are given at the institution. Comprehensive faculty evaluation systems attempt to improve existing informal and perhaps unstructured procedures by developing an objective, systematic, and fair set of criteria based on numerical values. It should also be noted that faculty consistently reduce the evaluation of complex student learning achievement to numbers, and, based on those numbers, colleges award credit and degrees. As a profession, we are not inexperienced in the process of summarizing evaluations of complex human behaviors as numerical values.

Establish a faculty development and evaluation center or office, preferably not located in the office of the vice president or dean. One efficient and cost-effective way to do this is to combine the media center, test scoring office, and any other instructional development and support office into one organizationally integrated unit. This unit should be directed by someone trained in evaluation and instructional development or educational psychology, and, most important, someone who has an affable, nonthreatening manner that inspires confidence. Remember, the objective is to facilitate the self-directed change in the behavior of faculty and administrators. The person in charge of the faculty development and evaluation facility should be able to grasp and deal with this concept in a positive manner.

Establish a faculty advisory board. Although the faculty evaluation and development unit will ultimately report to a dean or vice president, it helps to have a faculty advisory board. The board can be elected by the faculty or faculty senate or appointed by an appropriate administrator. In any case, there should be some mechanism for faculty to have input into the policy development affecting the operation of the center and the program, even if that input is only advisory.

Consider using a consultant. An outside consultant can play an important role in the process of overcoming faculty and administrative resistance. The consultant serves as a valuable conduit between faculty and administration by communicating concerns, suspicions, and fears expressed by the faculty to the administration. The consultant can also assure administrators that other institutions have been able to implement successful programs. The function of serving as a conduit between faculty and administrators is often critical in the early stages of faculty resistance. The consultant can act as a lighting rod for all complaints, criticism, and confessions that might not ordinarily be expressed to a local colleague.

One of the most effective means of using a consultant for this purpose is to hold an open faculty meeting where, with the appropriate administrators present, the consultant presents an outline of the proposed faculty evaluation and development program and then responds to questions and comments. Often in this forum, the faculty criticize the ideas presented by the consultant, or criticize the planned program, as if the consultant were solely responsible for the entire effort. What is really being communicated in this setting is a concern or an expression of opposition to the administration's proposals or practices without a direct confrontation with the administration. Breakthroughs in faculty resistance often occur in such forums. This approach also gives the administration the opportunity to present proposals which can receive perhaps a more honest appraisal by the faculty than they ordinarily might, with little risk being taken by either the faculty or the administration.

Integrate faculty evaluation and faculty development programs. Make certain that for every element of the faculty evaluation program there is a corresponding and concomitant element in the faculty development program. For example, if an instructor's syllabus is going to be evaluated as part of the overall evaluation of teaching, make sure that workshops, seminars, or materials are available in the faculty development program to show an instructor how to construct a good syllabus. This approach ensures that faculty have institutionally supported recourse when the evaluation system detects a weakness in their performance.

Use a variety of sources in the evaluation system. Make certain that the faculty evaluation system includes and uses input from such sources as peers, self, and administrators, as well as students. It is important to specify the impact each of these various sources of information has on the total evaluation. The following sections in this handbook describe in detail the process for doing this.

Make every effort to ensure that the faculty evaluation program is functionally valid. The aspects of faculty performance being evaluated should be ones that both the faculty and the administration believe *ought* to be evaluated. In establishing the program's functional validity, it is important to remember that the process of evaluation requires that a set of data be weighed against a set of values. If the data show that the performance of an individual corresponds to the values being used or assumed by the evaluation system, that individual is evaluated favorably. If the faculty member's performance is at odds with the evaluation system's assumed values, an unfavorable evaluation results. The issue of the importance in determining values in the development of a faculty evaluation system is discussed in greater detail in Step 2 of the process described in this handbook.

To the extent that faculty are either unsure of, or disagree with, the assumed value structure of the faculty evaluation program, they will consider the program not to be valid and will thus resist it. Functional validity, or the extent to which the faculty believe in the fairness and utility of the faculty evaluation program is, in large measure, a function of the degree to which they are aware of, and agree with, the assumed values in the evaluation program. A number of specific and effective steps can be taken to establish the *functional validity* of a faculty evaluation program and these are described in detail in the following chapters.

Make certain that detailed faculty evaluation information is provided primarily and exclusively to the instructor. Policies may be established that call for mandatory periodic review of the evaluation information by an administrator, but the issue of the initial control of the information must be resolved early so that the faculty evaluation and development unit does not come to be seen as a watchdog agency for the administration. If this occurs, the development or self-improvement function of the program is severely diminished. The faculty evaluation and development programs *must* be correctly seen as being confidential resources for faculty to use in improving and documenting the quality of their own performance.

Establish a facilitative reward structure. Establish policies that treat documented faculty development efforts in a fashion similar to those of publication and research efforts. Successful faculty development and instructional improvement efforts should contribute meaningfully to promotion, tenure, and, where possible, merit pay decisions.

Tie promotion, tenure, and merit pay decision-making procedures as directly to the faculty evaluation and development program as possible. This last suggestion is critical if the program is to succeed. Once we dispense with those few faculty who have a passionate drive for discovering truth through research regardless of cost, those who teach for the sheer love of teaching and would do so even if they were not paid, and those who are bent on a never-ending quest for self-actualization, self-development, and self-improvement, we are left with the great majority of faculty who are profoundly influenced in their professional performance by those aspects of job security, prestige, colleague respect, and monetary reward that their institution controls. If faculty perceive that decisions concerning their careers are still going to be carried out by an administrator who may or may not use faculty evaluation and development data in a systematic, fair, and predictable manner, the program will ultimately fail. This is true no matter how benevolent the administration may be.

Only when faculty realize that (1) obtaining the rewards their profession and institution have to offer is a function of their performance and thus under their control and that (2) the faculty evaluation and development program is a valuable tool in helping them both identify and overcome the obstacles standing between them and these rewards will the program have a chance of success.

Only when the administration realizes that well constructed faculty evaluation and development programs do not diminish its ability to direct the course and quality of the institution, but rather enhance and strengthen it, will a truly successful faculty evaluation and development program have been established.

CHAPTER REFERENCES

Arreola, R. A. (1979). Strategy for developing a comprehensive faculty evaluation system. *Engineering Education,* (December), 239–244.

Grasha, A. F. (1977). *Assessing and developing faculty performance: Principles and models.* Cincinnati, Ohio: Communication and Education Associates.

Milton, O., & Shoben Jr., E. J. (1968). *Learning and the professor.* Athens, Ohio: Ohio University Press.

O'Connell, W. R., & Smartt, S. H. (1979). *Improving faculty evaluation: A trial strategy, a report of the SREB faculty evaluation project.* Atlanta, Ga.: Southern Regional Education Board.

Seldin, P. (1980). *Successful faculty evaluation programs.* Cruger, N.Y.: Coventry Press.

3

Step 1:
Determining the Faculty Role Model

An important issue often overlooked by those involved in designing questionnaires, forms, or procedures for faculty evaluation systems is that the design and implementation of a successful program is as much a political process as it is a technical or psychometric one. Much time and effort is spent examining and discussing the validity of student ratings, the validity of peer evaluations, and the validity of the entire evaluation process. The literature abounds with research efforts to validate one form or another (see Chapters 14 and 15). Although these are serious and important questions, the most important form of validity for a faculty evaluation system is *functional validity*. That is, regardless of the statistical and psychometric characteristics that a form or procedure might possess, if it is not accepted and used by the faculty, it has no functional validity.

Establishing the functional validity of the forms and procedures of a comprehensive faculty evaluation system should be the first objective in our plan. Once the program's functional validity has been established and the system is operating, the issue of the psychometric validity of its various components can be tackled with accepted measurement and statistical techniques. If we take these steps in reverse order, as is often the case, we stand a very good chance of becoming bogged down by technical arguments which can defeat the necessarily political process of developing an acceptable faculty evaluation system.

Thus, the first step in developing a truly comprehensive faculty evaluation system is to determine which of the many activities faculty engage in *should* be evaluated. That is, the *faculty role model* for the institution must be determined. The quick and common answer as to what constitutes the faculty role model for an institution is teaching, research, and service. However, to make any educational institution run, faculty must engage in a wide variety of activities. In addition to teaching, conducting research, and performing various service activities, faculty also advise students, publish articles and books, serve on committees, administer programs, and perform many other essential duties (Table 1). Thus, a simple teaching, research, and service role model may be insufficient to adequately encompass the full range of legitimate faculty activities. Miller (1972) provides a more comprehensive treatment of activities which define possible roles in an academic institution.

It is important to begin the process of determining your faculty role model by itemizing the many activities required of the faculty at your institution (Figure 1). At this point, develop a list of activities without regard as to how you would evaluate them. The listing and categories you identify will serve as the starting point for the process of developing the faculty role model for your institution. Obviously, the brief listing of activities and categories you develop cannot be considered complete definitions of each role. To develop such definitions, it is best to set up committees or workshops to systematically gather information from the faculty as to which activities and categories are considered appropriate for defining each role.

Table 1   Partial List of Possible Roles with Suggested Defining Faculty Activities

Teaching

Instruction
1. Teaching regular course offerings
2. Developing course materials
3. Developing replicable systems of instruction
4. Developing new courses/labs
5. Coordinating clinical teaching/independent study/tutorials

Advising
1. Advising students on programs of study
2. Sponsoring or advising student groups
3. Chairing master's or doctoral supervisory committees
4. Serving on master's or doctoral supervisory committees

Scholarly Research/Creative Endeavors

Publications
1. Books
2. Journal and magazine articles
3. Monographs, etc.
4. Presenting recitals and exhibitions
5. Staging, directing or acting in musical, theatrical and dance productions
6. Exhibiting paintings, sculptures, and other creative arts
7. Developing software/media
8. Reviews
9. Nonrefereed material
10. Citation counts
11. Invited/contributed presentations
12. Invited/contributed papers
13. Poster sessions

Ongoing Research
1. Basic scientific investigations, both theoretical and applied
2. Investigations of educationally relevant problems

Professional Recognition
1. Awards, honors, or invited presentations
2. Achieving advanced degrees, certification, etc.

Service

Faculty Service
1. Serving on departmental, college, or university committees
2. Serving on the faculty senate
3. Chairing any committee (student, faculty, etc.)
4. Serving as a sponsor for student activities/groups

Professional Service
1. Activity in professional organizations (holding office, serving on committees or boards)
2. Consulting to organizations or corporations
3. Consulting to universities/colleges, etc.

Public or Community Service
1. Participating in local, state, or national civic activities and organizations
2. Applying academic expertise in the local, state, or national community without pay or profit

Arreola, R.A. (1995). *Developing a Comprehensive Faculty Evaluation System.* Bolton, MA: Anker Publishing Co., Inc.

Figure 1   Faculty Role Model Worksheet

Below list the various specific activities in which the faculty engage as part of their overall professional responsibilities at your institution.

1. _____

2. _____

3. _____

4. _____

5. _____

6. _____

7. _____

8. _____

9. _____

10. _____

(Use additional sheets if necessary to continue list of activities.)

Indicate the role categories into which the activities listed above may be grouped (e.g., teaching, scholarly research/creative endeavors, faculty service, public/community service, professional service). List the numbers of the activities which define each role.

Role 1: _____

Activities (numbers): _____

Role 2: _____

Activities (numbers): _____

Role 3: _____

Activities (numbers): _____

Role 4: _____

Activities (numbers): _____

Role 5: _____

Activities (numbers): _____

Arreola, R.A. (1995). *Developing a Comprehensive Faculty Evaluation System.* Bolton, MA: Anker Publishing Co., Inc.

CHAPTER REFERENCE

Miller, Richard I. (1972). *Evaluating faculty performance.* San Francisco: Jossey-Bass, Inc.

4

Step 2:
Determining Faculty Role Model
Parameter Values

Once the decision has been made which roles the faculty play *ought* to be evaluated, the second step is to determine how much value or weight should be given each role. Assume that teaching, scholarly research/creative endeavors, faculty service, and public/community service are the four main roles of the faculty role model for a given institution. Which of these roles is valued the most? Which the least? What is the priority order of this set of roles for the institution? Generally, teaching is said to be the most valued role. However, in reality, when it comes time for promotion, tenure, and other personnel decisions, we may find that scholarly research is valued more than teaching—or at least more than was originally thought. Therefore, it is important to establish, in some more rigorous and specific fashion, the relative values of these different roles.

ESTABLISHING PARAMETER VALUES

Within any institution, a wide variety of opinions or positions concerning the relative value of the roles which faculty play will exist. Some will hold teaching to be of primary importance, others will hold faculty service to be of greatest importance, and others still will maintain that scholarly research/creative endeavors is the most important function of the institution. Obviously, all of these values must be encompassed in the operation of the institution. However, a consensus must be reached in developing a value structure for the evaluation system. The best approach is to establish parameter values for each role. That is, determine the maximum and minimum weights that could be assigned to a role in your institution.

Figure 2 shows the parameter values for a hypothetical faculty role model. Notice that teaching ranges in weight from a minimum of 50% to a maximum of 85%. This would be interpreted to mean that, in the evaluation of a faculty member's overall performance, teaching performance would count *no less* than 50% of the overall evaluation and *no more* than 85%. This does NOT mean that a faculty member may have a 50% to 85% teaching load. Rather, these numbers are an expression of how much impact or weight performance in the role of teaching will have on the faculty member's overall evaluation. The teacher may or may not have a full-time teaching load, but the value associated with teaching performance in this evaluation system would range from 50% to 85%.

Figure 2   **Sample Faculty Role Model**

Minimum Weight (%)		Maximum Weight (%)
50	Teaching	85
0	Scholarly Research	35
10	Faculty Service	25
5	Community Service	15

Arreola, R.A. (1995). *Developing a Comprehensive Faculty Evaluation System.* Bolton, MA: Anker Publishing Co., Inc.

This model clearly communicates that a faculty member's total evaluation will be based not only on teaching, but on some other factors as well. Thus, we communicate to the faculty that simply doing well in their teaching assignment is not enough. Obviously, between 15% and 50% of the evaluation will be based on something else. In our example (Figure 2), that something else includes scholarly research/creative endeavors (abbreviated to scholarly research), faculty service, and public/community service (abbreviated here to community service). Here, scholarly research can count as little as 0% and as much as 35%. The 0% minimum weight communicates that activities which define scholarly research are not required. The 35% maximum weight communicates that such scholarly research activities cannot constitute the entire, or even the majority, of the activities on which a faculty member will be evaluated. The minimum and maximum weights for faculty service (10% - 25%) and community service (5% - 15%) communicate the fact that these two activities or roles are expected of everyone to some degree—although neither of these roles can constitute the primary or majority activity for a faculty member, insofar as the evaluation system is concerned.

Using the Weighted Faculty Role Model Worksheet (Figure 3), list the roles you identified in Step 1 and indicate your best estimate as to the minimum and maximum weights for each. The procedure for determining your final maximum and minimum weights is explained on the worksheet.

DETERMINING INSTITUTIONAL PARAMETER VALUES

In practice, determining the actual parameter values for your faculty role model is a political process which involves consensus building between faculty and administration. The minimum and maximum weights should reflect both the values and priorities of the administration as well as the general sentiment of the faculty. This is best accomplished by having faculty respond to an individual questionnaire that asks them to indicate their values or priorities relative to the roles in the faculty role model. The following steps should be taken to gather and summarize this data:

1. Set up special faculty meetings to discuss the issue of setting values for the faculty role model.

2. Distribute questionnaires that ask faculty to assign a maximum and minimum weight for each agreed upon faculty role. This questionnaire should include questions outlined in Step 3. Steps 2 and 3 should be carried out concurrently. (See Step 3 for a sample questionnaire.)

3. Determine the mean, median, and modal maximum and minimum values for each role. Use the values that seem most representative of the faculty given the range. If there is great variability among the values, then additional meetings and discussions may have to be held to reach some measure of consensus.

4. The final values assigned should reflect both the faculty's input as well as the values and priorities of the administration. Therefore, the final values may not be simply the average of the maximums and minimums indicated by the faculty. For example, many faculty may feel that community service should not be required and will indicate a minimum weight of 0. However, the administration may believe that community service is a mission of the institution, and thus all faculty bear some responsibility in providing service to the community. As a compromise, the institution may set a minimum of 5% for this role to reflect the administration's values and priorities.

5. Publish a report from the faculty evaluation committee to the faculty which delineates the adopted faculty role model for the institution. This report should include not only the minimum and maximum values but the role definitions determined in Step 3.

Figure 3   Weighted Faculty Role Model Worksheet

WEIGHTED FACULTY ROLE MODEL FOR

_____

Name of Institution

Minimum %	Role	Maximum %
_____	_____	_____
_____	_____	_____
_____	_____	_____
_____	_____	_____
_____	_____	_____
_____	_____	_____
_____	_____	_____
_____	_____	_____
_____	_____	_____
_____	_____	_____

Setting Minimum and Maximum Weights

A. List the roles you have identified as being appropriate for your faculty evaluation system.

B. Indicate, by means of a minimum and maximum weight for each role, how much a faculty member's performance in that role should count in the overall faculty evaluation system.

C. Make sure the total of all your minimum weights does not exceed 100%. Ideally, the total of all your minimum weights should be some value between 40% and 70% (author's subjective values).

D. Add the maximum weight of your first role to the minimum weights of the remaining roles. If the total is 100% or less, proceed to the next step. If the total exceeds 100%, you must reduce the value of one or more of the weights. Reduce either the maximum weight of the first role or one or more of the minimum weights in the remaining roles.

E. Repeat step D, above, using the maximum weight of each role in turn and the minimum weights of _all_ the remaining roles.

Arreola, R.A. (1995). _Developing a Comprehensive Faculty Evaluation System._ Bolton, MA: Anker Publishing Co., Inc.

5

Step 3:
Defining Roles in the Faculty Role Model

The third step in the process of developing a comprehensive faculty evaluation system should be carried out concurrently with Step 2. In one sense, Step 3 should occur before Step 2, as will be explained below. In any case, these two steps are part of the overall process of defining the faculty role model for the institution—that is, determining what should be evaluated and how much each activity should count in the overall evaluation. As noted earlier, it is assumed that a faculty evaluation committee or similar committee coordinates the detail work associated with this project. Step 3 involves coming to a consensus as to how each of the roles identified is defined. For example, teaching as a role will readily be agreed upon. However, different faculty mean different things when they use the word "teaching." Teaching a lecture course is different from teaching a lab course is different from teaching a vocational course in air conditioner servicing and repair. Teaching a graduate course is different from teaching an undergraduate course. Some faculty assume meeting and counseling with students is part of teaching. Librarians consider the orientation seminars they give to students and new faculty as teaching. Thus, to say we are going to evaluate teaching doesn't necessarily mean the same thing to everyone—even though we may all agree that it is important to evaluate it.

The next several pages are devoted to providing an example of the development of the definition of one role. Because teaching is a role that is included in virtually all faculty evaluation systems, a working definition will be developed. Throughout the remainder of this handbook, the definition of teaching derived here will be used in all examples. You may not agree with the definition of teaching developed below, or you may develop a more comprehensive definition. In any case, a consistent definition for each role in your faculty role model must be developed as Step 3 of the process.

PERSPECTIVES ON
THE DEFINITION OF TEACHING

In the broadest sense, we can define teaching as involving an interaction between a teacher and a student such that learning occurs on the part of the student. Of course, the crux of the matter in defining teaching is to specify what kind of interaction occurs between teacher and student. Over the years, we seem to have evolved three different perspectives or philosophical positions on what does, or should, occur when a teacher interacts with a student. These perspectives are founded on different assumptions that significantly affect how we approach the evaluation of teaching. Let's look closer at these different perspectives with an eye toward assessing their implications on faculty evaluation. The first perspective defines teaching as

an interaction between a teacher and a student conducted in such a way that the student is provided with the opportunity *to learn.*

Notice that this definition implies the assumption that a student has the responsibility for learning and that a good teacher simply must provide the student with the appropriate opportunity to learn.

The second perspective on teaching defines it as

an interaction between a teacher and a student conducted in such a way as to enable *the student to learn.*

This perspective of teaching still assumes that a student has the primary responsibility for learning. However, implied in this perspective is the assumption that a teacher has *some* responsibility for student learning, because now the teacher has the task of facilitating or enabling that learning.

Finally, the third perspective on teaching defines it as

an interaction between a teacher and a student conducted in such a way as to cause *the student to learn.*

This is the most severe definition of teaching insofar as teacher responsibility is concerned. This definition clearly implies that the teacher has the primary, if not the sole, responsibility for student learning.

Virtually every educator's conception as to what constitutes good teaching involves one, or some combination, of these three assumptions. If we choose any one of these definitions as the right one, we can easily demonstrate how these incomplete assumptions have led us astray in our efforts to develop a generally acceptable means for defining teaching for the purpose of evaluation.

Teaching as Providing the Opportunity to Learn

If we accept the first definition in which it is the teacher's responsibility to simply give the students the *opportunity* to learn (a very popular definition among college faculty), then the defining characteristic of a good teacher would simply be content expertise. Under this definition, the teacher's primary responsibility would be to continuously sharpen content expertise, primarily through research, and to share this expertise with students. The act of teaching would consist primarily of sharing knowledge, insights, hypotheses, and professional experiences through lectures, seminars, presentations, and individual consultations. The primary role of the teacher would be that of scholar, knowledge generator, knowledge resource, role model, and, ideally, mentor.

Obviously, with this definition of teaching, student ratings or so-called "student evaluations" would be at best useless, and at worst insulting, degrading, and humiliating. Students, by definition, would not have the teacher's content expertise and would thus not be qualified to make any sort of evaluative statements or conclusions concerning the teacher's competence. The faculty criticism of student ratings which says, "If students were competent to evaluate me, *they* would be up here teaching the course!" would be entirely correct and justified under this assumed definition of teaching. If this definition is assumed, then peer evaluation or department head evaluation becomes the only really acceptable type of evaluation. It would be assumed that these individuals would be content experts and thus qualified to adequately assess the instructor's expertise.

Teaching as Enabling Learning

If we choose the second definition of teaching in which the teacher *enables* students to learn, then teaching becomes more complex. Under this definition, students still have the primary responsibility for learning, but the teacher has the responsibility for promoting or facilitating that learning. As

with the first definition of teaching, the teacher must still be the source of knowledge and must possess content expertise, but now must also be capable of creating an environment that is conducive to learning.

Implicit in this definition is the idea that the teacher must have the kind of social or human interactive skills which can engender interest in students and motivate them to learn. Teaching, under this definition, implies not only content expertise, but affective or personality traits not always under the direct conscious control of the teacher. People assuming this definition often say, "Good teachers are born and not made" or "Teaching is an art" or "You either have it or you don't." Such comments or beliefs reflect a heavy emphasis on the affective or personality component of this definition of teaching.

Peer or department head evaluations would still be considered to be most important. However, under this definition, student ratings could be viewed as having some use, because students can report how interested or motivated the teacher made them feel. Faculty subscribing to the first definition of teaching (i.e., providing the *opportunity* to learn) who encounter other faculty who subscribe to this second definition will often charge that student ratings are "just a popularity contest."

Teaching as Causing Learning

Finally, if we assume that definition of teaching wherein the teacher has the primary responsibility for student learning, we are led to a somewhat different set of defining characteristics of a good teacher. This, of course, affects the ways in which we would set about evaluating teaching. Under this definition, the simplistic *sine qua non* of good teaching is student learning: A good teacher is one who produces the most learning in students.

In this case, if one wished to evaluate how good a teacher was, one would simply test the students. Those teachers whose students performed the highest on some prescribed test would be, *ipso facto*, the best teachers. The appeal of this definition, especially to the lay public and state legislators in particular, is so strong that we need to address it in more detail.

Because, in some measure, the entire faculty evaluation movement grew out of the larger issue of accountability in education, it is apparent that, for the foreseeable future, teachers at all levels will be assumed to be responsible for student learning to one degree or another. This is not necessarily a bad thing.

AN INTEGRATED DEFINITION OF TEACHING

If we take our three partially right, partially wrong, definitions of teaching and try to integrate them into a coherent

18

whole, we might get a more useful definition which will enable us to do a more effective job of evaluating teaching.

From our examination so far, it should be apparent that the total teaching act involves three broad interactive dimensions:

1. Content expertise

2. Instructional delivery skills and characteristics

3. Instructional design skills

Teachers must know the subject matter being taught, must be able to present that subject matter in such a way that students are encouraged to learn, and must be able to design instructional events in such a way that there is some assurance that learning will occur when they are experienced by students. Of course, teachers must also successfully deal with the myriad of bureaucratic tasks involved in managing a course. Drop/add slips must be turned in on time, as must final grades; field trips must be arranged; office hours must be posted and maintained; arrangements for guest lecturers must be made; etc. Thus, a fourth dimension—course management skills—could reasonably be added to the overall definition of teaching. However, before we can develop the specific definitions of each of these dimensions of teaching, we must carefully define what we mean by *instruction* and, even before that, what we mean by *learning*.

Defining Learning

Any text in educational psychology can provide us with a number of definitions of learning. However, because we want to develop definitions that will facilitate the ultimate objective of defining teaching in such a way as to make it more amenable to effective evaluation, we will define "learning" as *a persistent, measurable, specified change in the behavior of the student resulting from an experience*

designed by the teacher. Such a definition, of course, has its limitations. A teacher who hits a student on the knee with a bat in such a way that the student walks, forevermore, with a limp, fits this definition of learning. So, for our purposes we will assume that the experience designed by the teacher is intended to promote the achievement of specified goals and objectives of a course or other approved instructional unit.

Defining Instruction

Next, "instruction" is defined as *presenting a set of experiences which induces student learning*. With this definition, we take into account the responsibility of the teacher in causing learning to occur. Notice that by this definition, *instruction* has not occurred unless *learning* has occurred. With these two terms defined, we can go on to develop our definitions of the three broad dimensions of teaching.

Defining the Content Expertise Dimension

The "content expertise dimension" is defined as *that body of skills, competencies, and knowledge in a specific subject area in which the faculty member has received advanced experience, training, or education*.

From the point of view of evaluating this component, we can readily agree that, with the exception of advanced doctoral candidates or postdoctoral fellows, students are generally not competent to assess the degree to which a teacher is competent or knowledgeable in a field. In fact, rarely does a student rating form used in a faculty evaluation system ask students to evaluate the content expertise of the teacher. However, students *are* competent to report the degree to which the faculty member *appears* to be knowledgeable in the subject matter being taught. The issue of real and apparent content expertise is an important one in faculty evaluation and deserves a closer look. Figure 4 relates the issues of real and apparent competence to whether a teacher is rated good or not.

Figure 4   Categories of Teachers Based on Content Expertise versus Instructional Delivery Skills

	Truly Competent	Not Competent
Appears Competent	**Type A**	**Type C** (Dr. Fox)
Does Not Appears Competent	**Type B**	**Type D**

Arreola, R.A. (1995). *Developing a Comprehensive Faculty Evaluation System*. Bolton, MA: Anker Publishing Co., Inc.

Ideally, we would like instructors to be both competent in the subject being taught and to *appear* competent to students. This type of teacher is Type A (Figure 4). Some research has suggested that, given two instructors who are equally competent in their content area, students tend to learn more from the one who appears most competent (Sullivan & Skanes, 1974; Leventhal, Perry & Abrami, 1977; Ware & Williams, 1975; Williams & Ware, 1976). This stands to reason because, on the whole, students are likely to pay more attention to those whom they believe know what they are talking about than they would to someone whom they think does not. Thus, from an evaluative point of view, faculty members who are competent in their content area but do not appear so to their students (Type B) could not be considered to be performing at the same level in their overall role as teachers. Type B teachers are ideal candidates for faculty development programs. Already expert in their content field, all Type B teachers might need is some assistance in becoming more effective in their presentational or instructional delivery skills to move into the Type A category.

On the other hand, Type C teachers (i.e., faculty members who do not possess the desired level of content expertise) can, in certain instances, appear to be more competent than they really are by virtue of their superior presentation skills. This phenomenon is generally referred to as the Dr. Fox effect (Perry, Abrami & Leventhal, 1979; Meir & Feldhusen, 1979; Abrami, Leventhal, & Perry, 1982; Marsh & Ware, 1982).

Finally, we may have instructors who are not competent in their content area and do not appear competent to their students. This type of instructor is labeled Type D. When tenured, such faculty are generally resistant to institutional faculty evaluation program development, personal faculty development, or administrative career outplacement efforts.

Insofar as the evaluation of content expertise is concerned, students should be able to provide information on the degree to which a faculty member *appears* competent in a given subject area. However, it should be kept in mind that this information may not necessarily reflect the true competence of an instructor as a content expert. Obviously, the true content expertise of an instructor, if it is to be evaluated at all, must be assessed in some other way, perhaps by peers. But to the degree that it is important to know how knowledgeable the instructor *appears* to the students, student rating forms, appropriately constructed, should be able to provide useful and reliable information.

Defining the Instructional Delivery Skills Dimension

The second dimension of teaching—instructional delivery skills—can be defined as

those human interactive skills and characteristics which (1) make for clear communication of infor-

mation, concepts, and attitudes, and (2) promote or facilitate learning by creating an appropriate affective learning environment.

Such characteristics as clarity in exposition, demonstrated enthusiasm, the ability to motivate, the ability to capture and hold the interest and attention of students, as well as the ability to engender an overall learning environment appropriate to the content being taught are included in this dimension. Interestingly, it is from this dimension that a great deal of the confusion and misconceptions concerning the validity and utility of student ratings originates.

We can readily agree that some teachers are better classroom performers than others. Someone with a clear and pleasant speaking style, an ability to set a class at ease when appropriate, who can motivate and capture the interest of students, and who demonstrates an enthusiasm toward both the subject matter and student learning would be a highly prized teacher—if that person were also competent in the subject matter being taught and if the students taking the course actually learned the subject material! Certainly, such a person would be preferable to one who, though equally competent in the subject matter and whose students learned equally as much, was perceived by those students as uncaring or unenthusiastic and left the students feeling as if they had had an unpleasant experience in the course. It is interesting to note that if we define teaching as consisting of only instructional delivery skills, it becomes clear why we might see a lot of good teaching going on but very little learning occurring. Having good instructional delivery skills but little or no content expertise is analogous to gunning the engine in your car but not putting it in gear. It sure sounds like you're racing along, but in reality you're not getting anywhere.

Student rating forms used in faculty evaluation systems almost always include items that ask students to provide information concerning the instructional delivery skills and characteristics of the instructor, although the forms may not label such items that way. From this fairly common practice has grown the often-heard charge that student ratings are "just a popularity contest." This charge generally comes from those faculty who tend to assume that the first dimension, content expertise, is the sole defining characteristic of teaching. However, taken in its proper perspective in an overall faculty evaluation program, the popularity of an instructor relative to the appropriate instructional delivery skills used in the classroom is important information to have if we are to obtain a comprehensive picture, and thus produce a fairer evaluation, of the instructor's total teaching performance.

There appears to be an underlying assumption in such charges that if an instructor is a good performer, he or she must not really be a good teacher (i.e., possess a high level of content expertise). Fortunately, or unfortunately, depending on your perspective, such assumptions are not generally true. Teachers who are popular because they are good performers in the classroom are not necessarily poor in their content expertise, although we must watch out for the occasional Type C teacher on the faculty.

For the instructional delivery skills dimension, we can generally consider students competent to report their reactions to the performance characteristics of a faculty member relative to classroom presentations. Asking students to rate those human interactive skills and traits which, in and of themselves, do not produce learning, but rather create an environment or affective situation which promotes and facilitates it, is a valid endeavor. It should be noted that charges by faculty that student ratings can be raised by making classroom presentations more entertaining *do* have a basis in fact. To the extent that a faculty member becomes a better performer, those elements of student ratings which reflect instructional delivery skills will be affected, as they should be. The danger in this arises, however, when student rating forms are overloaded with items that measure only instructional delivery skills or when the tacit assumption is made by those reviewing the ratings that good instructional delivery skills are the predominate defining characteristic of good teaching. Of course, more sophisticated approaches besides student ratings can be taken in attempting to evaluate this dimension. Using television to videotape classroom presentations for later analysis by professionals, peers, and the instructor, have been found to be highly effective. Classroom visitation by peers, on the other hand, has not necessarily proven itself to be the most *efficient* means of evaluating this dimension of teaching (Aleamoni, 1982; Centra, 1979; Cohen & McKeachie, 1980).

Defining the Instructional Design Skills Dimension

The third dimension, instructional design skills, rounds out our definition of the overall act of teaching. This dimension is defined as

> *those technical skills in (1) designing, sequencing, and presenting experiences which induce student learning and (2) designing, developing, and implementing tools and procedures for assessing student learning outcomes.*

The relationship between the definition of this dimension and the definitions of *learning* and *instruction* is direct and intentional. If *instruction* is defined as an activity which induces learning, and if *learning* is defined as a specified change in student behavior which must persist and be measurable, then the teacher must possess the necessary skills to execute these tasks correctly. Such skills as designing tests; preparing learning objectives; developing syllabi, handouts, and other such supportive materials; properly

using media and other forms of instructional technology; as well as organizing lectures and presentations for maximal instructional impact are included in this dimension.

Unfortunately, with the exception of those faculty whose area of content expertise encompasses educational psychology, instructional design, or teaching methodology, most college faculty have had little or no formal training in these areas. All too often faculty simply use the teaching and testing strategies that were inflicted on them as students. It is ironic that most college faculty have never received even minimal formal exposure to two of the broad dimensions of teaching, namely instructional delivery skills and instructional design skills.

In evaluating instructional design skills, we find that several sources of information are available to us. Again, although students would not generally be considered competent to evaluate the correctness of the instructional design of the course, they could report their observations, perceptions, and reactions to certain aspects of the design of the course. For example, if students report their opinion that the course examinations did not appear to be related to the course objectives, this reaction could serve as a flag for the instructor, department head, and/or peer review committee that there may be some problem with the instructional design of the course. Likewise, if the students report that the course appeared to be too difficult, this could serve as a flag that perhaps the material was inappropriate for the level of the course or that important connecting information between topics was missing or even that a curriculum problem existed such that students were not being adequately prepared prior to taking the course being evaluated. In any case, as a general principle, department heads and/or other instructional leaders and peers in the department would most likely be the best evaluators of this dimension. A more detailed and expert analysis could be conducted by these and other qualified people of the syllabus, tests, handouts, content, and general instructional design of the course, as well as make appropriate interpretations of the flags put up by the students' responses on the rating forms concerning this dimension.

Again, it is important to note that students, when they complete rating forms, are not evaluating the instructor in the sense that they are passing final judgment on the overall quality of the teaching in its entirety. Rather, student rating forms, if they are carefully designed and used, can solicit observations, opinions, reactions, and perceptions from students, which others, who *are* qualified, can examine and draw inferences from concerning the performance of the instructor.

Defining the Course Management Skills Dimension

As noted earlier, the activities surrounding the management of a course in and of themselves comprise an important dimension of teaching. For our purposes here, course management is defined as

> *those bureaucratic skills in operating and managing a course including, but not limited to, timely grading of examinations, timely completion of drop/add and incomplete grade forms; maintaining published office hours; and generally making arrangements for facilities and resources required in the teaching of a course.*

From this discussion, we can conclude that the total teaching act involves four, broad interactive dimensions:

1. Content expertise

2. Instructional delivery skills

3. Instructional design skills

4. Course management skills

By defining the total teaching act in terms of these four broad components or dimensions, it becomes clear that the evaluation of teaching cannot be accomplished by using simply one form or another. Nor can it be done solely on the basis of the judgment of one individual administrator or peer committee based on a few classroom visits. No one person or group can have a sufficiently detailed and complete view of the entire process of teaching. A more accurate and valid perception of teaching performance would, of necessity, involve information from students on their opinions and reactions to the instructor's instructional delivery skills and characteristics, information from peers, and perhaps informed experts, on the instructor's instructional design skills, information from peers and department heads on the instructor's content expertise (if such information was required), and information from the department head, or perhaps even the departmental secretary, on the instructor's course management skills. Additionally, we would want information from students concerning the instructor's *apparent* content expertise as well as their reactions to several aspects of the course operation from which we could make inferences about the instructor's instructional design skills. Thus, the key to more effective evaluation of teaching is to carefully take all the parts of this mosaic and put them together in such a fashion that it accurately reflects the faculty member's overall teaching competence. The remaining steps in this handbook detail a procedure for doing just this.

DETERMINING ROLE DEFINITIONS FOR YOUR FACULTY ROLE MODEL

The purpose of Step 3, then, is to reach some agreement about defining the various roles which have been adopted

as the formal faculty role model of the institution. To give your faculty evaluation system a measure of objectivity, or to at least control the effects of the unavoidable subjectivity, it is important to define each of the roles in terms of *observable or documentable achievements, products, or performances*. This is obviously easier said than done. It is not reasonable to expect faculty to readily come up with concise definitions of the roles adopted in the faculty role model if they do not have the benefit of some prior thought on the matter. The discussion presented above on the development of the definition of the teaching role demonstrates the kind of work the faculty evaluation committee may wish to undertake in considering each role. Therefore, it is recommended that the faculty evaluation committee, as one of its first efforts, develops preliminary definitions of the roles in the proposed faculty role model. In this way, when the questionnaire soliciting faculty values (Step 2) and their role definitions (Step 3) is distributed, it will contain some definitions to which the faculty can refer in expressing their own views.

Using the separate Role Definition Worksheet (Figure 5), develop some preliminary definitions of the roles you identified in Step 1. Give careful thought to your definitions and try to keep in mind the differing views that may be represented on your campus relative to each role. Remember that the ultimate objective is to arrive at a definition that will be generally acceptable to everyone who will be subject to the evaluation system. This may mean that you may have several subdefinitions. For example, you may have to define teaching differently for vocational education courses than you might for the traditional academic curriculum. You may have to define scholarly research/creative endeavors differently for faculty in the arts than you would for faculty in the sciences. There is no hard and fast rule, and no single definition will necessarily work for all institutions. The important issue here is the process of developing these definitions by consensus so that the evaluation system will be seen as functionally valid by the faculty. That is, it will be seen as measuring something that they agree *ought* to be measured.

The following pages also include a sample questionnaire (Figure 6) that may be used to solicit role definitions and parameter values from the faculty. The questionnaire may be administered at the department, college, or institutional level. Ideally, such a questionnaire should be administered to departments separately and the data from the various departments in a college used to define the faculty role model for that college. Likewise, the faculty role models from the various colleges should be combined to form the institutional faculty role model. Accordingly, the sample questionnaire is constructed to be administered at the departmental level.

Figure 5 Role Definition Worksheet

Role	Definition
_____	_____
	_____
	_____
_____	_____
	_____
	_____
	_____
_____	_____
	_____
	_____
_____	_____
	_____
	_____
_____	_____
	_____
	_____
_____	_____
	_____
	_____
_____	_____
	_____
	_____

Arreola, R.A. (1995). *Developing a Comprehensive Faculty Evaluation System.* Bolton, MA: Anker Publishing Co., Inc.

Figure 6   Sample Questionnaire for Gathering Faculty Role Model Weights and Definitions.

MEMORANDUM

TO: Faculty of the Department of _____

FROM: Committee on Professional Evaluation and Development

RE: Faculty Evaluation System

The Committee on Professional Evaluation and Development is charged with developing a faculty evaluation system which reflects the priorities and values of the faculty in each department. It is our view that, for a fair and valid faculty evaluation system to be developed, it must be based on information that permits us to address the following issues:

1. Which of the many roles faculty play do you think *ought* to be evaluated in your departmental evaluation system?

2. How should these roles be defined so that, when they *are* evaluated, our faculty are confident that the appropriate activities have been examined and/or observed in arriving at the evaluation?

3. For each role, what is the range of specific values or weights you believe to be appropriate for your department in reaching an overall evaluation of a faculty member?

As a first step, a preliminary set of roles and sample definitions have been developed by the Committee. These roles and definitions are not final but are merely meant to serve as a reference as you consider your responses to the questions above. In Part 1, below, please list the roles which you think *ought* to be evaluated as part of our evaluation system. In Part 2, define the roles you identify in Part 1. The attachment to this memo includes a number of possible roles and some preliminary definitions to assist you in considering these issues. If you find any of the role categories and their definitions useful, please feel free to include them either as is or modify them in any way you see fit. If there are other roles you believe ought to be evaluated, please be sure to list them.

Also in Part 1, you are asked to indicate a minimum and maximum weight for each role. For example, considering the teaching role, should performance in teaching count at least 50% of the overall evaluation of a faculty member? Should it count at least 75%? In other words, what should be the minimum weight that teaching performance should count in the overall evaluation system? Likewise, what should be the maximum teaching should count? 85%? 95%? 100%? Should a faculty member's entire evaluation be allowed to be based only on teaching performance (e.g., 100% maximum)? Or should a faculty member be evaluated in some other activities besides teaching in arriving at an overall evaluation? The answers to all these questions reflect your values concerning the various roles to be evaluated. We need to have your values expressed so that the final evaluation system reflects the faculty as a whole.

Arreola, R.A. (1995). *Developing a Comprehensive Faculty Evaluation System.* Bolton, MA: Anker Publishing Co., Inc.

PART 1

Below, please write in the roles you think should be evaluated and the minimum and maximum weights each role should carry in the overall evaluation.

Minimum	Role	Maximum
_____	_____	_____
_____	_____	_____
_____	_____	_____
_____	_____	_____
_____	_____	_____
_____	_____	_____
_____	_____	_____
_____	_____	_____
_____	_____	_____

PART 2

Please list and define each of the roles indicated in Part 1. Your definition should be in terms of activities, products, or performances which can be readily observed for evaluative purposes.

_____

_____

_____

_____

_____

_____

_____

_____

_____

_____

_____

_____

_____

Thank you for your assistance with this important project.

Arreola, R.A. (1995). *Developing a Comprehensive Faculty Evaluation System.* Bolton, MA: Anker Publishing Co., Inc.

CHAPTER REFERENCES

Abrami, P. C., Leventhal, L., & Perry, R. P. (1982). Educational seduction. *Review of Educational Research,* 52, 446–64.

Aleamoni, L. M. (1982). Components of the instructional setting. *Instructional Evaluation,* 7, 11–16.

Centra, J. A. (1979). *Determining faculty effectiveness.* San Francisco: Jossey-Bass Publishers.

Cohen, P. A. & McKeachie, W. J. (1980). The role of colleagues in the evaluation of college teaching. *Improving College and University Teaching,* 28, 147–154.

Leventhal, L., Perry, R. P., & Abrami, P. C. (1977). Effects of lecturer quality and student perception of lecturer's experience on teacher ratings and student achievement. *Journal of Educational Psychology,* 69, 360–374.

Marsh, H. W., & Ware, J. E. (1982). Effects of expressiveness, content coverage, and incentive on multidimensional student rating scales: New interpretations of the Dr. Fox effect. *Journal of Educational Psychology,* 74(1), 126–134.

Meier, R. S., & Feldhusen, J. F. (1979). Another look at Dr. Fox: Effect of stated purpose for evaluation, lecturer expressiveness, and density of lecture content on student ratings. *Journal of Educational Psychology,* 71, 339–345.

Perry, R. P., Abrami, P. C., & Leventhal, L. (1979). Educational seduction: The effect of instructor expressiveness and lecture content on students' ratings and achievement. *Journal of Educational Psychology,* 71, 107–116.

Sullivan, A. M., & Skanes, G. R. (1974). Validity of student evaluations of teaching and the characteristics of successful instructors. *Journal of Educational Psychology,* 66, 584–590.

Ware, J. E., & Williams, R. G. (1975). The Dr. Fox effect: A study of lecturer effectiveness and ratings of instruction. *Journal of Medical Education,* 50, 149–156.

Williams, R. G., & Ware, J. E. (1976). Validity of student ratings of instruction under different incentive conditions: A further study of the Dr. Fox effect. *Journal of Educational Psychology,* 68, 48–56.

6

Step 4:
Determining Role Component Weights

At this point, you will have developed definitions for the various roles in your faculty role model. You will also have determined the relative impact or parameter values that the different roles can take in the overall evaluation of a faculty member. It now becomes important to consider how much weight or relative importance the various *components* of each role should have in the overall evaluation of that specific role. In our example in Step 3, we defined teaching as involving four components: instructional delivery skills, instructional design skills, content expertise, and course management. The issue now is to determine how much weight or relative importance each of these four defining components of the teaching role should have. Of course, as you develop your various role definitions, it is

possible that some roles may not have any separate defining components. *In the event a role is defined in such a way that it stands as a complete singular statement, it is not necessary to develop separate role component weights.*

It is important at this stage in the development of a comprehensive faculty evaluation system that we begin using one of several matrices which will play an important part in the final design of our system. The first matrix to be developed is the Source Impact Matrix, which provides the tool with which we can control the effect of the subjective data gathered as part of the overall evaluative process. Figure 7 shows an example of a partially completed Source Impact Matrix for teaching. Note that the sources of information

Figure 7   Component Weights of the Teaching Role

Source Impact Matrix for		TEACHING			
Sources					
Role Components					Component Weight
Instructional Delivery Skills					(30 %)
Instructional Design Skills					(40 %)
Content Expertise					(25 %)
Course Management					(5 %)
Total Source Impact Weights					= 100 %

Arreola, R.A. (1995). *Developing a Comprehensive Faculty Evaluation System.* Bolton, MA: Anker Publishing Co., Inc.

have not yet been determined and are simply left blank. In this example, the instructional delivery skills component is weighted as 30%, the instructional design skills component as 40%, the content expertise component as 25%, and the course management component as 5%. These weights reflect the relative importance that the various defining components of the teaching role hold for the faculty in our hypothetical institution. Thus, whatever the rating or evaluation outcome is for the instructional delivery skills component for a given faculty member, that rating will count only 30% of the total evaluation of the teaching role. Likewise, the rating or evaluative outcome of the instructional design skills component will count 40%, and so on. The weights used in this example are entirely subjective. Actual weights for your institution may vary considerably from these examples.

It is necessary at this point in our procedure to begin ascertaining the relative importance or weights *your* institution would hold for the different components for each role. On the following page is a master blank Source Impact Matrix (Figure 8) forms for making working copies. Begin one matrix for each role by first listing the role components down the left side and assigning role weights down the right side. *Note that the total of all component weights for each role must equal 100%.* When you have completed one matrix for each role for which you have developed defining components, place it aside. These matrices will be completed in Step 6. At this time, do not enter anything into the other cells in each matrix.

Figure 8   Source Impact Matrix Worksheet Master

Source Impact Matrix for _____
                              (Role)

Sources

Role Components

Component
Weight

(%)

(%)

(%)

(%)

(%)

(%)

(%)

(%)

= 100 %

Total Source
Impact Weights

Arreola, R.A. (1995). *Developing a Comprehensive Faculty Evaluation System*. Bolton, MA: Anker Publishing Co., Inc.

7

Step 5:
Determining Appropriate
Sources of Information

In Steps 1–4, we focused on determining and defining the roles that *should* be evaluated, how much weight or value should be placed on the performance of each role in the overall evaluation, and how much weight the individual components of each role contribute in the evaluation of that role. The next step is to come to an agreement as to *who* should provide the information on which the evaluations will be based. Too frequently students are automatically selected as the sole or primary source of the information used in a faculty evaluation system. Students are certainly appropriate sources of information for certain kinds of activities, but they are by no means the best source of information for *all* the activities in which faculty engage and on which they may be evaluated. The most important principle in identifying and selecting sources of information is to make certain that the source identified has *first-hand knowledge* of the performance being evaluated. Too often peers or administrators are included in the evaluation of a faculty member's classroom performance when they have never, or rarely, seen that performance. However, peers and various administrators believe they have a good idea of the quality of such performance. The question is where did these sources get their information? The answer is almost always "from students." If you are ultimately going to depend upon students for information, go directly to the source—don't rely on second-hand information. Using second-hand information may give the random, or nonsystematically obtained, input of a few students an inordinate effect on a faculty member's evaluation.

Here we will need to develop another working matrix, the Source Identification Matrix, for each of our roles. That is, we need to begin determining, by means of an analysis of the specific component activities which define each role, who are the most appropriate sources of information concerning each of those activities. Figure 9 shows a complet-ed Source Identification Matrix appropriate for the teaching role as defined in our earlier example (Figure 7).

As can be seen in Figure 9, teaching has previously been defined in terms of four components: instructional design skills, instructional delivery skills, content expertise, and course management. Depending on the definition developed for your institution for the teaching role, you may have three, four, five, or more defining components for teaching. These components are listed down the left side of the matrix. A number of possible sources of information are listed across the top of the matrix. In our example, we have listed only students, peers, and the department head. However, other sources such as self, alumni, parents, external consultants, etc., are also possible.

In completing the matrix, "Yes" or "No" decisions are made as to whether a particular source of information should be tapped for the role component in question. In Figure 9, teaching is defined, in part, as consisting of instructional delivery skills. These skills would include those human interaction and communication skills which the students experience every time they are in class. Obviously, in this situation, students would be a good source of information, so a "Yes" is entered in the appropriate cell. However, note that a "No" has been entered for peers and department head as sources for instructional delivery skills. Making a decision to enter a "Yes" in these cells would have important implications that must be considered. In this case, unless the department is willing to undertake a peer visitation program or the department head is willing and able to regularly sit in on a faculty member's class, neither of those sources would really have first-hand information concerning instructional delivery skills and should probably thus not be included. However, in our example, teaching has been defined, in part, as also consisting of instructional design skills. This includes those technical skills in designing the course, developing tests, selecting references, setting up laboratory experiences, etc. For these kinds of skills, peers may be an excellent source of evaluative information; thus, a "Yes" has been entered in the appropriate cell. Students, too, could provide certain kinds of information about these skills as they are exhibited in the course.

Proceeding in this way through each role's defining components, it is possible to make rational decisions and determinations as to what sources of information would be appropriate and acceptable to the faculty. Again, the important principle to follow in identifying sources is to always select the source who has the best opportunity to observe *first-hand* the performance to be evaluated.

The process of developing the source identification matrices for each of the roles in your institution's faculty role model is best accomplished by the faculty evaluation committee. Appropriate input from the faculty at large may be solicited and, in fact, the committee may wish to send out a questionnaire asking faculty to indicate their preferred sources of information for each activity which defines a given role. However, this becomes cumbersome and can delay the process considerably. Rather, the committee, through a series of discussions and meetings with faculty groups, can determine what source or sources would be most appropriate for each of the roles' defining activities.

On the following page is a blank Source Identification Matrix Worksheet Master form (Figure 10) for making working copies. Using the definitions of the roles which you developed earlier, make a preliminary decision as to which sources of information would be appropriate and acceptable for each component of each role. Write the sources of information across the top of the matrix and enter the defining components along the left-hand side. As you consider each cell in the matrix, write either a "Yes" or a "No" in that cell.

Figure 9   Source Identification Matrix for the Teaching Role

Source Identification Matrix for _____ TEACHING _____

Sources

Role Components	Students	Peers	Dept. Head	
Instructional Delivery Skills	Yes	No	No	
Instructional Design Skills	Yes	Yes	No	
Content Expertise	No	Yes	Yes	
Course Management	No	No	Yes	

Arreola, R.A. (1995). *Developing a Comprehensive Faculty Evaluation System.* Bolton, MA: Anker Publishing Co., Inc.

Figure 10   Source Identification Matrix Worksheet Master

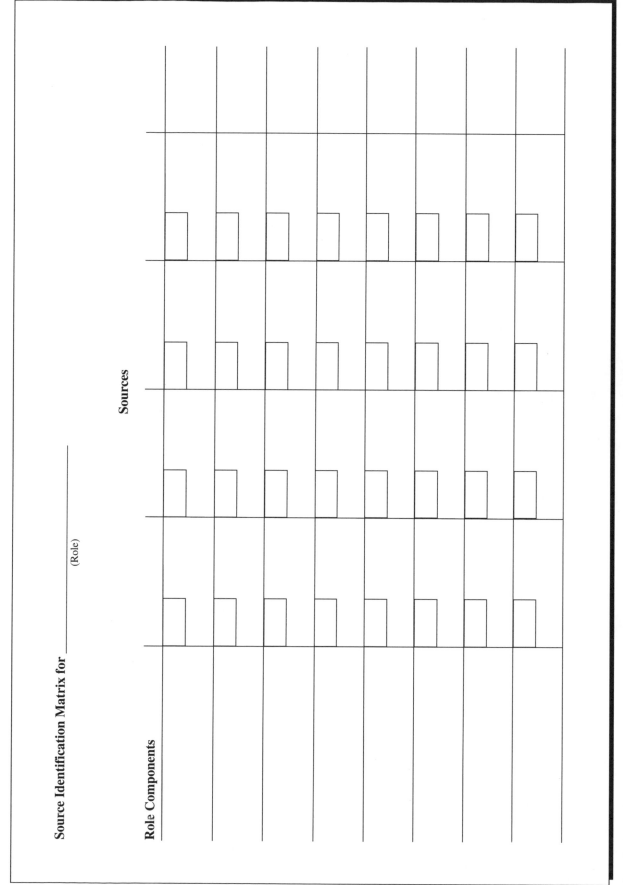

Source Identification Matrix for _____
(Role)

Sources

Role Components

Arreola, R.A. (1995). *Developing a Comprehensive Faculty Evaluation System.* Bolton, MA: Anker Publishing Co., Inc.

Step 5: Determining Appropriate Sources of Information

8

Step 6:
Determining Information Source Weights

In any faculty evaluation system, judgments and evaluations will be based on information derived from a number of sources. This information will concern various elements or components of the roles being evaluated. The issue of the appropriateness of those sources was addressed in Step 5. Having determined where the information to be used in the evaluation system will come from, the issue of credibility of those sources now needs to be addressed.

DETERMINING THE SOURCE WEIGHTS

In many faculty evaluation systems, the most common sources of information are students, peers, and administrators at various levels. This is true whether data from these sources are systematically gathered or randomly acquired. Depending on the situation and the performance being evaluated, however, the credibility of the information coming from these sources varies. For example, students may be a credible source of information concerning classroom performance but not as credible for information concerning the faculty member's research activities. Likewise, peers may be a credible information source concerning the professional standing and publication record of an individual but not as credible for information concerning classroom teaching style. The credibility of any information source in a faculty evaluation system depends as much on the opportunity that source has to be a *first-hand* observer of the performance in question as it does on the *willingness of the person being evaluated to accept and believe what that source has to say.* Thus, our next step in developing a comprehensive faculty evaluation system is to arrive at some consensus as to the credibility of the various sources of information that have been previously identified and to determine and define the impact the information from these sources will have on the overall evaluation of an individual. The tool used for this is another matrix, the Weighted Source by Role Component Matrix. Figure 11 shows an example of a completed Weighted Source by Role Matrix.

Figure 11   Source Weights for Teaching Role Components

Role Components	Sources			
	Students	Peers	Dept. Head	
Instructional Delivery Skills	100%	0%	0%	
Instructional Design Skills	25%	75%	0%	
Content Expertise	0%	80%	20%	
Course Management	0%	0%	100%	

Arreola, R.A. (1995). *Developing a Comprehensive Faculty Evaluation System.* Bolton, MA: Anker Publishing Co., Inc.

Note the values for each source for every defining role component in the example (Figure 11). In this hypothetical situation, following the "Yes" and "No" decisions made in completing the Source Identification Matrix (Figure 9), the faculty have determined that whatever information students provide concerning the instructional delivery skills component of the teaching role will be *all* the information that will be considered in the evaluation of that component because it was decided that neither peers nor the department head would be sources of information for this component. Thus, the total weight for student input on the instructional delivery skills component is 100%.

In completing your own Weighted Source by Role Component matrix for each role (i.e., teaching, community service, etc.), make certain that the sum of the weights for any given role component equals 100%.

In Figure 11, because students and peers have been determined to be appropriate sources of information for the instructional design skills component, the task is now to divide the 100% total weight across these two sources. This decision is a subjective one which is based, in large measure, on how these elements of teaching are defined and weighted (Steps 3 and 4) and how much credibility these two sources have with the faculty relative to the activities defining instructional design skills. If we can assume that instructional design skills speak more to the technicalities of course design (i.e., test construction, appropriateness of the readings, currency of content, etc.), then it might be considered appropriate to place the bulk of the weight (75%) on the input from faculty peers and 25% of the weight on input from students. However, as noted earlier, this is a subjective decision.

Following this procedure does not guarantee an objective evaluation system. However, it does clearly delineate and circumscribe the subjectivity which is inherent in any system. On the following page is a blank Weighted Source by Role Component Matrix Worksheet master (Figure 12) for use in making working copies.

Complete one form for each role by following the steps below:

1. Write the name of the role at the top of the form.

2. Indicate the sources across at the top of the columns, leaving any extra columns blank.

3. List the defining components for the role down the left side.

4. Be sure to "zero out" those cells in the matrix for which you previously determined no information would be gathered. For example, previously we determined that no information would be gathered

from students concerning the content expertise component of the teaching role. Therefore, enter a "0" in the cell formed at the intersection of the student column and the content expertise row.

5. Once you have zeroed out the empty cells, indicate the weight or value for each source for every component. Note that the sum of all the source weights across a given component row must total 100%.

In actual practice, of course, these values would have to be determined by gathering overall faculty input and then combining this input to arrive at a consensus as to the specific values or weights for each defining component of each role. An example of the type of questionnaire that could be used in gathering this information is shown in Figure 14.

DETERMINING THE SOURCE IMPACT

To this point, we have reflected the credibility of various sources of information by completing the Weighted Source by Role Component Matrix. Further, in Step 4 we reflected the relative importance of each of the defining components for every role by determining the role component weights and recording them down the right side of a Source Impact Matrix for each role. The purpose of these exercises was to lead us to the point of determining (and thus permitting us to specify and control) the impact information from each source will have on the overall evaluation of a faculty member. We now return to the Source Impact Matrices and complete them to determine our source impact weights.

Figure 13 shows an example of a completed Source Impact Matrix for the teaching role. In this example, the information recorded on the Weighted Source by Role Component Matrix for teaching has been entered into the small boxes in the corresponding cells of the Source Impact Matrix for the teaching role (see Figure 13). By multiplying the source weights for each cell by the row weight for that role component, it is possible to obtain a clear indication of the impact any one source of information will have on the overall evaluation of a role.

For example, in Figure 7, a value of 40% was assigned to the instructional design skills component of teaching. In Figure 11, it was determined that 75% of the information concerning instructional design skills would be provided by peers, so 75 has been entered in the small box of the upper left-hand corner of the peer instructional design skills cell of the Source Impact Matrix. Thus, as shown in Figure 13, by multiplying 40% by 75%, we get a source impact weight of 30% for peers which is recorded in larger numbers in that cell. By adding all the source impact weights in each column, we compute the total impact weight for the information coming from each source. It is

Figure 12   Weighted Source by Role Component Matrix Worksheet Master

Weighted Source by Role Component Matrix for _____
(Role)

Source Weights

Role Components					
					= 100%
					= 100%
					= 100%
					= 100%
					= 100%
					= 100%
					= 100%
					= 100%

Arreola, R.A. (1995). *Developing a Comprehensive Faculty Evaluation System.* Bolton, MA: Anker Publishing Co., Inc.

Figure 13 Completed Source Impact Matrix for the Teaching Role

	Sources				
Role Components	Students	Peers	Dept. Head		Component Weight
Instructional Delivery Skills	100 / 30	0 / 0	0 / 0		(30 %)
Instructional Design Skills	25 / 10	75 / 30	0 / 0		(40 %)
Content Expertise	0 / 0	80 / 20	20 / 5		(25 %)
Course Management	0 / 0	0 / 0	100 / 5		(5 %)
Total Source Impact Weights	40	50	10		= 100 %

Arreola, R.A. (1995). *Developing a Comprehensive Faculty Evaluation System.* Bolton, MA: Anker Publishing Co., Inc.

clear from the values shown in the Source Impact Matrix (Figure 13) that peer input will account for 50% of the overall evaluation of teaching, student input will account for 40%, and department head input will account for 10%. These values should be reported back to the faculty. If the values do not correspond to the expressed values of the institution, adjustments can now be made to bring the total final weights into agreement with the faculty's collective value structure. Note that the sums of both the component weights and source impact weights must each total 100%.

At this point, you should complete your Source Impact Matrix forms for each role by following the steps below:

1. For each role for which you have previously completed a Weighted Source by Role Component Matrix, copy the source weights from that matrix into the small boxes in the upper left-hand corner of the corresponding cells in the Source Impact Matrix.

2. At this point, your Source Impact Matrix should contain both component weights down the right side and source weights in the small boxes in the upper left-hand corner of each cell. Multiply the values in the small boxes in the upper left hand of each cell by the component weight for the row of that cell. Write the resulting product (source impact weight) in the larger portion of each cell.

3. Compute each of the column totals of the source impact weights and record them at the bottom of the matrix. These column totals are the total source impact weights for the given role. *Note that both the*

sum of the component weights and the sum of the source impact weights must each equal 100%.

GATHERING SOURCE AND SOURCE IMPACT VALUES FROM FACULTY

It should be remembered that the essence of a workable faculty evaluation system is that the value structure implicit in the system be clearly evident and agreed to by the majority of the faculty being evaluated. If this is not the case, the system, no matter how technically correct its structure, has little chance of long-term success. Thus, in determining the impact weights for the various sources which are to provide information for the components of each role, it is best to follow the same procedure described in earlier steps. That is, a simple questionnaire should be constructed and distributed to the faculty. At this point, building on the information gathered earlier, the questionnaire should list the various roles, their defining components, and the identified and agreed upon sources. A suggested form for the questionnaire is shown in Figure 14.

It is *not* recommended that the faculty be asked to fill in the entire matrix as shown in Figure 13. Rather, the first part of the questionnaire simply asks faculty to indicate the credibility each source of information has for them for each of the roles as previously defined, and the second part asks them to indicate the relative value of the defining components of each role. Although it would be possible to ask them to complete the detailed matrix, experience has shown that this task is more cumbersome and complex than most faculty care to deal with on a questionnaire. Thus, in order to maximize the return and ensure that the system reflects the values of the greatest number of faculty, it is recommended that the questionnaire be kept in its simpler form, as shown.

COMPILING THE DATA

The task before the committee at this point is to aggregate and combine all the data to most appropriately reflect the expressed values of the faculty within a department. This is best done by making a rough distribution of the data for each cell and determining whether to use the mean, median, or modal value for the final institutional value. This determination is made, in part, by considering the range of the distribution. If the range is extremely wide or if the distribution is bimodal, these are signs that considerable disagreement exists among the faculty and must be resolved. However, if the greatest bulk of the faculty responses appear to cluster together, the mean or average may be used.

College-wide values should be determined by a similar consideration of the departmental values for that college. Ideally, the college-wide values should encompass and subsume each of the separate departmental value ranges. Thus, although individual departments may have different values associated with specific roles, reflective of their different emphases or cultures, the college value system as a whole should accommodate these differences. For example, the college-wide range for scholarly research may be 0% to 45%. However, a research-oriented department may have as its values for this role a range of 25% to 45%. Similarly, a nonresearch-oriented department may have the values of 0% to 15% for the same role. Both ranges are encompassed by the college-wide value range of 0% to 45% for scholarly research.

Once the committee has received all the questionnaire data and has arrived at college-wide figures for the various sources for each role, it is then appropriate to begin filling in the empty cells of the weighted role by source matrix. Referring once more to Figures 11 and 13, we can see that zeros (0%) have been entered into the cells for which it was determined in Step 5 that no data would be gathered from that source. Thus, 0% has been entered for *peers* and *dept. head* in the instructional delivery skills portion of the teaching role. It was determined earlier that unless a structured peer or department head visitation procedure was to be put into place, neither of these would be an appropriate source of information concerning the instructional delivery skills. Likewise, zeros are placed in the content expertise and course management cells under students, because it was determined in Step 5 that students would not be an appropriate source of information for these elements of the teaching role.

Given the component and source weights derived from faculty input, the committee is left with the task of computing the relative impact of each role for the Source Impact Matrix (Figure 13). Use the Weighted Source by Role Component Matrix forms (Figure 12) to work through your best estimate of the source weights and role component values based on the definitions and determinations made in the earlier steps. Finally, complete the Source Impact Matrix for each role by transferring the cell values to the appropriate small boxes and then multiplying the values as described above.

Figure 14   Sample Questionnaire for Gathering Weighted Source by Role Information

Memorandum

To: All Faculty

From: Faculty Evaluation Committee

Subject: Determining Weights for the Faculty Evaluation System

Previously, the faculty have indicated that our faculty evaluation system should address teaching, scholarly research, faculty service, and public/community service. Further, the faculty have provided specific definitions for these roles. The defining components of each role are shown on the next page. This questionnaire provides you with an opportunity to indicate (1) how much you wish each component of each role to count, and (2) what impact you want each of the sources of information to have in the final overall evaluation of each of the defined roles.

Part I: Determining Component Weights

To reflect the faculty's judgment about how much each element contributes to the overall impact of a given role, it is necessary to assign different weights to these elements or components. In the example shown below, teaching's four defining elements have been weighted as instructional delivery skills = 30%, instructional design skills = 40%, content expertise = 25%, and course management = 5%. Note the total of the individual weights of all defining components equals 100%.

Example (only): Component Weights for the Teaching Role

Components of Teaching:		
Instructional Delivery Skills	=	30%
Instructional Design Skills	=	40%
Content Expertise	=	25%
Course Management	=	5%
		100%

On the reverse side, indicate how much weight you believe should be assigned to each defining component of each role. Please make sure that the sum of the component weights you assign for any role equals 100%.

Arreola, R.A. (1995). *Developing a Comprehensive Faculty Evaluation System.* Bolton, MA: Anker Publishing Co., Inc.

Name:_____ Department:_____

Part 1: Role Component Values

   TEACHING:

      Instructional Delivery Skills   [_____]

      Instructional Design Skills   [_____]

      Content Expertise   [_____]

      Course Management   [_____]

      _____   [_____]

                                                                       100%

   SCHOLARLY RESEARCH/CREATIVE ENDEAVORS:

      _____   [_____]

      _____   [_____]

      _____   [_____]

      _____   [_____]

      _____   [_____]

                                                                       100%

   FACULTY SERVICE:

      _____   [_____]

      _____   [_____]

      _____   [_____]

      _____   [_____]

      _____   [_____]

                                                                       100%

   PUBLIC/COMMUNITY SERVICE:

      _____   [_____]

      _____   [_____]

      _____   [_____]

      _____   [_____]

      _____   [_____]

                                                                       100%

Arreola, R.A. (1995). *Developing a Comprehensive Faculty Evaluation System.* Bolton, MA: Anker Publishing Co., Inc.

Part 2: Determining Source Weights

In analyzing the definitions shown on the first page of this questionnaire, you may find that different sources of information are appropriate for each of the defining components for each role. Completing the next step will enable us to determine how much weight the information from each of these sources should have in the overall evaluation of any role. The example below shows how to record the weights *you* believe should be given to evaluative information from the various sources for each defining component of the teaching role.

Example (only): Source Weights for the Teaching Role

Defining Elements/Sources	Students		Peers		Dept. Head	
Instructional Delivery Skills	100%	+	0%	+	0%	= 100%
Instructional Design Skills	25%	+	75%	+	0%	= 100%
Content Expertise	0%	+	80%	+	20%	= 100%
Course Management	0%	+	0%	+	100%	= 100%

In this example, students, peers, and the department head are, in general, appropriate sources of evaluative information concerning teaching. However, the figures shown indicate, in part, that the faculty would wish 100% of the information on instructional delivery skills to come from students, 80% of the information on content expertise to come from peers, and 100% of the information concerning course management to come from the department head.

For each of the roles shown on the reverse side, indicate the weight you feel is appropriate for each source of information for each role element identified. Please make sure that each row of cells adds to 100%. Leave blank any cell containing 0%, because it has been previously determined that no input is to be gathered from that source for that role component.

Arreola, R.A. (1995). *Developing a Comprehensive Faculty Evaluation System.* Bolton, MA: Anker Publishing Co., Inc.

Name:_____ Department:_____

Leave blank those cells with 0%.

TEACHING

	Students		Peers		Dept. Head	
Instructional Delivery	[_____]	+	[0%]	+	[0%]	= 100%
Instructional Design	[_____]	+	[_____]	+	[0%]	= 100%
Content Expertise	[0%]	+	[_____]	+	[_____]	= 100%
Course Management	[0%]	+	[_____]	+	[_____]	= 100%

SCHOLARLY RESEARCH/CREATIVE ENDEAVORS

	External		Peers		Dept. Head		Dean	
_____	[_____]	+	[_____]	+	[_____]	+	[_____]	= 100%
_____	[_____]	+	[_____]	+	[_____]	+	[_____]	= 100%

FACULTY SERVICE

	External		Peers		Dept. Head		Dean	
_____	[_____]	+	[_____]	+	[_____]	+	[_____]	= 100%

PUBLIC/COMMUNITY SERVICE

	Business		Peers		Dept. Head		Dean	
_____	[_____]	+	[_____]	+	[_____]	+	[_____]	= 100%

PLEASE RETURN THIS COMPLETED QUESTIONNAIRE BY [date] TO:

Arreola, R.A. (1995). *Developing a Comprehensive Faculty Evaluation System.* Bolton, MA: Anker Publishing Co., Inc.

9

Step 7:
Determining How
Information Should Be Gathered

Now that the sources of the information for your evaluation system have been determined, we begin moving into the less political and more technical area of measurement. It is best at this point to enlist the aid of those people on your faculty whose area of expertise is tests and measurement. They will certainly be required in the next step, and it is generally a good idea to have this expertise represented on the faculty evaluation committee in the first place.

In this step, we set about determining *how* the information we have specified in our role definitions is to be gathered from the sources we have identified and agreed are appropriate. This is a relatively simple process. However, it does require a careful review of the roles and the development of an operational plan for the final faculty evaluation system.

In completing this step, we will make use of a new matrix worksheet, the Data Gathering Tool Specification Matrix. Figure 15, below, shows a completed Data Gathering Tool Specification Matrix for the teaching role.

The matrix follows the example that has been used throughout the handbook. Note that the cells that contained zeros (0%) in the previous Source Impact Matrix (Figure 13) completed in Step 6 are blanked out on this matrix. Because we will not be gathering data from those sources for these elements, we will not need to specify the tools or means for doing so. In the cells that are *not* vacant, however, we are faced with the task of determining *how* we will gather information from students, peers, and the department head. For example, if we wish to gather information from students

Figure 15   Data Gathering Tool Specification Matrix for the Teaching Role

Role	Sources		
Teaching	Students	Peers	Dept. Head
Instructional Delivery Skills	Questionnaire		
Instructional Design Skills	Questionnaire	Peer Review of Materials	
Content Expertise		Peer Analysis of Course	Interview
Course Management			Checklist/ Grade Report

Arreola, R.A. (1995). *Developing a Comprehensive Faculty Evaluation System.* Bolton, MA: Anker Publishing Co., Inc.

concerning a faculty member's instructional delivery skills, there are several possible alternatives:

1. Interview each student.

2. Interview a random sample of students from each class.

3. Administer a questionnaire to each student.

4. Administer a questionnaire to a random sample of students from each class.

Unless the classes are unusually small and an appropriate team of individuals can be identified to serve as nonthreatening interviewers, interviewing students is generally not done. However, if that approach *were* desired, then an appropriate interview protocol would have to be developed. In our example (Figure 15), as is commonly the case, a questionnaire has been identified as the way in which student information is to be gathered. This does not mean that some system that uses both questionnaires and a form of follow-up interview could not also be implemented. Only by discussing what is desired, what is acceptable, and what is feasible and affordable can an appropriate determination be made as to the best way the information for each role is to be gathered.

Following our example, note that peers have been identified as appropriate sources of information for both the instructional design skills and the content expertise components of the teaching role. For instructional design skills, peers will review the course materials. That is, the course syllabus, tests, handouts, text selected, and general design of the course will be assessed by a group of knowledgeable peers. Likewise, the peer source will provide information as to the content expertise of the faculty member. This may involve a careful analysis and review of the course in terms of the currency of the content, as well as the sequencing of the material. Note that gathering the information required for a given role or role component may require a form, a set of forms, a specified procedure or protocol, or some combination of forms and procedures.

On the following page is a blank Data Gathering Tool Specification Matrix Worksheet Master (Figure 16) for making copies. Using the information developed to this point, make a preliminary judgment as to what means will be used to gather the information from each source. Develop a brief explanation and rationale for the data gathering approach you identify for each cell.

Figure 16   Data Gathering Tool Specification Matrix Worksheet Master

Data Gathering Tool Specification Matrix for _____
(Role)

Sources

Role Components

Arreola, R.A. (1995). *Developing a Comprehensive Faculty Evaluation System.* Bolton, MA: Anker Publishing Co., Inc.

10

Step 8:
Completing the System—
Selecting or Designing Forms and Protocols

We now arrive at the last step in developing a comprehensive faculty evaluation system—designing the questionnaires and other forms. It should be apparent at this point that designing forms without first having (1) clearly identified what is to be measured (steps 1 and 4) and (2) deciding from whom the information will be gathered (Step 5) could lead in directions we may not ultimately wish to go. Unfortunately, many institutions make designing a questionnaire, usually a student rating form, their first step in the process of developing a faculty evaluation system. This is a serious error that can stymie the entire process. Committees charged with such tasks can argue interminably over specific questions to be included on the questionnaire or rating form and the resultant product is almost always universally criticized.

However, because we have clearly defined what it is we wish to measure, from whom we wish to get the information, and how we are going to gather the information, the design of the forms and procedures becomes a relatively straight-forward matter. There is no specific recipe for accomplishing the development of your forms and procedures. Rather, what is provided here is simply a word of caution and some resources.

The word of caution is, "Don't reinvent the wheel." Many questionnaires have already been developed and are used in faculty evaluation systems around the country. In addition, there are a number of commercially available forms and systems are available. The *Student Rating Form Selection and Development Kit* portion of this handbook (Chapters 14, 15, 16 and 17) contains a complete description and critical review of a number of the better commercially available student rating forms. Also a sample manual is provided in the Appendix as an example of a faculty evaluation manual from a college which has used the procedure outlined in this handbook to develop its system.

It is recommended that the task of designing a final set of forms be accomplished by a small team of faculty with expertise in tests and measurement under a contract format rather than by the full committee. The full committee has determined all the specifications as to *what* is to be measured and *who* is to be tapped for the information. This specification provides sufficient directions for the technical team to follow in developing the questionnaires, protocols, etc. Experience has shown that if the full committee takes on this task, previous agreements can unravel once the item-by-item determination of the forms and questionnaires gets under way. Faculty unfamiliar with the principles of psychological measurement are likely to overlook the fact that well-designed questionnaires may include questions that, when taken in isolation, may be argued, but when taken in the aggregate provide valid and reliable measures of the characteristic or role component in question.

It is necessary to clarify one assumption before we move to actually constructing the forms, questionnaires, protocols, etc. We must assume that all information gathered from each source will be reported on a common scale. That is, regardless of whether we use a questionnaire, an interview schedule, or some other technique in gathering evaluative information from the various sources identified, that data will be reported on the same scale. For example, we may agree to assume that all information will use a scale of 1 to 4 where 1 is a low rating and 4 is a high one. That is, student ratings of instructional delivery skills would be reported on a scale from 1 to 4. Likewise, peer ratings of instructional design skills would be reported on a scale from 1 to 4, and so on. Thus, the faculty evaluation committee would need to specify the scale *before* the various questionnaires, forms, and protocols were developed.

Faculty Evaluation
Tools and Procedures

The following is a summary of a number of tools and procedures that have been used in evaluating faculty performance. Each summary contains a brief overview of the strengths, weaknesses and characteristics of the particular tool or procedure. This listing is by no means exhaustive but, rather, summarizes a number of more commonly used tools and procedures in faculty evaluation systems.

Student Ratings

Students rate an instructor's performance through a structured or unstructured questionnaire or interview.

Strengths of This Approach. Can produce extremely reliable and valid information concerning faculty classroom performance, because students observe the teacher every day. Instructors are often motivated to change as a result of student feedback. Results show high correlation with other peer and supervisor ratings if a *professionally designed* student rating form is used. Assessments are reliable and not affected by grades if well-designed form is used.

Weaknesses. Unless a professionally developed student rating form is used, factors other than teacher performance (e.g., class size, time of day) may inappropriately contribute to student ratings. Students may tend to be generous in their ratings.

Conditions for Effective Use. Need student anonymity. Need teacher willingness to accept student feedback. Instruments must be carefully developed by appropriate reliability and validity studies.

Nature of Evidence Produced. Student perceptions of what they have learned, how they have changed. Student opinions of how various teaching acts affected them. Student reaction to instructor actions. Student perceptions of what they like and dislike about an instructor.

Purposes for Which Most Highly Appropriate. Help instructors improve. Identify faculty for merit recognition. Make personnel decisions.

Tests of Student Performance

Measures of what students have learned or how they have changed over a period of time in working with the instructor.

Strengths of This Approach. Student attainment of objectives a legitimate source of data on faculty performances. Measures impact of instructor on students over a period of time.

Weaknesses. Difficulty of designing appropriate tests. Gains on standardized tests are often an inadequate measure of performance. Other factors may considerably affect performance (e.g., student intelligence, family background, previous schooling).

Conditions for Effective Use. Must have systematic and comprehensive data collection plan. Need personnel skilled in collecting performance data.

Nature of Evidence Produced. Student work samples. Test results (standardized and others). Attitude measures.

Purposes for Which Most Highly Appropriate. Improve student learning. Identify teachers for merit recognition.

Simulated Teaching

Brief teaching unit on content normally *not* taught by the instructor to a special selected group of students; pre- and posttest measure student gains.

Strengths of This Approach. Evaluates instructor skills in terms of student learning. Provides short-term feedback. Increases control over nonteacher variables assumed to influence student.

Weaknesses. Does not allow for assessing student growth over time. Expensive to conduct. Not a normal classroom situation.

Conditions for Effective Use. Need personnel trained in design of controlled situation evaluations and in student performance testing. Requires extra teacher preparation time.

Nature of Evidence Produced. Evidence on student learning under controlled conditions.

Purposes for Which Most Highly Appropriate. Improve student learning. Make personnel decisions.

Self-Evaluation

Instructor uses various means to gather information to assess performance relative to own needs, goals, and objectives.

Strengths of This Approach. May be used as part of a program of continuous assessment. Faculty are most likely to act on data collected on themselves. The data collected are more clearly related to a faculty member's own goals and needs.

Weaknesses. Results not consistent with other raters. May be unwilling to collect and/or consider data relative to own performance. Tend to rate themselves higher than students do.

Conditions for Effective Use. Instructor must have self-confidence and security. Need skills in identifying goals and collecting appropriate data. Must not be weighted highly in the determination of personnel decisions (promotion, tenure, merit pay, etc.)

Nature of Evidence Produced. Information on progress toward one's own goals.

Purposes for Which Most Highly Appropriate. Help instructors improve. Determine best assignments.

Supervisor or Department Head Observation
Administrators evaluate an instructor's performance through classroom observation, review of student learning data, feedback from students.

Strengths of This Approach. Supervisor is familiar with college and community goals, priorities, and values and may often have additional information about faculty performance. Can compare instructors within the college, school, division, or department. Requires minimal resources for observation, feedback, follow-up. Have legal responsibility for evaluation and related decision-making.

Weaknesses. Bias due to previous data, personal relationships, reason for observation, own values, and favored teaching methods. Situation being observed is, by definition, not normal because the observer is present.

Conditions for Effective Use. Supervisor needs adequate time and observational and review skills. Observation must focus on characteristics of teaching that research has established relates to desired student outcomes.

Nature of Evidence Produced. Comments on relations between instructor acts and student behaviors. Information on how instructors compare on certain factors. Comparison with methods supervisors consider to be good. Directions on changes to be made.

Purposes for Which Most Highly Appropriate. Guide professional growth and development. Information produced should *not* be used for personnel decisions unless supervisor is a part of a team of observers who use a standardized observation tool and who have been trained and have made sufficiently frequent observations to produce interrater reliability of the data.

Peer Evaluation
Other faculty evaluate an instructor's performance through classroom observation, review of instructional materials, course design.

Strengths of This Approach. Familiar with college (departmental, divisional) goals, priorities, values, and problems faculty face. Encourages professional behavior (e.g., motivation to help upgrade own profession). Can be chosen from instructor's subject area and thus may be able to give specific suggestions.

Weaknesses. Bias due to previous data, personal relationships, or peer pressure to influence evaluation. Relation-ships among peers may suffer. Possible bias due to evaluator's preference for own teaching method.

Conditions for Effective Use. Requires high degree of professional ethics and objectivity. Requires training in observational and analysis skills. Need time for multiple reviews.

Nature of Evidence Produced. Comments on relations between instructor acts and student behaviors. Comparison with methods peers consider to be good. Suggestions for instructors on methods, etc., to use.

Purposes for Which Most Highly Appropriate. Guide professional growth and development. Information produced should *not* be used for personnel decisions unless peer is a part of a team of observers who use a standardized observation tool and who have been trained and have made sufficiently frequent observations to produce interrater reliability of the data.

Visiting Team of Experts
People external to the system recognized as qualified in faculty (teacher) evaluation procedures observe faculty performance and/or review student learning data.

Strengths of This Approach. Can select evaluators with special skills. External to politics, problems, and biases of the college (school). Provides reliable data through pooling of independent ratings.

Weaknesses. Bias of evaluators due to own values, preferences, etc. Evaluators not accountable to the academic unit (college, school, division, department, etc.)

Conditions for Effective Use. Experts must be properly selected, oriented, and trained. Need time for multiple observations and reviews. Must use a standardized observer rating form on which team has been trained.

Nature of Evidence Produced. Comments on relations between instructor acts and student behaviors. Comparison with methods experts consider to be good. Suggestions for teachers on methods, etc., to use.

Purposes for Which Most Highly Appropriate. Guide professional growth and development. Aid in making personnel decisions. If data are to be used for personnel decisions, the team of experts must have been trained and have made sufficiently frequent observations to produce interrater reliability of the data.

TIMETABLE FOR DEVELOPING A COMPREHENSIVE FACULTY EVALUATION SYSTEM

Once the questionnaires, protocols, checklists, and other forms have been designed, the system is ready to be implemented. This assumes, however, that the appropriate support systems have been developed and put in place as noted earlier in Chapter 2.

The following timetable has been found to be typical in the successful development of a comprehensive faculty evaluation system:

Month 1   Appoint faculty evaluation committee. Familiarize committee with system development procedure. Hold general faculty meeting, sponsored by the committee, where procedure is presented and explained.

Month 2–6   Committee distributes questionnaires to faculty to develop the faculty role model, weights for the roles, definitions of roles, sources of information, and weights for each source.

Month 7   Committee reports to the general faculty the total value structure and role definitions as determined by their input.

Month 7–12   System forms and protocols are designed, selected, and developed. Policy decisions concerning confidentiality and the use of the information in promotion, tenure, and merit pay decisions finalized.

Month 12–24   Trial run of system. Time of stress because decisions of promotion, tenure, and merit pay during this time will still have to be based on old system. Debug system, make adjustments.

Month 25   Full implementation of system.

11

Using the System:
Combining Data to Generate
an Overall Composite Rating

In developing your comprehensive faculty evaluation system as specified in steps 1 through 8, you have made the following determinations:

- What faculty roles should be evaluated.

- What the defining activities or components are for each role.

- How much weight each component contributes to overall role definition.

- How much the evaluation of any one role may impact the total evaluation of an individual.

- Where information concerning each role is to be gathered and how much that information will impact or influence the total evaluative outcome.

- The methods and forms by which the information specified will be gathered from the sources agreed upon.

At this point you are ready to begin using the system. The task now is to combine all the data resulting from the system in a usable form. Previously it was determined that all information gathered from each source would be reported on a common scale. That is, regardless of whether a questionnaire, an interview schedule, or some other technique has been used in gathering evaluative information from the various sources identified, that data will be reported on the same scale. In our examples below, the scale of 1 to 4 will be used where 1 is the lowest rating and 4 is the highest. That is, student ratings, peer ratings, and department head ratings will all be reported on a scale of 1 to 4.

COMPUTING THE COMPOSITE ROLE RATING

Having determined and specified the weights to be assigned to various activities and sources in the overall faculty evaluation system, it is now possible to compute an overall rating for each role which reflects the collective values of the faculty. This rating will be referred to as the "composite role rating," because it will be derived from various sources, with each source providing information concerning various components of each role and with the information from each source and component weighted in ways which reflect the collective value structure of the institution. The following is an example of how the composite role rating for teaching would be computed.

In Figure 13, we determined that the information students provided concerning the faculty member's instructional delivery skills would impact the overall rating of the teaching role by 30%. Likewise, student information concerning the instructional design skills component would count 10%, and peer information would count 30%. We also determined that peer input on content expertise would count 20%, and department head input would count 5%. Finally, it was determined that department head input concerning course management would count 5% of the overall rating on teaching.

Figure 17 shows these weights along with the rating each source has given each role component. Note that all ratings, shown in brackets, use the common scale of 1 to 4. Here the students rated the instructor 4 in instructional delivery skills. Because it was determined in Figure 13 that whatever data the students provided concerning the instructional delivery skills component would count 30%

of the overall evaluation of the teaching role, we simply multiply the rating of 4 by 30% to arrive at a weighted rating of 1.2. In a similar fashion, the ratings provided by the various sources on the different components of the teaching role are multiplied by their impact weights. Finally, all weighted ratings are added together to form a composite role rating of 3.45. For ease of computation, the ratings in Figure 17 are shown as whole numbers. In practice, the ratings will be averages and will thus include decimal values.

Note that the composite role rating of 3.45 was not assigned by any one student, peer, or administrator. Rather, this value represents a mosaic of information concerning activities the faculty agreed should be evaluated, collected from sources that were agreed to be appropriate, and weighted to reflect both the credibility of the sources and the relative importance of each component of the entire role. Although the composite role rating does not represent an objective measure, the subjectivity involved in computing it has been carefully controlled and prescribed by the values assigned to the the sources and role components. A similar procedure would be followed in determining the composite role ratings for the other roles (e.g., research, faculty service, community service).

INDIVIDUALIZING THE EVALUATIONS

As a first step in developing a comprehensive faculty evaluation system, a faculty role model was developed with minimum and maximum parameter values, reflecting the collective values of the faculty and the institution, assigned to each role. These minimum and maximum values were expressions of the variability that may appropriately occur in faculty assignments. Using the matrices and values developed to this point, it is now possible to begin individualizing the evaluations of different faculty.

Assume that Professor Gray has received the composite role ratings shown in Figure 18.

Figure 17   Composite Role Rating for Teaching

TEACHING	Students	Peers	Dept. Head	Weighted Rating
Instructional Delivery	30% x [4]			1.20
Instructional Design	10% x [3]	30% x [3]		1.20
Content Expertise		20% x [4]	5% x [3]	.95
Course Management			5% x [2]	.10
COMPOSITE ROLE RATING				= 3.45

Figure 18   Composite Role Ratings for Professor Gray

Role	Composite Role Ratings
Teaching	3.45
Research	3.20
Faculty Service	3.60
Community Service	2.60

Arreola, R.A. (1995). *Developing a Comprehensive Faculty Evaluation System.* Bolton, MA: Anker Publishing Co., Inc.

The individual composite role ratings shown for Professor Gray were computed as shown in Figure 17. That is, each composite role rating is the result of gathering specific information from specified sources, weighted in ways that reflect the value system of the faculty and the institution. Of course, it is possible to stop at this point and use the various composite role ratings separately. However, using them in isolation does not permit us to reflect the specific nature of Professor Gray's assignment.

Assume that Professor Gray has an assignment as reflected in Figure 19. Recall that the faculty role model for our hypothetical institution (Figure 2) allowed a minimum of 50% weight on teaching and a maximum of 85%. Likewise, the minimum and maximum weights were 0% and 35% for scholarly research, 10% and 25% for faculty service, and 5% and 15% for community service.

In Figure 19, the 50% weighting for teaching for Professor Gray does not necessarily mean a 50% teaching load.

Rather, it simply reflects the fact that, given the particular roles the faculty member is engaged in, it has been agreed that whatever rating Professor Gray receives for the teaching role will count 50% of the comprehensive overall rating.

To combine Professor Gray's several separate composite role ratings into an overall composite rating, we simply multiply each composite role rating by the assignment weights shown in Figure 19 and compute the total. These computations are shown in Figure 20.

Note that Professor Gray's overall composite rating of 3.34 was not determined by any single individual or group. Rather, the overall composite rating can be thought of as a singular "index of success," because it was assembled by gathering information from various sources, weighted in ways that reflect the credibility of those sources, and further weighted by the assignment emphasis for this faculty member. That is, given the particular assignment Professor Gray had this year, the various appropriate sources provided

Figure 19 Assigned Role Weights for Professor Gray

Teaching	50%
Research	35%
Faculty Service	10%
Community Service	5%
TOTAL	100%

Figure 20 Computation of Professor Gray's Overall Composite Rating

Role	Assigned Weight	x	Composite Role Rating	=	Weighted Composite Rating
Teaching	50%	x	3.45	=	1.73
Research	35%	x	3.20	=	1.12
Faculty Service	10%	x	3.60	=	0.36
Community Service	5%	x	2.60	=	0.13
OVERALL COMPOSITE RATING				=	3.34

Arreola, R.A. (1995). *Developing a Comprehensive Faculty Evaluation System.* Bolton, MA: Anker Publishing Co., Inc.

a mosaic of information which is expressed in the overall composite rating. This approach permits us to more fairly compare the ratings of two faculty who may have considerably different assignments. For example, look at the overall composite rating computation for a different faculty member, Professor White (Figure 21).

The assigned role weights for Professor White differ considerably from those of Professor Gray. Professor White did not engage in any scholarly research, as indicated by the absence of that role. In contrast, however, Professor White placed the maximum weight (85%) on the teaching role. Yet, if we consider the overall composite rating to be an index of success, it can readily be seen that both Professor Gray and Professor White, with overall composite ratings of 3.34 and 3.35, respectively, were rated as essentially equally successful in accomplishing their assignments. Again, it should be noted that no one individual assigned these rating values to professors Gray and White. Rather, their overall composite ratings were the results of information gathered from a number of appropriate sources, weighted in such ways as to reflect the value structure of the institution as well as the individual faculty.

The development of the overall composite rating as a single numerical index representing a summary evaluation of a faculty member's professional performance provides the academic decision-maker, in fact, with the kind of numerical evaluative index that student rating averages are often used as, but never really are. That is, a singular value has been determined which represents a complex set of behaviors and performances and which *takes into account the interaction* between the values of the evaluator and the person being evaluated. Although the assignment of a singular numerical index to represent complex human performance can be criticized, it is a practice used throughout society and in education especially. Colleges and universities routinely make critical decisions and award degrees on the basis of summary singular numerical indices of complex human behavior (i.e., student GPAs.) As a profession, we are not unfamiliar or unskilled in this practice.

Criticisms may also be made that using a singular numerical index such as the overall composite rating can fool us into making significant decisions on the basis of insignificant differences, such as in the examples of professors Gray and White whose ratings differed by only 0.01. This criticism would be valid if the careful definition and delineations of the role weights, role component weights, identified sources, source weights, and individual assignment weights had not been determined and accounted for. The response to this criticism is to point out that it is generally preferable to make significant decisions on the basis of small differences along relevant and appropriate dimensions than to make significant decisions on the basis of larger differences along irrelevant and inappropriate dimensions.

With the computation of an individualized overall composite rating, which can be correctly characterized as an index of perceived success, we now possess a tool which may be appropriately applied to decisions concerning promotion, tenure, continuation, and merit pay.

Figure 21   Computation of Professor White's Overall Composite Rating

Role	Assigned Weight	x	Composite Role Rating	=	Weighted Composite Rating
Teaching	85%	x	3.53	=	3.00
Faculty Service	10%	x	2.00	=	.20
Community Service	5%	x	2.90	=	.15
OVERALL COMPOSITE RATING				=	3.35

Arreola, R.A. (1995). *Developing a Comprehensive Faculty Evaluation System.* Bolton, MA: Anker Publishing Co., Inc.

12

Using the System:
Making Personnel Decisions
Based on Faculty Evaluation Data

Computing an overall composite rating in the manner described to this point greatly simplifies the use of faculty evaluation information in making personnel decisions such as promotion, tenure, merit pay, and continuation. An essential administrative principle must be recognized at the outset. In general, personnel decisions are based on information that clearly demonstrates the pattern of performance of a faculty member over a length of time. The particular student ratings for one class, the peer critiques of a single article, or similar such specific data are rarely appropriate for decision-making. The professional academic administrator recognizes this. Thus, for a faculty evaluation system to be truly effective for personnel decisions, it must gather an aggregate of *relevant* performance data and demonstrate a *pattern of performance* over some specified length of time. Generally, positive personnel decisions are based on a body of evidence which says, in essence, "no matter what the assignment, this faculty member achieves a certain level of success time after time." The system you will have developed up to this point using the model in this handbook can provide the academic decision-maker with relevant information concerning the pattern of performance and level of success of a faculty member over time.

PROMOTION DECISIONS

Making decisions on whether to promote a faculty member are significantly simplified using the overall composite rating. It is assumed, of course, that the institution has policies concerning the length of time faculty members must be in a given rank or level before they are eligible for promotion to the next rank or level. One such policy, using the overall composite rating, could read as follows:

Promotion Policy Statement (Example)
Promotions from one rank to the next are based on achieving a specified minimum overall composite rating for a specified number of years.

To be promoted from assistant professor to associate professor, the applicant must have served as an assistant professor, or the equivalent, for at least four years and must have achieved a minimum overall composite rating of 2.75 for the three consecutive years prior to consideration for promotion.

Note this policy statement specifies that the applicant must have served a minimum of four years as an assistant professor and must have achieved a minimum overall composite rating of 2.75 or higher. The minimum number of years in rank in this example is arbitrary, as is the value of 2.75. However, the point is that such a policy statement makes it clear that the applicant must achieve and sustain a certain level of "success" for the three years prior to applying for promotion from assistant to associate professor. It is the pattern of performance over time that is important. Also, by specifying a minimum overall composite rating, one can ensure that, regardless of the assignment given, this faculty member is able to consistently experience a level of success that is comparable to faculty already at the associate professor level. One suggested approach to determining what the value of the minimum overall composite rating should be for promotion from assistant to associate professor is to determine the *average* overall composite rating for associate professors and set the minimum entry level at one standard deviation below that average. Similar policy statements could be developed for promotion from associate to full professor.

Even more than promotion decisions, tenure or continuation decisions need to be based on the complete performance history of an individual as it relates to the prediction of future performance. Whereas promotion decisions may be based on an individual's achieving and sustaining a specified level of performance in the three years prior to application for promotion, tenure decisions need to be based on the overall performance of the individual over the entire span of time he or she may have been employed at the institution. The following is an example of the type of policy statement that applies the overall composite rating to tenure decisions:

> *Policy for Awarding Tenure (Example)*
> The awarding of tenure is determined, in part, on achieving of an average overall composite rating of 2.5 for the entire length of time the faculty member has been employed by the college. Generally, no faculty member may be awarded tenure before the completion of five years of employment with the college. However, credit may be given for previous employment. Because the number of applicants for tenure in any given year may exceed the number of available tenure positions as determined by the Board of Regents, achieving the required average overall composite rating in the faculty member's fifth year does not automatically ensure the granting of tenure at that time.

This policy statement specifies a level of success as indicated by the average overall composite rating for the entire length of time the faculty member has worked at the institution. This implies that one or two bad years does not automatically disqualify the person from applying for and being awarded tenure. Again, it is the pattern of performance over time that is being used to make the decision. What this policy says is that, regardless of what assignment this faculty member has had, regardless of the normal ups and downs that affect most careers, *on the average* the faculty member is able to perform at such a level that the college is willing to make a long-term commitment for continued employment.

Also with this approach, no single person makes the tenure decision. Here the decision-making rationale of the administration has been codified, and it is clear what conditions must be met before tenure may be granted. The same holds true for the promotion decisions described in the previous section. It must be emphasized that this procedure does not restrict, or in any way limit, the decision-making authority of the administration. The values and decision-making rules used are simply built into the procedure for using the the faculty evaluation data.

In this section a merit pay raise is defined to be that increase in pay which may be given based on evidence of meritorious performance. This section does not address cost of living pay raises or raises associated with promotions.

Developing a comprehensive faculty evaluation system that results in an annual overall composite rating for every faculty member significantly simplifies the process of determining merit pay raises. The discussion that follows assumes that the amount of merit money available in the merit raise pool has been determined in the customary fashion for a given institution. State-supported institutions may have their merit pay pool determined by state legislators, while private institutions may have their merit pay pool determined by their board of governors. In any case, it is assumed that a merit pay raise pool of funds is available for distribution.

In computing the merit pay raise for a faculty member based on evidence provided by the faculty evaluation system, it is desirable to make the merit raise a direct function of the faculty member's overall composite rating (OCR). The first step in this process is to compute what can be called the merit unit amount (MUA). Computation of the MUA assumes that

1. The academic unit within which all meritorious faculty will receive a merit raise has been determined. The academic unit may be a department, division, college, or an entire university.

2. A pool of merit raise money has been made available by whatever process is customary at the institution.

3. A specified OCR value has been set which defines the eligibility of faculty for merit raises.

If the assumptions above are met, the MUA may be computed in several ways, depending upon the position the institution takes relative to how much differentiation should be made between those faculty who are barely meritorious and those who are highly meritorious. Below are three different options for computing merit raises which represent the range of positions that an institution may take relative to the distribution of merit raise monies.

Option 1 assumes that not all faculty who fall into the meritorious category are equally meritorious. Thus, faculty who attain the highest meritorious levels will be rewarded to a greater degree than those who barely make it into the meritorious category.

Option 2 assumes that all faculty who achieve the meritorious category should be rewarded as *being* meritorious, with only fine differences being reflected in their merit raises.

Option 3 assumes that fine discriminations between meritorious faculty should not be made. Under this option, faculty are placed in blocks or groups of meritorious performance, and all faculty within the same block receive the same merit raise.

The following examples demonstrate the use of the OCR in computing the merit raise amounts to be distributed to eligible faculty under the assumptions of each option described above. In each case, it is also assumed that the faculty evaluation system has used a common 1 - 4 rating scale for all data.

Option 1

Under this approach, the merit unit amount would be computed as follows:

MUA = Total funds available in merit raise pool*
 Grand total of excess OCRs of eligible faculty

 * The academic unit may be a department, division, or entire college.

Example:
Assume that a policy has been established which states that only faculty who achieve an OCR of 3.00 or greater on our four-point scale are eligible for a merit raise. With our definition of merit raises, such raises are given *in addition* to any cost of living or across the board raises. Further assume that our academic unit is a department with ten faculty, and $10,000 has been made available for its merit raise pool. The faculty in this department, with their various different assignments, have achieved the following OCRs for the year just completed:

Prof. Gray	3.34	Prof. White	3.35
Prof. Green	2.89	Prof. Brown	4.00
Prof. Jones	3.01	Prof. Smith	2.99
Prof. Downs	3.77	Prof. Maple	3.96
Prof. Dean	2.45	Prof. Yews	3.63

As can be seen, professors Green, Smith, and Dean do not qualify for merit raises this year, because their OCRs are less than 3. The first step under this option is compute how much the seven remaining eligible faculty members *exceeded* the minimum OCR cutoff for merit raise eligibility. This is computed by simply subtracting the OCR cutoff value of 3.0 from each faculty member's individual OCR:

Name	OCR	Cutoff		OCR Excess
Prof. Gray	3.34	- 3.00	=	.34
Prof. Brown	4.00	- 3.00	=	1.00
Prof. Jones	3.01	- 3.00	=	.01
Prof. Downs	3.77	- 3.00	=	.77
Prof. Yews	3.63	- 3.00	=	.63
Prof. Maple	3.96	- 3.00	=	.96
Prof. White	3.35	- 3.00	=	.35
Total OCRs in excess of		3.00	=	4.06

The merit unit amount for this department is then computed as

$$MUA \quad = \quad \frac{\$10,000}{4.06} \quad = \quad \$2,463$$

The merit raise for each faculty member is then computed by multiplying the OCR excess by the MUA as follows:

Name	OCR Excess		MUA		Merit Raise
Prof. Gray	.34	x	$2,463.00	=	$ 837.42
Prof. Brown	1.00	x	2,463.00	=	2,463.00
Prof. Jones	.01	x	2,463.00	=	24.63
Prof. Downs	.77	x	2,463.00	=	1,896.51
Prof. Yews	.63	x	2,463.00	=	1,551.69
Prof. Maple	.96	x	2,463.00	=	2,364.48
Prof. White	.35	x	2,463.00	=	862.05

Note the large difference between the merit raise of Professor Jones, who barely makes it into the meritorious category, and Professor Brown who is at the top of the meritorious category.

Option 2

This approach takes the position that those who barely make it into the meritorious range are still meritorious and should receive more than token merit raises. With this approach, the merit unit amount is computed as follows:

MUA = Total funds available in merit raise pool*
 Grand total of OCRs of eligible faculty

 * The academic unit may be a department, division, or entire college.

Example:
In this situation, as before, assume that only faculty who achieve an OCR of 3.00 or greater on our four-point scale are eligible for a merit raise. Assume that our academic unit is a department which has been given $10,000 for its merit raise pool.

Once again, the faculty in this department, with their various different assignments, have achieved the following OCRs for the year just completed:

Name	OCR	Name	OCR
Prof. Gray	3.34	Prof. White	3.35
Prof. Green	2.89	Prof. Brown	4.00
Prof. Jones	3.01	Prof. Smith	2.99
Prof. Downs	3.77	Prof. Maple	3.96
Prof. Dean	2.45	Prof. Yews	3.63

As before, professors Green, Smith, and Dean do not qualify for merit raises this year because their OCRs are less than 3. Under this option, we simply add up all the OCRs for the eligible faculty and divide that total into the raise pool to compute our MUA:

Faculty Eligible for Merit Raises

Name	OCR
Prof. Gray	3.34
Prof. Brown	4.00
Prof. Jones	3.01
Prof. Downs	3.77
Prof. Yews	3.63
Prof. Maple	3.96
Prof. White	3.35
Total OCR	25.06

Under this option, the MUA is computed as:

$$\text{MUA} = \frac{\$10,000}{25.06} = \$399.04$$

Computing the individual merit raises then becomes a simple matter of multiplying each faculty member's OCR by the MUA for the department. The resulting merit pay raises, which are now computed as a direct function of the faculty member's OCR, are

Name	OCR		MUA		Merit Raise
Prof. Gray	3.34	x	$399.04	=	$1,332.79
Prof. Brown	4.00	x	399.04	=	1,596.16
Prof. Jones	3.01	x	399.04	=	1,201.11
Prof. Downs	3.77	x	399.04	=	1,504.38
Prof. Yews	3.63	x	399.04	=	1,448.52
Prof. Maple	3.96	x	399.04	=	1,580.20
Prof. White	3.35	x	399.04	=	1,336.78

Under this option, there is less variability among raises. Professor Jones receives a merit raise of $1,201.11 for an OCR of 3.01, whereas in Option 1 the computed merit raise was only $24.63. Which approach you choose to use depends upon the particular value system of your institution.

Option 3
Another approach is to simply group the eligible faculty into blocks based on their OCR and give the same raise to everyone within a given block. For example, we could arbitrarily decide to give everyone who receives an OCR between 3.0 and 3.5 a merit raise of $1000. In our example below, three faculty would get $1000 merit raises. This would leave $7000 to be distributed among the remaining four faculty. Dividing $7000 by 4 gives us $1750, and so everyone who received an OCR greater than 3.5 gets a merit raise of $1750.

Name	OCR		Merit Raise
Prof. Jones	3.01	=	$1,000.00
Prof. Gray	3.34	=	1,000.00
Prof. White	3.35	=	1,000.00
Prof. Yews	3.63	=	1,750.00
Prof. Downs	3.77	=	1,750.00
Prof. Maple	3.96	=	1,750.00
Prof. Brown	4.00	=	1,750.00

Option 3 is not generally recommended, because it tends to significantly water down the usefulness of an evaluation system that produces an overall composite rating. In addition, setting cutoff points for inclusion into various groups is fraught with political danger. However, it is recognized that in some cases this approach may be more politically acceptable, especially when the faculty evaluation system is first put into place. The example shown above grouped meritorious faculty into only two groups. Obviously, any number of groups can be defined. A generalized procedure for computing the merit raise amount for any number of groups is shown below.

Multiple Groupings

The following steps should be taken in computing merit raise amount for blocks or groups of meritorious faculty:

1. Decide how many meritorious levels or groups you wish to have.

2. Decide the values of the OCR cutoffs for each meritorious level.

3. Divide your meritorious faculty into groups based on the cutoffs established and count the number of people in each group. Label the lowest group (the baseline group) as Group 1, the next higher group as Group 2, and so on up to the highest group.

4. Using the lowest group as the baseline group, decide how much more (percentage) the faculty in Group 2 will receive over those in Group 1 (the baseline group); decide how much more (percentage) Group 3 will receive over those in the baseline group, and so on.

5. Use the following general formula to compute the MUA:

$$MUA = \frac{\text{Total Money Available in Merit Raise Pool}}{[G_1 + G_2(1 + P_1) + \dots + G_i(1 + P_{i-1})]}$$

Where: N = the total number of groups

i = 1, 2, 3, …, N

G_i = the number of faculty in the i th group

P_{i-1} = the percentage increase over Group 1 Group i is to receive. This value must be expressed in its decimal equivalent. [It is apparent that $P_{1-1} = P_0 = 0.0$. That is, the percentage increase which Group 1 is to receive over itself is 0%.]

6. Compute the merit raises for the faculty in each group. The general formula for computing the merit raise amount (MRA) for a given group is:

MRA for Group i = $MUA (1.00 + P_{i-1})$

where i = 1 to N and P_0 is defined as being equal to zero (0.0).

Example:
Let's assume once again we have $10,000 in our merit raise pool and that we have divided our faculty into three groups with the OCR cutoffs for Group 1 set at 3.00–3.50 and the OCR cutoffs for Group 2 set at 3.51–3.80. All faculty with OCRs higher than 3.80 fall into Group 3. The cutoff points are subjectively determined using the natural breaks method often used to set cutoff points for different grades.

Prof. Jones	3.01	
Prof. Gray	3.34	Group 1
Prof. White	3.35	
Prof. Yews	3.63	Group 2
Prof. Downs	3.77	
Prof. Maple	3.96	Group 3
Prof. Brown	4.00	

Group 1 (the baseline group) contains three faculty, Group 2 contains two faculty, and Group 3 contains two faculty. Further assume that we have decided that faculty in Group 2 will receive 50% more than those in the baseline group (Group 1), and faculty in Group 3 will receive 75% more than those in the baseline group (Group 1). As with the cutoff points for the groups, these percentage increases are subjectively determined.

Thus, in terms of our formula for the MUA

N = 3 (Number of Groups)

G_1 = 3 (Number of faculty in Group 1)

G_2 = 2 (Number of faculty in Group 2)

G_3 = 2 (Number of faculty in Group 3)

P_0 = 0.0 (By definition)

P_1 = 0.50 (Faculty in Group 2 will get 50% more)

P_2 = 0.75 (Faculty in Group 3 will get 75% more)

Then, computing

$$MUA = \frac{\text{Total Money Available in Merit Raise Pool}}{[G_1 + G_2(1 + P_1) + \dots + G_i(1 + P_{i-1})]}$$

$$MUA = \frac{\$10,000}{[3 + 2(1.50) + 2(1.75)]}$$

$$MUA = \$1,052.63$$

Using the formula MRA = MUA x $(1 + P_{i-1})$, we compute the merit raises for each group as follows:

Group 1: MRA = $1,052.63 x (1 + 0.0) = $1,052.63

Group 2: MRA = 1,052.63 x (1 + .50) = 1,578.95

Group 3: MRA = 1,052.63 x (1 + .75) = 1,842.10

Thus, the three faculty in Group 1 would each receive a merit raise of $1,053.63, the two in Group 2 would each receive $1,578.95, and the two in Group 3 would each receive $1,842, for a grand total of $9,999.99 or $10,000.

			Merit Raise
Prof. Jones	3.01		$1,052.63
Prof. Gray	3.34	Group 1	1,052.63
Prof. White	3.35		1,052.63
Prof. Yews	3.63		$1,578.95
Prof. Downs	3.77	Group 2	1,578.95
Prof. Maple	3.96		$1,842.10
Prof. Brown	4.00	Group 3	1,842.10
TOTAL			$9,999.99

Note that in each of the examples above, no single administrator or decision-maker determined the merit raise of any given individual. Each merit raise was a direct function of the performance of the individual as reflected by the OCR or index of success. The use of the OCR in determining merit raises or in making any other personnel decision does not eliminate the ability of an administrator or administration to be arbitrary. The setting of cutoff values, the determination of merit pool amounts to be given to any particular department, and similar decisions may all still be arbitrary. What the OCR and its application *do* constrain is capriciousness—that is, the inconsistent application of agreed-upon criteria, standards and procedures in making personnel decisions. Conversely, although the use of the OCR in this way does not eliminate faculty complaints and grievances, it *does* tend to protect the administration from unwarranted charges of prejudice, bias, and unfairness in making personnel decisions.

13

Issues in Designing and Operating
a Faculty Evaluation System

The literature in the field of faculty evaluation contains an abundance of research concerning the theoretical and psychometric underpinnings of a variety of forms, questionnaires, and procedures for use in a faculty evaluation system (See Chapters 14 and 15). However, less attention has been paid to the fundamental, practical, everyday issues and problems that face those responsible for actually operating a fully functioning faculty evaluation program. This chapter addresses a number of practical issues related to designing, developing, and operating a large-scale faculty evaluation system in various academic settings.

PURPOSE OF THE SYSTEM

From a practical standpoint, any faculty evaluation system must ultimately serve both a formative and a summative purpose. That is, the system must provide both the rich diagnostic information for improving or enhancing faculty performance, as well as for providing accurate, reliable, and relevant data on which to base personnel decisions. Faculty evaluation systems that start out ostensibly as formative (i.e., designed to provide feedback to facilitate professional growth and development) almost always end up serving a summative purpose as well. Sooner or later, a faculty member will submit evaluation data as part of the evidence in support of a promotion, tenure, or merit pay decision. Or, conversely, an administrator will ask for certain evaluative data to assist in making a difficult personnel decision concerning a faculty member.

In practice, a singular faculty evaluation system *can* be made to serve both formative and summative purposes. The key to developing and operating such a system is to carefully determine and prescribe the type of data to be gathered and what is to be done with it. The faculty evaluation system should be constructed in such a way that detailed, frequently gathered data are provided in confidence only to the faculty member for diagnostic and feedback purposes. Specified formats for summarizing the detailed data should be developed. See the sample manual in the Appendix for several examples. These formats, which will be used for administrative purposes, should reflect only aggregated data which provide a clear picture of the faculty member's *pattern of performance over time.* In no case should any particular term's detailed evaluative information concerning a faculty member be used for administrative decision-making. The detailed data should provide the basis for self-improvement or faculty development efforts only. The principle to be followed in preparing summative data for administrative purposes is to make certain that the summative data convey a sense of a faculty member's overall performance across time and not just a single term's performance, whether that performance was good or bad.

DATA STORAGE AND CONFIDENTIALITY

Virtually any faculty evaluation system will gather information from students, peers, and administrators, as well as various other sources, depending upon the specific design of the system. From a practical standpoint, a way must be developed for maintaining confidentiality while the data are stored. There are basically two approaches to this: the centralized department file and the individualized portfolio.

Centralized Departmental Files
A number of institutions place the responsibility of gathering and storing faculty evaluation data on the departmental or division head. In this system, a centralized file location is specified, and the department head (or the departmental secretary) controls access to the files. This approach places the responsibility for security and confidentiality on a limited

number of people, namely, the department head and the department secretary.

The advantage to this approach is that it is relatively unlikely that anyone will systematically violate the integrity of the information stored for a given individual faculty member. However, there are a number of disadvantages. First and foremost, it creates a great deal of work for the department head, especially if the department is relatively large. Second, if faculty perceive the central files as the primary evidence on which the administration will make decisions, there is a pronounced tendency for them to put voluminous amounts of material in their files, just to be safe. Finally, faculty may feel that the confidentiality of the information has already been compromised because the department head, as an administrator, will have already seen it. However, if the department head is serving as the chief faculty development officer, as is sometimes the case, this approach can be very effective, especially in relatively small departments.

Portfolio System
A system for accumulating and storing faculty evaluation information which appears to be gaining popularity is the so-called "portfolio system." Under such a system, faculty members themselves are responsible for assembling and maintaining their own files in a specified style and format to create their faculty evaluation portfolio. In some instances, the institution has special three-ring binders produced for the portfolio. The portfolio generally contains clear, step-by-step instructions concerning gathering the faculty evaluation data. Sometimes special file pockets are provided within which to store certain types of documentation, such as published articles, syllabi, and examples of tests. Various summary and data recording sheets are provided so that the faculty member may assemble, in a consistent standardized fashion, the aggregate statistical data which are to be used for personnel decisions. Peter Seldin (1991, 1993) has charted the growth of the portfolio approach to evaluating teaching and has developed a concise and highly effective procedure for assembling and using teaching portfolios to both improve faculty performance and provide data for personnel decisions.

The advantage of the portfolio approach is that individual faculty members are responsible for assembling and maintaining their own evaluation data. No one person must assemble the data for all faculty, as is the case in the centralized filing system. However, this approach assumes a high level of trust between the faculty and the administration, because personnel decisions may rely heavily on the summary or aggregate data assembled in the portfolio.

PEER EVALUATION ISSUES

In many faculty evaluation systems, peer review or peer evaluation plays an important political, if not psychometric, role. Although the idea of peer review is appealing to many faculty, peer review systems are touchy and complicated at the very least. In actual practice, peer review components of faculty evaluation systems provide one of the biggest sources of problems and confusion.

The first step in developing a peer evaluation system should always be the careful review and consideration of the purpose of the system, proposed methods of implementing the system, and the expected outcomes. Distinctions should be made especially between the use of peer evaluation for formative (improvement) versus summative (judgmental) purposes. Although a system may be adequate for formative development of faculty, it may not fulfill administrative needs or legal requirements for summative purposes. Ideally, this first step is tempered by the study of reports of existing systems and the research literature on peer evaluation. Systems that are developed hastily are seldom adequate or effective.

What Should Peers Evaluate?
The first consideration in developing a peer evaluation system should involve the definition of *what* should be evaluated by peers. Typically, three broad components of faculty activity are defined: teaching, research, and service. Within each of these components, however, numerous activities of the faculty member are potentially available for inclusion in the evaluation process. It is especially important to realize that the ultimate validity of a peer system rests directly on what faculty activities are chosen for review by peers. That is, peers may be excellent judges of certain activities but very poor judges of other activities. Therefore, the development of a good peer evaluation system requires that careful consideration be given to those activities or elements that are to be judged by peers, by students, etc. For example, most experts agree (Aleamoni, 1982; Centra, 1979; Cohen & McKeachie, 1980) that teaching should not be evaluated by peers as classroom observers. A more cost-efficient and reliable use of peer judgments of teaching effectiveness would be in reviewing written documentation (e.g., instructional plans, course materials and examinations, instructional methods). Therefore, an important initial step in developing a peer evaluation system is the complete specification of the faculty activities to be reviewed by peers. This specification process is not unlike creating instructional objectives for teaching a course or the specification process that occurs in designing and reporting an experiment. For the purposes of reliability and to conform with recent legal decisions, this

specification process should result in an explicit, written protocol that defines exactly what activities are to be reviewed by peers and what weights are assigned to each activity reviewed (i.e., some faculty activities may be deemed more important than others.)

How Should Peer Input be Gathered?

A second consideration involves *how* peer judgments are to be elicited, categorized, and summarized. Several methods of peer evaluation have been used, including surveys and questionnaires, rating and ranking systems, and open-ended written questions and comments. In designing methods for a peer evaluation system, the developer should be concerned primarily with the objectivity and reliability of the method chosen. That is, the particular method chosen is much less important than the development of procedures that will ensure impartial, less subjective, and reliable peer judgments. This process is facilitated to the extent that written documentation is submitted for peer review. For example, peer review of written course materials (e.g., course syllabus, course outline, texts and reading assignments, handouts, homework) is more likely to result in less subjective and more reliable peer judgments of teaching effectiveness than peer responses to a general attitude or opinion survey.

The research literature is quite consistent in reporting a strong positive bias in any peer evaluation system. The peer system must, therefore, be designed to ensure the reli-

able differentiation of different levels of faculty performance. This process is aided by explicitly defining criteria for evaluation and by establishing minimum standards for each criterion. For example, peer review of the adequacy of an instructor's course materials might focus on several criteria for judgment: comprehensiveness, organization, relation to course and learning objectives, currency, etc. Ideally, each criterion must be defined explicitly and accompanied by a minimum standard of performance. For example, the currency of course materials might be accompanied by a standard requiring that at least 20% of course content is based on recent developments (last five years, perhaps) in the field.

Care must also be exercised in designing peer evaluation systems to ensure that peer judgments are not influenced or confounded by irrelevant factors. A common difficulty in many instruments used for peer evaluation is the inadequacy of the response or rating scales. To reduce these difficulties, descriptions used to label points on a response scale should be relevant for the item and should define each point on the scale. Such scales should always be accompanied by explicit instructions and, whenever possible, the minimum standard for each scale point.

Two examples of peer review documents that are unlikely to produce consistent and accurate judgments are presented in Figure 22.

Figure 22   Examples from Two Peer Review Documents That Do Not Allow for Consistent and Accurate Judgments

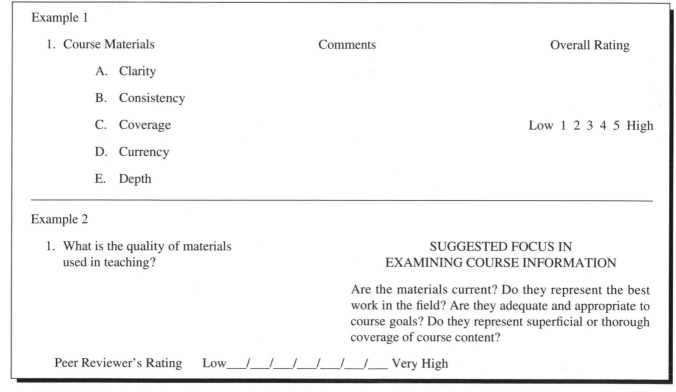

Arreola, R.A. (1995). *Developing a Comprehensive Faculty Evaluation System.* Bolton, MA: Anker Publishing Co., Inc.

Several difficulties may arise with an instrument like that presented as Example 1. First, no standards are provided to allow the reviewers to judge the degrees of, for example, clarity and consistency relative to departmental requirements. Additionally, without explicit definitions of these criteria, reviewers may not agree in their interpretation of the criteria. The overall rating scale is also not well defined. The labels are only marginally relevant to several of the criteria. Furthermore, the interior points of the scale are not labeled. This allows the possibility of divergent definitions of these points by different respondents.

The potential for difficulties in Example 2 is similar to that in Example 1. In both of these examples, it is left to the whim of the reviewer to determine what standards to use in making a qualitative judgment. Such poorly developed systems may therefore result in judgments that are based on questionable or irrelevant information. For example, Centra (1979) reports a study in which peer ratings of teaching effectiveness were related to office location! Such approaches to peer evaluation may result in little more than popularity ratings.

Who are Peers?

A third major consideration in developing peer evaluation systems involves those included in the peer judgment process. Some peer evaluation systems include all members of a department in the judgment process. In such a system, each faculty member would evaluate all other departmental faculty. This approach is very expensive in time expended. Furthermore, such approaches are often less reliable and less effective than alternative approaches. For example, Centra (1975) reported an average correlation of only +0.26 among ratings of faculty by all peers in a department. Additionally, many peer evaluation systems attempt to guard against several potential problems of peer review by selecting smaller numbers of peer judges. For example, several systems attempt to avoid problems arising from direct competition for promotion and tenure by using only tenured faculty in the peer review process. For the purposes of obtaining reliable measurement, a minimum of three peers is necessary. It also appears from the research literature that the use of more than six peer evaluators does not improve the quality of evaluation and may, in some cases, be a detriment to valid and reliable measurement.

A second issue in considering who conducts the evaluation relates to whether reviewers should be anonymous. As with student ratings of faculty, anonymity is more likely to produce candid and meaningful peer evaluation. In fact, if peer evaluation is not anonymous, the positive bias of peers may result in undifferentiated, high evaluations of faculty.

Many different methods have been used to select peer evaluators. Several systems have used departmental standing committees for peer evaluation and others have formed committees by general departmental election. Neither approach safeguards against problems of committee composition (positive or negative bias, etc.). Several systems that do provide some safeguards for composition include procedures for the selection of peers by the faculty member and also by the dean or department head.

PEER REVIEW AND EVALUATION COMMITTEES

Generally, peer review components of faculty evaluation systems involve a committee, sometimes made up of all the tenured faculty, all the senior faculty, or some like combination. The function of such a peer committee is to review all the evidence (e.g., student rating form printouts, letters of recommendation, other peer or colleague comments, and articles published) and make a decision or recommendation to the administration. When there are a number of faculty submitting their materials for review at the same time, the task can be daunting. In addition, such committees can often bring subjective impressions, friendships, and hostilities into the decision-making process. Such an approach also has the unfortunate side effect of giving second-hand information or hearsay evidence much greater impact than should be the case. Committee members may bring to the deliberations positive or negative opinions concerning the faculty member's teaching performance based on random or limited student comments. This approach may be considered as a *traditional hierarchical peer review model* (Figure 23).

Note that in the traditional hierarchical peer review model, there is repeated processing of the same material. That is, the peer committees, the department head, and the dean all have the opportunity to examine all of the information available in the faculty member's file: student ratings; peer or colleague reports concerning research, teaching, or college service; self-reports; as well as the reports of others such as alumni, employers of graduating students, etc. With the traditional hierarchical peer review model, opportunities exist at each level for the entry of new or anecdotal information that may or may not be relevant to the decision being made. Such information may have the effect of biasing the recommendations made at each level. In these situations, it is possible for a faculty member to be recommended positively at each level for promotion, tenure, or some other personnel action, yet be turned down at the highest level. The converse is also possible, although less frequent. This result is possible in the traditional hierarchical peer review model, because different value systems may be applied to the evaluation of the data provided. What a peer review committee or administrator at one level finds good and valuable performance, a peer review committee or an administrator at another level may find to be of little or no value.

Figure 23   Traditional Hierarchical Peer Review Model

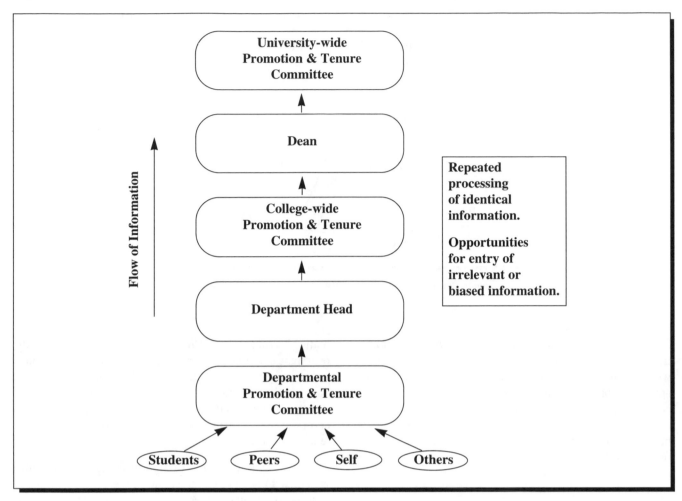

Arreola, R.A. (1995). *Developing a Comprehensive Faculty Evaluation System.* Bolton, MA: Anker Publishing Co., Inc.

If the value structure of the institution has been determined and carefully integrated into the construction of the faculty evaluation system as specified in earlier chapters, peer review can assume a much more consistent and valuable role. In a faculty evaluation system where the values assigned to teaching, research, and service by the department, college, and university have been determined and specified; where the value or weight to be placed on the information provided by the sources has been agreed to; and where the performance levels which qualify for promotion, tenure, continuation, or merit pay have all been determined and placed into policy statements, an alternate and potentially much fairer peer review model becomes possible (Figure 24).

In this model, the peer review committee that examines all the information for all faculty and then forwards it to the next level administrator is replaced by what may be called the institutional/college/departmental value filter. That is,

as noted in earlier chapters, all constituencies to the faculty evaluation system—students, peers, self, department head, dean, and others—have been identified and the appropriate information gathered from each. That information has been weighted in accordance with the consensus value structure of the institution and combined with all other information to form the overall evaluation. This process of gathering, weighting, and combining information can be thought of as the application of the value filters for the department, college, and entire institution. The outcome of such a process may then be interpreted through the previously determined set of policies governing promotion, tenure, etc. These policies form the decision-making rule system for the institution. Notice that with this approach the power and authority of the administration is neither diminished nor diluted. Rather, the decision-making rule system followed by the administration is simply codified in advance so everyone knows what it is. This approach does not keep administrators from being *arbitrary*. However, it does constrain them

Figure 24   Lateral Peer Review Model

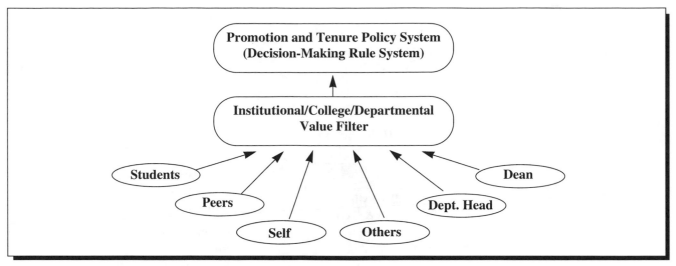

Arreola, R.A. (1995). *Developing a Comprehensive Faculty Evaluation System.* Bolton, MA: Anker Publishing Co., Inc.

from being *capricious*. The administration may still arbitrarily determine procedures, criteria, and standards by which faculty performance will be judged. However, this approach constrains the administration to apply these procedures, criteria, and standards *consistently* to all faculty because the decision-making rule system is codified and built into the evaluation system. In this model, the peers are represented by a peer review committee or several peer review committees using the triad peer review committee structure described later.

Early in this handbook, we noted that faculty evaluation requires the careful combination of both political and psychometric requirements. Therefore, it should be recognized that, for political reasons, it may be necessary to have a peer review oversight committee somewhere in the faculty evaluation system. Figure 25 shows an alternate lateral peer review model which accommodates this requirement.

In this variation, it is recommended that the peer review oversight committee limit its work to simply ensuring that due process has been followed in gathering and assembling the information from the various sources and that the appropriate value filter has been correctly applied to the data. If the oversight peer review committee concerns itself with reevaluating all the data provided by the various sources, we are once again faced with the possibility of the entry of irrelevant or biasing information into the decision-making process. However, this possibility is somewhat less than in the traditional hierarchical peer review model (Figure 23). If a strong need is felt to have an oversight peer review committee, the question must be asked, What information is the committee going to consider that has not been considered earlier by someone closer to the source of infor-

mation? What criteria for judging the information is the oversight peer review committee going to apply that have not been applied to the data earlier? If some new criteria, values, or information needs to be considered by the oversight peer review committee, then those criteria, values, and information requirements should be built into the system at an earlier level.

The primary need for an oversight peer review committee generally grows out of the situation where the values and criteria for evaluating faculty performance at the departmental or college level differs markedly from that at the institutional or university-wide level. If the process for developing a comprehensive faculty evaluation system described in earlier chapters has been followed, such differences should have already been resolved and the need for an oversight peer review committee obviated.

Peer Review: The Best Source Principle
In practice, peer input should be provided as simply one of several sources of information in a comprehensive faculty evaluation system. A peer review component of a faculty evaluation system should limit itself to using colleagues or peers to provide information which requires a professional perspective or for which peers are the primary, best source of information. If peer input is to be gathered concerning a faculty member's classroom teaching performance, then the faculty evaluation system should specify a classroom visitation policy or procedure. Guidelines must be developed which clearly specify what behavior or performance is to be observed and rated. Ideally, a training program should be set up to prepare faculty peers to be accurate and reliable observers.

Developing a Comprehensive Faculty Evaluation System

Figure 25   Alternate Lateral Peer Review Model

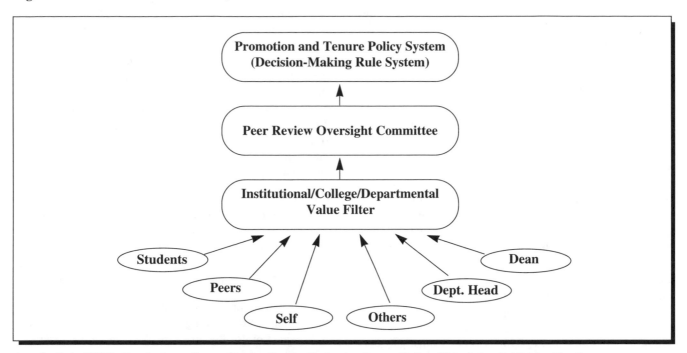

Arreola, R.A. (1995). *Developing a Comprehensive Faculty Evaluation System.* Bolton, MA: Anker Publishing Co., Inc.

Practical experience leads one to suggest that faculty peer evaluation restricts itself to those areas of professional performance requiring knowledge of the content field of the faculty member: for example, assessing the correctness and completeness of the content in a given course or judging the contribution a given article makes to the literature in the faculty member's content field. In any case, the principle recommended concerning peer evaluation is to gather only that information from faculty peers for which they are the primary or best source. Peer evaluation systems which ask a peer committee to review the ratings of students or other such evaluative information and come forth with another, singular evaluation based on their deliberations tend to create more problems than they solve.

Peer Review: The Triad Model

If separate peer review committees are required and tasked with making such summary judgments, a good form to follow is the three-member, or triad, peer committee structure (Figure 26). In the triad peer review committee model, a three-person committee is appointed for every faculty member. One member of the committee is selected by the department head, one member is selected from a group of peers recommended by the faculty member being evaluated, and one member is appointed from the faculty at large, perhaps by the dean. In this way, no one faculty member will have to sit on more than three peer review committees, and each committee will concern itself with only one faculty member.

Under this triad approach, the third member appointed from the faculty at large does not necessarily have to be from the same content field as the person being evaluated. The primary function of the at-large third member is to ensure that the proper deliberative process, prescribed by the faculty evaluation system, is followed. It is assumed that the other two members will adequately represent the perspective of professionals from the content field. Also, because the faculty being evaluated will have one person on the committee that he or she nominated, it is unlikely that any negative biases on the part of the other two members will unduly

Figure 26   Triad Peer Review Committee Model

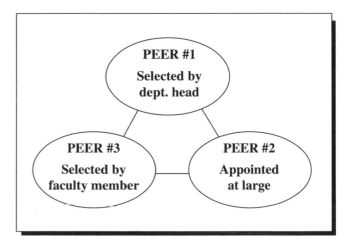

affect the the outcome of the committee's deliberations. Likewise, any unwarranted positive biases by the two content peers will be off-set by the assumed neutrality of the at-large member.

Because the triad peer review committee concerns itself with only one faculty member, it is much easier to assign it more detailed and evaluatively relevant tasks. Such tasks may include in-depth assessment of course design, course materials, examinations, published articles, professional development, or any of a host of other activities and roles which only peers may be best qualified to judge. Separate triad peer review committees may be assigned to provide evaluative information on different aspects of a faculty member's performance. For example, one triad committee may provide information concerning the instructional design of the courses being taught. Another committee may provide information concerning the faculty member's research performance, and yet another on the college or community service provided by the faculty member. In any case, the operational principles to be followed here are (1) each triad committee considers the performance of only *one* individual, and (2) the triad committee members be selected on the basis of the *best source* principle noted earlier.

PRACTICAL CONSIDERATIONS IN OPERATING STUDENT RATING SYSTEMS

Easily the largest and most visible component of a faculty evaluation system is the student rating form and its computerized output. Over the years, for good or ill, student ratings have come to be the single most important component of faculty evaluation systems. Unfortunately, this has led to the development of a plethora of student rating instruments by faculty, students, administrators, and faculty evaluation committees. While this situation is not necessarily endorsed, from a practical perspective it must acknowledged in dealing with the problems that arise from designing and operating a large-scale student rating system.

In keeping with the concept of designing and operating the faculty evaluation system in such a way as to serve both formative and summative purposes, several guidelines related to student rating systems may be stated. First, it must be recognized that the value of any student rating system relies on the confidence the students have that their input will (1) cause them no harm, and (2) have some effect on the instructor (Arreola, 1987). In actual practice, operating a student rating system requires a careful balancing of the needs and concerns of the students, faculty, and administration. These needs and concerns are sometimes antithetical to one another. This can often place the person in charge of the office or agency running the student rating system in a very difficult and tricky situation.

On the one hand, faculty may be fearful and distrustful of the administration. Faculty go through a predictable set of stages in resisting or attempting to escape from a faculty evaluation system as noted earlier. On the other hand, students are fearful of retribution by the faculty if they give negative ratings and don't believe the faculty or the administration will pay any attention to what they say anyway. Finally, the administration may desperately want any kind of quantitative or hard data on which to base difficult personnel decisions. Long experience with these circumstances leads to the following practical guidelines pertaining to running a student rating system:

1. If at all possible, *do not* locate a student rating coordination or processing agency in the office of a dean, vice president, or other major administrator. Such placement only reinforces the idea that the student rating system and the faculty evaluation office are simply watchdog agencies of the administration.

2. Try to locate the student rating form processing office in a test scoring center, computer center, media center, or, ideally, in a faculty development center.

3. Arrange the processing schedule so that the completed analyses of the student rating forms are not available until after final grades have been reported.

4. Maintain student credibility. Conduct a program to maintain the credibility of the students in the student rating system. Include regular contacts with student government, appoint student representative(s) to the faculty evaluation development committee, include stories concerning use of student ratings in student newspapers at least once each term. A constant communication campaign with the students must be maintained which informs them that the faculty member will not see the student rating results until after grades have been reported and that the student ratings are taken seriously by the faculty and the administration (Arreola, 1983). Without such a campaign, the student rating system will experience serious problems, including refusal of the students to complete forms, completing forms by simply marking the same response for all items, and covering the forms with various types of graffiti. The GIGO (Garbage In Garbage Out) principle applies here.

5. Make it clear that the student rating form processing office is a service to the *faculty* and not the administration or the student government. *Do not* automatically send results of the ratings to the administration or the student newspaper, even though written permission has been given by the instructor. Such actions will forever taint the credibility of the processing office. Require anyone wanting information

concerning the student ratings of a faculty member to get them from *that* faculty member. See 6, below.

6. Make certain that the issue of the distribution of copies of faculty evaluation printouts is a matter between the administration and the faculty or between the students and the faculty. Provide the faculty member with multiple copies of the student rating form analyses or other results; do not keep copies in the processing office. Make it physically difficult to recover or reconstitute a given faculty member's computer analysis. The best approach is to maintain only raw data files on disk or tape. Then, if a request is received by the processing office to provide copies of a particular faculty member's evaluation results, it can truthfully be said that the processing office has no copies but that the faculty member has several.

The issue of the confidentiality and distribution of student rating or faculty evaluation results should be a matter between the faculty member and the administration and not between the processing office and the administration. The processing office must not be perceived as an arm of a "big brother" administration.

DESIGNING A STUDENT RATING FORM

The following is an outline of the steps that should be taken in designing a student rating form. Chapter 16 contains a more detailed description of these steps.

Determine the purpose of the form. That is, determine if the form is to serve as a *formative*, a *summative*, or *both a formative and a summative* evaluation tool. The types of questions asked and the design of the data analysis and distribution depend greatly on the purpose of the form.

Specify the elements to be addressed in the form.

Course:	organization, structure, objectives, difficulty, pace, relevance, content, usefulness, etc.
Instruction:	instructor characteristics, instructor skill, clarity of presentation, instructor rapport, method of presentation, student interaction, etc.
Learning:	student satisfaction, student perceived competency, student desire to continue study in the field, etc.

Identify or select appropriate types of items to be used. The *accuracy* of the rater's responses and the *meaningfulness* of the ratings to the instructor depend upon the appropriateness of the item response formats. Considering the intended use for the form, determine what combination of the following types of items are best suited for measuring each element.

High inference:	used for summative decisions and employs scales such as partial-fair, autocratic-democratic, or dull-stimulating
Low inference:	used for formative decisions and uses frequency ratings on scales such as gesturing, variation in voice, asking questions, or praise and encouragement
Open-ended:	free-response items usually produce a colorful array of responses in the student's own words but provide very little representative (consensus) information for the instructor to use in formative evaluation
Close-ended:	limited-response items can provide accurate counts on the types of responses to each item

1. Type of close-ended responses is largely determined by the type of question being asked. If one is not careful, incongruous and unreliable responses will result.

2. Example: "Was the instructor enthusiastic?" dictates a Yes or No response, not an Agree Strongly to Disagree Strongly response.

3. Neutral or Don't Know responses should be used only if they represent necessary options; otherwise many will choose them rather than make a considered response.

4. Do not use a continuum response format with only the end points anchored. Example:

   GOOD_/_/_/_/_/_/_/_/_ BAD

5. If behaviorally anchored response scales are to be used, make certain that the behavioral descriptions along the continuum are elaborated clearly and concisely.

Prepare/select items.
1. Prepare appropriate item types for the elements to be measured.

2. Have items edited by someone other that the item writers.

3. Have the items independently reviewed by other competent colleagues.

4. Rewrite the items based upon the results of the editorial review.

5. When selecting items, if possible draw them from existing questionnaires or item pools rather than writing them from scratch.

6. Conduct a careful content analysis of the selected items.

Organize items in the questionnaire.
1. Determine if grouping and labeling of the items is appropriate or necessary.

2. Mix positive and negative items to guard against the response set phenomenon.

3. Determine if subscales should be identified on the form.

Determine the reliability and validity of the questionnaire through experimental administration.
1. Administer the form to sufficiently large groups to provide an adequate basis for the appropriate statistical analysis.

2. Conduct a factor analysis of the trial responses and determine if the factor structure matches the intended rating elements. If the structure does not match or has weak factor loadings, select alternative items and readminister.

3. Estimate the reliability of the items, subscales, and entire questionnaire by using the appropriate statistical analyses.

4. Determine the validity of the total questionnaire.

5. Conduct a pilot study using the completed questionnaire.

TYPES OF
STUDENT EVALUATION RATING SYSTEMS

Keeping in mind the steps for designing a student evaluation rating instrument and the necessity of conducting reliability and validity studies on the resulting instrument, several different student evaluation rating systems that may be considered.

Instructor-Constructed

The least defensible type of system is the one made up by a particular instructor for a particular course. Such a situation really does not constitute a rating system but rather is generally the result of an attempt to do something about responding to pressure to have a student rating system—without really doing anything.

Instructor-Selected

A more defensible type of system is one where the instructor may select from a finite pool of items made available by the institution for use in evaluating teaching. The students respond to these items on a standardized rating form that includes a common set of general items used by all instructors. One of the earliest examples of such a pool is the Purdue Cafeteria System, which provides a 200-item catalog. Instructors select their items, which are then computer-printed on an optically scanned answer sheet along with five standard general items. Normative data are provided only for the five general items. Derry (1977) reported that the average reliability of a cafeteria rating form was 0.88. Other similar examples of this type are the Instructor and Course Evaluation System (ICES) of the University of Illinois at Urbana-Champaign, the Instructor Designed Questionnaire (IDQ) of the University of Michigan, and the Student Perceptions of Teaching (SPOT) of the University of Iowa (Abrami & Murphy, 1980).

Standard Form—Optional Items

The most defensible type of student rating system is one that has a standard section of items applicable to almost all courses and instructors with additional optional item sections that allow the instructor to select supplementary (or more diagnostic) items from a catalog. One of the earliest and continuing examples is the Course/Instructor Evaluation Questionnaire (CIEQ) system which provides a standard section of 21 items on which normative data are provided by item and five subscales and two optional 21-item response sections that allow instructors to select up to 42 additional items from a 373-item catalog. Aleamoni and Stevens (1986) reported test-retest reliabilities for the 21 standard items from 0.81 to 0.94 and for the subscales and total from 0.92 to 0.98. Other examples of this type are the Instructional Development and Effectiveness Assessment System (IDEA) of Kansas State University, the Student Instructional Report (SIR) of Educational Testing Service, and the Student Instructional Rating System (SIRS) of Michigan State University (Abrami & Murphy, 1980).

Multiple Standard Forms

Another type of system is one that consists of multiple standard forms. The instructor's only choice here is the type of form, not the items. The University of Washington Instructional Assessment System (IAS) provides six forms to their faculty, one for small lecture/discussion courses, one for large lecture courses, one for seminar courses, one for problem-solving courses, one for skills-oriented or practicum courses, and one for quiz sections. Reliabilities from 0.15 to 0.34 for single raters to 0.88 and above for classes of 40 students have been reported (Abrami & Murphy, 1980).

Administration of Student Evaluation Rating Systems

After an appropriate instrument has been developed or selected, administration procedures need to be established. As noted earlier, if possible the responsibility for managing and directing a campus-wide program of administering student ratings should be placed in the hands of instructional development, evaluation, or testing personnel. One should avoid placing such responsibility either in the hands of students or faculty in individual departments or colleges, because its application would be restricted and the possibility of a lasting program would be reduced. As a last option, the responsibility may be assumed by the office of the chief academic officer of the institution. However, the danger of having the program perceived as a watchdog program of the administration is increased in such cases.

The method of administering and gathering student responses can determine the quality of the resulting data. It is advisable to administer the instrument in a formalized manner in the classroom by providing a standard set of instructions and enough time to complete all the items. If the instrument is administered in an informal manner, without a standard set of instructions and a designated time to fill it out, the students tend not to take it seriously and possibly do not bother to turn it in. Furthermore, if the students are permitted to take the instruments home to fill them out and return them at the next class meeting, very few instruments will be returned.

The following practical procedures have been successfully used in managing large student rating systems. These procedures assume that the faculty member will not be the primary person administering the rating forms in class to the students.

1. Set up a log system for maintaining control of student rating form distribution and collection. This log should contain the name of the faculty member, the number of the course, and the enrollment. Such information is generally available from the registrar's office.

2. Prepare student rating packets with at least five more sheets than the official number enrolled in the course. Log in the actual number of sheets sent to the instructor.

3. In addition to the student rating forms, the packet should contain a standardized script to be read when administering the forms and a proctor identification form (PIF). Upon receipt of the packet, the faculty member should remove the PIF and indicate the name of the student in the class who has been selected to administer the rating forms. The faculty member must sign the PIF and return it separately to the processing office. The processing office should log in the date of the receipt of the form and the name of the student proctor.

4. After removing the PIF, the faculty member should give the student rating form package to the chosen student proctor. The student proctor removes and distributes the student rating forms and removes and reads a special form identified as the proctor administration form. It contains the standardized script for administering the student rating form. In addition to the standard information concerning the use of a #2 pencil to record student responses, the script should note that

   a. The faculty member is not in the room.

   b. The results of the rating will not be returned to the instructor until after final grades have been turned in.

   c. The students' responses will be an important part of the information considered in improving the course or making promotion, tenure, retention, and merit pay decisions.

5. The proctor must sign the proctor administration form, certifying that the student rating forms were administered in accordance to the instructions, that the script was read as part of the administration, and that the faculty member was not in the room.

6. Finally, cross-checking items should be included on the student rating forms that ask such questions as, Was the instructor in the room when this form was administered? Did the proctor read the administration directions out loud to the class? and, Do you have confidence that your responses will make a difference?

7. After the forms are completed and returned to the proctor, they should all be placed in the envelope, along with the signed proctor administration form, and dropped in the campus mail to the processing office.

8. Upon receipt of the packet, the date of receipt should be logged in, the name on the proctor administration form should be checked against the name reported by the instructor on the proctor identification form. A count is made of the incoming completed student rating forms to make sure that the number does not exceed the official enrollment figure for the class. This latter step is designed to discourage stuffing of completed student rating packets by either students or, in certain instances, the faculty themselves.

9. Before machine processing, the student rating forms must be visually scanned for stray marks. Often the students doodle in the margins or simply cross out an incorrect response rather than erase it. These types of marks must be erased before the sheets can be processed. Experience has shown that the student rating processing office would be well advised to buy electric erasers rather than using the eraser end of a pencil. The time and staff size required to carry out this necessary step is often much larger than would first be anticipated. This is especially true if the system is new and the students are not yet familiar with the rating forms.

10. Finally, log the date when the completed computer analysis and student rating forms were returned to the faculty member.

OPTIONS FOR ADMINISTERING RATING FORMS IN CLASS

The steps above assume that a student proctor, selected from the class itself, administers the rating form. Other options, some less desirable than others, are possible.

Self-Administered

In systems where instructors administer their own questionnaires, they also should read the standard set of instructions after the forms have been distributed and then remain in the front of the room until all forms have been completed. The instructor may then select a student from the class to gather the completed forms and deposit them in the campus mail. As before, the statement read should specify that the instructor will not see the results until after the term grades have been turned into the Admissions and Records Office. The exception to this procedure is when the instructor has informed the students that their responses will be used in a formative way to improve the current course.

Student Government Administered

Another option is to have representatives of the student government association administer the instruments if the faculty and department or college administrators are willing or request them to do it. The students administering the instruments should also read a similar standard set of instructions and request that the instructor leave during the administration. The student organization could use the campus newspaper to announce when the instruments are going to be used and how they will be administered as a final cross-checking procedure.

Staff-Administered

If an administrator decides to designate a staff member to administer the instrument, then the same procedures should be followed as suggested above. This option should be avoided, however, unless there is no other way to ensure a common administration of the instruments. As noted earlier, faculty and students tend to feel threatened if they know that an administrator is controlling and directing the administration or processing of the instruments.

When the rating instrument is administered, the students should have all necessary materials. Students should generally fill out the forms in their regular classroom near the beginning of a particular class session. Above all, the students must be left with the impression that their frank and honest comments are desired and not that this is their chance to get back at the instructor. If the students get the impression that the instructor is not really interested in their responses, they will not respond seriously. If the students feel the instructor is going to see their responses before final grades are in, they will respond more positively and write very few comments. This is especially true if the students are asked to identify themselves on the instrument. If the instrument is administered immediately before, during, or after the final examination (or any other meaningful examination), the students tend to respond in an inconsistent manner. If students are allowed to discuss the course and instructor while filling out the forms, then biases will enter into their ratings.

REPORTING STUDENT RATING RESULTS

One of the most important aspects of any program is the method of reporting the results. If the results are not reported in an appropriate, accurate, and timely manner, the usefulness of the instrument and the system as a whole will be seriously compromised. When tabulating and summarizing item responses, the following procedures should be considered:

1. The item responses should be weighted (that is, given numerical values) in order to calculate descriptive statistics, and the descriptive statistics should be reported.

2. The results should be reported by item and subscale, if appropriate.

3. The results should be summarized by class section, department, college, and so on.

Directionality of Numerical Scale

When items are presented with defined response scales, such as Agree Strongly, Agree, Disagree, and Disagree Strongly, they should be weighted to reflect direction and ideal response when the results are tabulated and summarized. For example, if the above response scale were weighted 4, 3, 2, 1, respectively, it would indicate that the item was positively stated with the ideal response being Agree Strongly. With such a weighting, it is possible to calculate a mean and standard deviation for each item for a given class of students. The mean value indicates their average rating and the standard deviation indicates how similar or dissimilar their responses were. With such a weighting scheme and the resulting means and standard deviations, the results can then be reported for both items and subscales. The results can also be summarized and reported by class section, course, selected courses, courses within a department, courses within a college, and courses within the university. Such complete reporting schemes permit meaningful comparisons when necessary.

Distributing Rating Results—Voluntary Systems

An important aspect of any system of reporting student evaluation rating results is who will or should actually see the results. If the administration of the instruments is completely voluntary, then only the faculty members themselves should receive the results. As noted earlier, the processing office is ill-advised to enter into an arrangement that places it between the faculty and the administration.

Distributing Results—Mandatory Systems

If the administration of the student rating form is mandatory, as is the case in many systems, then every effort should be made by the processing office to remove itself from the responsibility of distributing rating results directly. However, if the processing office has no choice and the system must be designed to provide faculty with the option of releasing copies of their results to other interested parties, great effort must be taken to ensure that the instructor feels no pressure to release the results. In such a circumstance, a procedure must be implemented that requires a formal written release by the instructor. The processing office in such a situation would be well-advised to consult with the college or university attorney in developing the wording of such a release. Every effort must be made to make faculty members aware of who is to receive copies of their results and how frequently. Under no circumstances, however, should students' written comments be reported to administrators or student organizations, because those comments tend to be susceptible to widely discrepant subjective interpretations by the reader.

Publishing Rating Results

If the faculty or administration has entered into an agreement with the campus student organization to publish the results of the student ratings, every effort should be made to ensure fair and accurate reporting of the results. Such results are usually reported in a book divided by discipline or content area. Student-published books are usually promoted as course and instructor guides for prospective student enrollees as well as vehicles to encourage instructional improvement. Unfortunately, due to the overzealousness of some student editors and the vendettas of others, such publications have tended to simply generate antagonistic relationships between the rated faculty and student editors.

One vehicle to disseminate student ratings of faculty to a wider segment of the student body is the student newspaper. The most effective way to present such results is to do so in a positive manner. For example, only the names or course numbers of the most highly rated are reported; the others are not mentioned. Whoever is responsible for publishing student ratings for mass consumption should remember that accentuating the positive, rather than focusing on the negative, results in better acceptance, continued participation, and potential instructional improvement on the part of the participating faculty members. Any attempt to be cute or to "get" an instructor usually results in short-lived systems with serious negative repercussions.

Format of the Student Rating Form Computerized Analysis Output

It has been assumed that virtually every operational student rating form system produces some form of computerized analysis output. This output may range from a simple frequency count for each response to each item up to a very sophisticated printout showing normative data of various sorts. Experience has shown that most faculty react to a sophisticated printout that contains page after page of indices, norms, graphs, and tables with something less than total enthusiasm. Although professional standards demand that the analysis of student rating data be accurate and statistically sound, it must be remembered that most faculty are not well-versed in the the intricacies of item analysis, measurement theory, or statistical analysis. Moreover, most faculty have no real desire to become well-versed in these areas. Thus, for the computerized analysis of student rating results to have the desired effect of providing useful information which may be acted upon by the faculty member for self-improvement, an effort must be made to make these computerized analyses user friendly. One way of doing this is to provide a verbal summary sheet which translates the statistical information into general statements.

For example, if the student rating form has four response choices per item, it is clear that a standard deviation exceeding 1.00 would indicate wide disparity of responses to the item. In such a case, the mean item would have little value other than to represent the numerical average of the responses. The computer program can be written to produce a statement such as the following:

On item 6 , the standard deviation was 1.3 . This can be interpreted to mean that there was **considerable disagreement** among the students on this item and thus the Average Response value should NOT be interpreted as representing a consensus rating by the class.

Or, the program could present a statement such as

On item __18__, the average response was __3.1__ and the standard deviation was __0.4__. This can be interpreted to mean that the students rated you as being **moderately high** on this item and there was a **high** degree of consensus among the students in this rating.

Ideally, such statements should be printed as either the first or the last page in a computer analysis so it is easily found. Obviously, the program must be written to make the proper interpretations of various combinations of data relative to the appropriate norms. The point, though, is that even though the processing office may produce reports which are statistically sophisticated and correct, one must never lose sight of the fact that for the analyses to be useful they must be understood and used by the faculty. Again, as a practical guideline, providing computerized, written interpretations of the statistical information listed in the printout is highly effective in helping to promote the effectiveness of the student rating information.

INTERPRETING AND USING STUDENT RATING RESULTS

Although we may wish our analyses to be user friendly, they must still present data of sufficient clarity and detail to permit sophisticated interpretations. How accurately and meaningfully the results of student ratings are interpreted and used depends on the type of information provided to the participating faculty member and other interested parties. The research on student ratings has revealed a definite positive response bias, which needs to be addressed when interpreting and using the results. That is, if students are asked to respond to positively stated items using a four-point scale of Agree Strongly, Agree, Disagree, and Disagree Strongly, the responses tend to be distributed as shown in Figure 27. To someone not familiar with statistics, the midpoint of the four-point scale (2.5) could easily be interpreted as average, and any rating higher than 2.5 could be interpreted as a positive rating. But, as Figure 27 shows, the easy interpretation that any rating of 2.5 or higher is good can be seen as being substantially in error. In fact, because the distribution of student ratings is skewed, the average or mean rating tends to fall closer to 3.0 than 2.5.

One effective way of reporting student rating data is to present decile information based on the appropriate norm base. In this way, the bias of the student rating distribution can be taken into account. Figure 28 shows one way of representing student rating data in deciles.

The use of comparative (normative) data, such as the deciles shown in Figure 28, when reporting results can serve to counteract the positive response bias and result in a more accurate and meaningful interpretation of the ratings. For example, comparative data gathered on freshmen level courses in the Anthropology Department allow the instructors to determine how they and their courses are perceived

Figure 27   Skewed Student Rating Response Curve

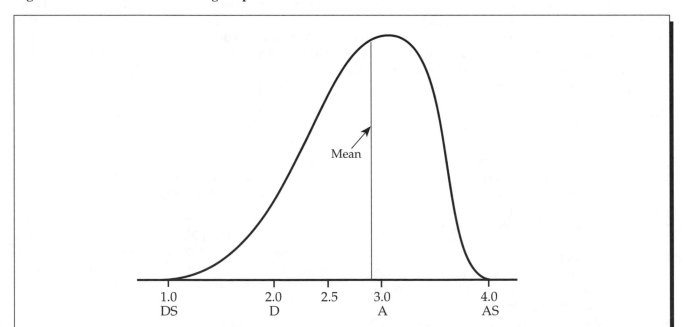

Arreola, R.A. (1995). *Developing a Comprehensive Faculty Evaluation System.* Bolton, MA: Anker Publishing Co., Inc.

in relation to the rest of the courses in the department. When such comparative data are not available, the instructor will be interpreting and using results in a void with very little substantiation for the resulting conclusions and actions taken.

Qualitative judgments can also be provided to the instructor by identifying course mean intervals in the comparative data, which can be defined as representing levels of excellence or needed improvement. For example, the comparative data for the freshmen courses in the Anthropology Department consisting of course means on student rating questionnaires could be divided into 10 equal portions. Each portion could be defined as representing a 10% interval of rated courses with a defined minimum and maximum course mean. These 10 intervals could then be defined as follows:

1. DNI = Definitely Need Improvement
   Any course mean falling in the lowest 10%, 20%, or 30% interval is defined as poor and indicates that improvement is definitely necessary.

2. NSI = Needs Some Improvement
   Any course mean falling in the 40% or 50% interval is defined as below average and indicates that some improvement is necessary.

3. NVLI = Needs Very Little Improvement
   Any course mean falling in the 60% or 70% interval is defined as good and needs little improvement.

4. DNNI = Definitely Needs No Improvement
   Any course mean falling in the upper 80%, 90%, or 100% interval is defined as very good and indicates that very little, if any, improvement is necessary.

This information could be provided to each participating instructor in a computerized format along with the appropriate interpretive materials. Or, as noted earlier, these values could be built into the computer program to produce appropriate written interpretive statements.

Further, the numerical values of 1, 2, 3, and 4 have been assigned to the labels DNI, NSI, NVLI, and DNNI, respectively. Thus, a raw student rating average of 3.2 may translate into either a decile of 8, a category rating of Definitely Needs No Improvement, or provide an appropriately norm-referenced summary qualitatively determined value of 4 since DNNI = 4.

Once established on a representative number of courses, the normative database should not change appreciably from year to year. Additional courses can be added to the normative database without significantly changing the distribution

Figure 28   Decile Interpretation of Student Ratings

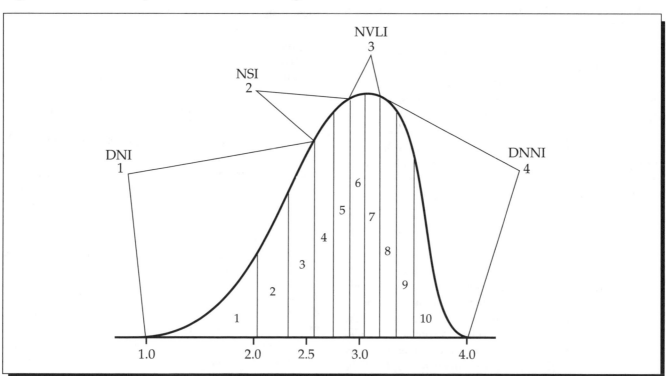

Arreola, R.A. (1995). *Developing a Comprehensive Faculty Evaluation System.* Bolton, MA: Anker Publishing Co., Inc.

and comparative judgments. For some of the sources of invalidity identified as nontrivial by research studies, such as class level and required-elective status, comparative data stratified by course level and required-elective status will provide meaningful interpretations of the results. Aleamoni and Stevens (1986) include particular examples.

Once faculty members are provided with both comparative data and interpretive materials, they are then ready to interpret their results. The comparative interpretations result from the normative data provided, and the subjective interpretations result from reflections on what had taken place in the classroom that could be related to the comparative interpretations. Using this procedure, in addition to a careful reading of the students' written comments (if available), each instructor should be able to generate diagnostic interpretations of instructional strengths and weaknesses in the course. If an instructor has results on two or more similar sections, then the ratings of one section may be compared to those of another section to determine what instructional behaviors may have led to the higher comparative ratings in one section.

If the faculty are not able to generate any diagnostic interpretations, they may need to talk with the department head, dean, or instructional development specialist about the results. This assumes, of course, that these individuals know how to interpret the results. Finding that this approach still does not adequately identify the source of instructional difficulty, the instructor may want to consider other procedures (such as the use of additional diagnostic optional items, classroom visitation, videotaping, etc.) in future evaluations.

After identifying their instructional strengths and weaknesses, instructors can use the information to plan an improvement strategy. In some instances, the strategy may simply require minor modifications in the course or teaching method. In other instances, the strategy may require a substantial commitment of time and resources on the part of both the faculty member and the department. It has been through a process such as this that instructors have been able to use student evaluation ratings to identify instructional problems and then rectify them. Obviously, the success or failure of such a venture rests solely with the instructors and their willingness to both gather and use the data provided.

If faculty members decide to submit copies of their student evaluation results to their department head or dean for rank, pay, and tenure considerations, then all of the appropriate interpretive materials should also be provided. Ideally, the student evaluation results should be interpreted by someone with expertise in the field of measurement and instructional development. Deans and department heads should be made aware of the necessity of using the comparative data to interpret the results rather than relying on the more subjective and highly unreliable written and oral comments of students. Interpretations of student rating results may also be carried out by peer review triads using several other assessments of instructional effectiveness such as self-evaluation, quality of student learning, and peer evaluation of content (Aleamoni, 1987).

Student course/instructor evaluation data should never be used alone in evaluating instructional effectiveness for rank, pay, and tenure decisions, because such data are not completely diagnostic of all elements in the instructional domain. How such student evaluation data should be used in a comprehensive system of instructional evaluation and how much weight they should carry is something that should be determined at the departmental level.

FACULTY EVALUATION AND FACULTY DEVELOPMENT

Experience has shown, time and again, that a faculty evaluation system implemented without reference or connection to a faculty development program will generate greater amounts of anxiety and resistance among the faculty than if it is part of a larger faculty development/instructional improvement effort. Likewise, experience has also shown that faculty development programs, operated in isolation or without reference to a faculty evaluation program, tend to attract mainly those faculty who need their services the least.

Ideally, a faculty evaluation system should be an integral part of a larger faculty evaluation/faculty development program. To achieve maximal benefit from these two programs, each element of the faculty evaluation system should have a corresponding and concomitant element in the faculty development program. Thus, if the faculty evaluation system is going to evaluate how well faculty teach courses or how frequently they publish scientific articles, there should be seminars, workshops, and instructional materials available to assist them in learning how to teach better or how to write manuscripts that are more likely to be accepted for publication. In short, the faculty evaluation system should provide diagnostic information on the strengths and weaknesses a faculty member possesses and then follow up with programs or materials to aid the faculty member in enhancing strengths or overcoming weaknesses.

Again, as a practical matter, the computerized report derived from student ratings should include written comments which not only highlight the major areas of concern but also provide information on where to seek assistance. For example, a computer printout could include a statement such as the following:

On the **testing and grading** section of the student rating form, the majority of the students (87%) indicated that your tests did not seem to relate well to the course objectives. The Office of Assessment and Professional Enrichment offers a seminar for faculty on Test Construction which may be of some interest. Call 555-1234 for information about the next seminar.

Thus, to be truly effective, a faculty evaluation program must work in concert with a faculty development program. Only in this way will both programs stand a reasonable chance of achieving the common goals of improving instruction and enhancing faculty performance.

CHAPTER REFERENCES*

Abrami, P. C., & Murphy, V. (1980). *A catalogue of systems for student evaluation of instruction.* Montreal, Canada: McGill University Centre for Teaching and Learning.

Aleamoni, L. M. (1982). Components of the instructional setting. *Instructional Evaluation, 7,* 11-16.

Aleamoni, L. M. (1987). Evaluating instructional effectiveness can be a rewarding experience. *Journal of Plant Disease, 71*(4), 377-379.

Aleamoni, L. M., & Stevens, J. J. (1986). *Arizona course/instructor evaluation questionnaire (CIEQ): Results interpretation manual.* Tucson, AZ: Office of Instructional Research and Development, University of Arizona.

Arreola, R. A. (1983). Establishing successful faculty evaluation and development programs. In A. Smith (Ed.), *Evaluating faculty and staff, new directions for community colleges,* No.41, March, San Francisco; Jossey-Bass, pp. 83-90.

Arreola, R. A. (1987). The role of student government in faculty evaluation. In L. M. Aleamoni (Ed.), *Techniques for evaluating and improving instruction,* New Directions for Teaching and Learning, No. 31, San Francisco: Jossey-Bass, Fall 1987, pp. 39-46.

Centra, J. A. (1975). Colleagues as raters of classroom instruction. *Journal of Higher Education, 46,* 327-337.

Centra, J. A. (1979). *Determining faculty effectiveness.* San Francisco: Jossey-Bass.

Cohen, P. A., & McKeachie, W. J. (1980). The role of colleagues in the evaluation of college teaching. *Improving College and University Teaching, 28,* 147-154.

Derry, J. O. (1977). *The cafeteria system: A new approach to course and instructor evaluation.* West Lafayette, Ind.: Purdue University.

Seldin, Peter. (1991). *The teaching portfolio.* Bolton, MA: Anker Publishing, Inc.

Seldin, Peter. (1993). *Successful use of teaching portfolios.* Bolton, MA: Anker Publishing, Inc.

---

* Portions of this chapter appeared earlier in the following publications. Used by permission.

Aleamoni, L. M. (1984). Peer evaluation. *Note to the Faculty, 15,* October. The University of Arizona, Tucson, Arizona.

Arreola, R. A., & Aleamoni, L. M. (1990). Practical issues in designing and operating a faculty evaluation system. In M. Theall & J. Franklin (Eds.), *Student Ratings of Instruction: Issues for Improving Practice, 43,* Fall, 37-55, Jossey-Bass.

Student Rating Form
Selection and Development Kit

14

Student Rating Form
Selection and Development Kit Part I:
Some Common Misconceptions and Beliefs

Student ratings are one of the most common features of faculty evaluation systems. More than 85% of all faculty evaluation systems make regular and routine use of student ratings (Seldin, 1993). Despite the continued recommendations in the literature that faculty evaluation systems use multiple sources of data, many working faculty evaluation systems continue to use student ratings of instructor and instruction as their *only* component. It is not surprising, therefore, that student ratings have tended to become synonymous with faculty evaluation. And, because the evaluation of faculty performance, especially for the purpose of making personnel decisions, is not always the most popular and well-received of administrative activities, faculty and administrators have generated and perpetuated a number of common beliefs (myths) concerning student ratings of instructors and instruction.

There have been more than 70 years of research on student ratings. Even today the design, development, use, and interpretation of student ratings continues to be one of the most heavily researched topics in the general area of faculty evaluation. The results of all this research have led to some fairly firm conclusions. At this point, it is helpful to review some of the more common perceptions and beliefs concerning student ratings and examine what the research has told us regarding the validity or truth of those perceptions and beliefs.

In examining the research findings relative to these common perceptions concerning student ratings, it is important to note that the conclusions drawn are based on the assumed use of professionally developed, valid, and reliable student rating forms. What the literature demonstrates to be a misperception of how student ratings work may, in fact, be true for student rating forms that have been "homemade" by either student, faculty, or administrative groups.

Such forms have generally not undergone the rigorous psychometric and statistical procedures required to construct a valid and reliable rating instrument and may, in fact, produce data that support the beliefs or misconceptions indicated below.

Common Belief #1: Students cannot make consistent judgments about the instructor and instruction because of their immaturity, lack of experience, and capriciousness.

Evidence dating back to 1924, according to Guthrie (1954), indicates that this commonly held belief is not true. The stability of student ratings from one year to the next results in substantial correlations in the range of 0.87 to 0.89. More recent literature on the subject, cited by Costin, Greenough, and Menges (1971), and studies by Gillmore (1973) and Hogan (1973) indicated that the correlation between student ratings of the same instructors and courses ranged from 0.70 to 0.87.

Common Belief #2: Only colleagues with excellent publication records and expertise are qualified to teach and to evaluate their peers' instruction.

There is a widely held belief (Borgatta, 1970; Deming, 1972) that good instruction and good research are so closely allied that it is unnecessary to evaluate them independently. Research is divided on this point. To be sure, weak positive correlations between research productivity and teaching effectiveness have been found by Maslow and Zimmerman (1956), McDaniel and Feldhusen (1970), McGrath (1962), Riley, Ryan, and Lipschitz (1950), and Stallings and Singhal (1968). In contrast, however, Aleamoni and Yimer (1973), Guthrie (1949, 1954), Hayes (1971), Linsky and Straus (1975), and Voeks (1962) found no significant relationship between instructors' research productivity and students' ratings of their teaching effectiveness. One study (Aleamoni & Yimer, 1973) also reported no significant relationship between instructors' research productivity and colleagues' ratings of their teaching effectiveness. Thus, no clear and consistent evidence has emerged in the literature to substantiate the belief that only good researchers can be good teachers and are the only people qualified to evaluate teaching, so the belief must be held to be essentially untrue.

Common Belief #3: Most student rating schemes are nothing more than a popularity contest, with the warm, friendly, humorous instructor emerging as the winner every time.

Studies conducted by Aleamoni and Spencer (1973), while developing and using the Illinois Course Evaluation Questionnaire (CEQ) subscales, indicated that no single subscale (e.g., Method of Instruction) completely overlapped the other subscales. This result meant that an instructor who received a high rating on the Instructor subscale (made up of items such as "The instructor seemed to be interested in students as persons") would not be guaranteed high ratings on the other four subscales (General Course Attitude, Method of Instruction, Course Content, and Interest and Attention). In reviewing both written and objective student comments, Aleamoni (1976) found that students frankly praised instructors for their warm, friendly, humorous manner in the classroom, but if their courses were not well organized or their methods of stimulating students to learn were poor, the students equally frankly criticized them in those areas. This evidence, in addition to that presented by Costin and associates (1971), Frey (1978), Grush and Costin (1975), Perry, Abrami, and Leventhal (1979), Ware and Williams (1977), and Arreola (1983), indicates that students are discriminating judges of instructional effectiveness.

Common Belief #4: Students are not able to make accurate judgments until they have been away from the course, and possibly away from the university, for several years.

This very popular belief is continuously bolstered by anecdotes passed from teacher to teacher. However, conducting research on this belief has proven to pose certain problems. For example, it is very difficult to obtain a comparative and representative sample in longitudinal follow-up studies. The sampling problem is further compounded by the fact that almost all student attitudinal data relating to a course or instructor are gathered anonymously. Most studies in this area, therefore, have relied on surveys of alumni and/or graduating seniors. Early studies by Drucker and Remmers (1951) showed that alumni who have been out of school 5 to 10 years rated instructors much the same as students currently enrolled. More recent evidence by Aleamoni and Yimer (1974), Marsh (1977), Marsh and Overall (1979), and McKeachie, Lin, and Mendelson (1978) further substantiated the earlier findings. Thus, the literature to this

point leads to the conclusion that this popularly held belief is not generally true.

Common Belief #5: Student rating forms are both unreliable and invalid.

Interestingly, this statement is true for most of the student rating forms used today. This derives from the fact that most student rating forms used in faculty evaluation systems are "home-made." That is, they have been developed by student, faculty, or administrative groups who have not followed the rigorous psychometric and statistical procedures required to produce a professional, well-developed student rating form. Well-developed instruments have been shown to be both reliable and valid. Costin and associates (1971) and Marsh (1984) reported reliabilities for such forms to be about 0.90. Aleamoni (1978a) reported reliabilities ranging from 0.81 to 0.94 for items and from 0.88 to 0.98 for subscales of the CIEQ. It should be noted, however, that wherever student rating forms are not carefully constructed with the aid of professionals, as in the case of most student- and faculty-generated forms (Everly & Aleamoni, 1972), the reliabilities may be so low as to negate completely the evaluation effect and its results.

Validity is much more difficult to assess than reliability. Most student rating forms have been validated by the judgment of experts that the items and subscales measure important aspects of instructor (Costin et al., 1971). These subjectively determined dimensions of instructional setting and process have also been validated using statistical tools, such as factor analysis (Aleamoni & Hexner, 1980; Burdsal & Bardo, 1986; Marsh, 1984). Further evidence of validity comes from studies in which student ratings are correlated with other indicators of teacher competence, such as peer (colleague) ratings, expert judges' ratings, graduating seniors' and alumni ratings, and student learning. The 14 studies cited by Aleamoni and Hexner (1980) in which student ratings were compared to (1) colleague rating, (2) expert judges' ratings, (3) graduating seniors' and alumni ratings, and (4) student learning measures all indicated the existence of moderate to high positive correlations, which can be considered as providing additional evidence of validity. This is in contrast to two studies (Bendig, 1953; Rodin & Rodin, 1972) that found a negative relationship between student achievement and instructor rating. The latter study, however, has been soundly criticized for its methodology by several researchers (Centra, 1973b; Frey 1973; Gessner, 1973; Menges, 1973).

Common Belief #6: The size of the class affects student ratings.

This is one of the oldest and most popular beliefs in education. Faculty members frequently suggest that instructors of large classes may receive lower ratings because students generally prefer small classes, which permit more student-instructor interaction. Although this belief is supported to some extent by the results of eight studies cited by Aleamoni and Hexner (1980), other investigations do not support it. For example, Aleamoni and Hexner (1980) cited seven other studies that found no relationship between class size and student ratings. Some investigations have also reported curvilinear relationships between class size and student ratings (Gage, 1961; Kohlan, 1973; Lovell & Haner, 1955; Marsh, Overall, & Kesler, 1979; Pohlmann, 1975; Wood, Linsky, & Straus, 1974). The research literature does not support the belief that a consistent relationship between class size and student ratings of any sort exists.

Common Belief #7: Gender of the student and the instructor affects student ratings. That is, students tend to rate higher those faculty who are of their same gender.

Conflicting results have been obtained when relating the gender of the student to student evaluations of instruction. Aleamoni and Thomas (1980), Doyle and Whitely (1974), Goodhartz (1948), and Isaacson, McKeachie, Milholland, Lin, Hofeller, Baerwaldt, and Zinn (1964) reported no differences between faculty ratings made by male and female students. In addition, Costin and associates (1971) cited seven studies that reported no differences in overall ratings of instructors made by male and female students or in the ratings received by male and female instructors. Conversely, Bendig (1952) found female students to be more critical of male instructors than their male counterparts; more recently, Walker (1969) found that female students rated female instructors significantly higher than they rated male instructors. In addition, Aleamoni and Hexner (1980) cited five studies that reported female students rate instructors higher on some subscales of instructor evaluation forms than do male students. Clearly, no consistent relationship between gender of the student and the instructor in student ratings has emerged in the literature.

Common Belief #8: The time of the day the course is offered affects student ratings.

The limited amount of research in this area (Feldman, 1978; Guthrie, 1954; Yongkittikul, Gillmore, & Brandenburg, 1974) indicates that the time of day the course is offered does not influence student ratings.

Common Belief #9: Whether students take the course as a requirement or as an elective affects their ratings.

Interestingly, the bulk of the literature tends to support this belief. Several investigators have found that students who are required to take a course tend to rate it lower than students who elect to take it (Cohen & Humphreys, 1960; Gillmore & Brandenburg, 1974; Pohlmann, 1975). This finding is supported by Gage (1961) and Lovell and Haner (1955) who found that instructors of elective courses were rated significantly higher than instructors of required courses. In contrast, Heilman and Armentrout (1936) and Hildebrand, Wilson, and Dienst (1971) reported no differences between students' ratings of required courses and elective courses.

Common Belief #10: Whether students are majors or nonmajors affects their ratings.

The limited amount of research in this area (Aleamoni & Thomas, 1980; Cohen & Humphreys, 1960; Null & Nicholson, 1972; Rayder, 1968) indicates that there are no significant differences and no significant relationships between student ratings and whether they were majors or nonmajors.

Common Belief #11: The level of the course (freshman, sophomore, junior, senior, graduate) affects student ratings.

The majority of studies on this issue tend to support this belief. Aleamoni and Hexner (1980) cited eight investigators who reported no significant relationship between student status (freshman, sophomore, etc.) and ratings assigned to instructors. However, they also cited 18 other investigators who reported that graduate students and/or upper division students tended to rate instructors more favorably than did lower division students.

Common Belief #12: The rank of the instructor (instructor, assistant professor, associate professor, professor) affects student ratings.

The literature on this issue, in general, does not support this belief, because no consistent relationship between faculty rank and student ratings has been found. Although some investigators reported that instructors of higher rank receive higher student ratings (Clark & Keller, 1954; Downie, 1952, Gage 1961; Guthrie, 1954; Walker, 1969), others reported no significant relationship between instructor rank and student ratings (Aleamoni & Graham, 1974; Aleamoni & Thomas, 1980; Aleamoni & Yimer, 1973; Linsky & Straus, 1975; Singhal, 1968). Conflicting results have also been found when comparing teaching experience to student ratings. Rayder (1968) reported a negative relationship, whereas Heilman and Armentrout (1936) found no significant relationship.

Common Belief #13: The grades or marks students receive in the course are highly correlated with their ratings of the course and the instructor.

This is the single most frequently researched issue on student ratings with over 400 studies on this question having been conducted to date. Considerable controversy has centered around the relationship between student ratings and their actual or expected course grades, the general feeling being that students tend to rate courses and instructors more highly when they expect to, or actually receive, good grades. Correlational studies have reported widely inconsistent grade-rating relationships. Some 22 studies have reported zero relationships (Aleamoni & Hexner 1980). Another 28 studies have reported significant positive relationships (Aleamoni & Hexner, 1980). In most instances however, these relationships were relatively weak, as indicated by the fact that the median correlation was approximately 0.14, with the mean and standard deviation being 0.18 and 0.16, respectively.

A widely publicized study by Rodin and Rodin (1972) reported a high negative relationship between student performance on examinations and their ratings of graduate teaching assistants. These results have been contested on methodological grounds by Rodin, Frey, and Gessner (1975). Subsequent replications of the study using regular faculty rather than teaching assistants and using more sophisticated rating forms have resulted in a positive rather than a negative relationship (Frey, 1973; Gessner, 1973; Sullivan & Skanes, 1974). The clear outcome from the studies on this issue is that, at best, the relationship between grades and ratings is extremely weak, with the average correlation across all studies being 0. Clearly, the belief that student ratings are highly correlated with their grades is not supported by the literature.

Common Belief #14: Student ratings on single general items are accurate measures of instructional effectiveness.

The limited amount of research in this area (Aleamoni & Thomas, 1980; Burdsal & Bardo, 1986) indicates that there is a low relationship between single general items and specific items and that the single general items had a much higher relationship to descriptive variables (gender, status, required-elective, etc.) than did the specific items. These findings suggest that the use of single general items should be avoided, especially for tenure, promotion, or salary considerations.

Common Belief #15: Student ratings cannot meaningfully be used to improve instruction.

Studies by Braunstein, Klein, and Pachla (1973), Centra (1973a), and Miller (1971) were inconclusive with respect to the effect of feedback at midterm to instructors whose instruction was again evaluated at the end of the term. However, Marsh, Fleiner, and Thomas (1975), Overall and Marsh (1979), and Sherman (1978) reported more favorable ratings from and improved learning by students by the end of the term. In order to determine if a combination of a printed report of the results and personal consultations would be superior to providing only a printed report of results, Aleamoni (1978b), McKeachie (1979), and Stevens and Aleamoni (1985) found that instructors significantly improved their ratings when personal consultations were provided. The key finding that emerges here is that student ratings *can* be used to improve instruction if used as part of a personal consultation between the faculty member and a faculty development resource person.

All this research points out that many commonly held beliefs concerning student ratings are, on the whole, myths or misconceptions. Faculty cannot "buy" good ratings by giving easy grades. Students do not generally rate faculty lower in classes taught early in the morning or right after lunch. Teaching a small class does not automatically guarantee high student ratings, nor does teaching a large class automatically guarantee low ratings. However, freshman students do tend to rate faculty more harshly than do sophomores, sophomores tend to rate more harshly than juniors, and so on, with graduate students tending to rate faculty most generously. Also, students in required courses tend to rate their instructors more harshly than students in elective courses. It is interesting to note that most large, required courses tend to be offered early in the curriculum of a college. Thus, most of the large required courses may be offered in the freshman and sophomore years, just the time when students tend to rate their teachers most harshly. It would be easy to conclude from personal experience with such courses that the problem lies with the size of the course when, in fact, the research indicates it is the level (freshman, sophomore, etc.) and the fact that the course is required that are the factors which contribute to generally lower student ratings. The important conclusion to be drawn at this point is the necessity to systematically incorporate these findings into the interpretation of student ratings.

CHAPTER REFERENCES*

Aleamoni, L. M. (1976). Typical faculty concerns about student evaluation of instruction. *National Association of Colleges and Teachers of Agriculture Journal, 20*(1), 16–21.

Aleamoni, L. M. (1978a). Development and factorial validation of the Arizona Course/Instructor Evaluation Questionnaire. *Educational and Psychological Measurement, 38,* 1063–1067.

Aleamoni, L. M. (1978b). The usefulness of student evaluations in improving college teaching. *Instructional Science, 7,* 95–105.

Aleamoni, L. M., & Graham, M. H. (1974). The relationship between CEQ ratings and instructor's rank, class size and course level. *Journal of Educational Measurement, 11,* 189–202.

Aleamoni, L. M., & Hexner, P. Z. (1980). A review of the research on student evaluation and a report on the effect of different sets of instructions on student course and instructor evaluation. *Instructional Science 9,* 67–84.

Aleamoni, L. M., & Spencer, R. E. (1973). The Illinois Course Evaluation Questionnaire: A description of its development and a report of some of its results. *Educational and Psychological Measurement, 33,* 669–684.

Aleamoni, L. M., & Thomas, G. S. (1980). Differential relationships of student, instructor, and course characteristics to general and specific items on a course questionnaire. *Teaching of Psychology, 7(4),* 233–235.

Aleamoni, L. M., & Yimer, M. (1973). An investigation of the relationship between colleague rating, student rating, research productivity, and academic rank in rating instructional effectiveness. *Journal of Educational Psychology, 64,* 274–277.

Aleamoni, L. M., & Yimer, M. (1974). *Graduating Senior Ratings Relationship to Colleague Rating, Student Rating, Research Productivity and Academic Rank in Rating Instructional Effectiveness* (Research Report No. 352). Urbana: University of Illinois, Office of Instructional Resources, Measurement and Research Division.

Arreola, R. A. (1983). Students can distinguish between personality and content/organization in rating teachers. *Phi Delta Kappan, 65(3),* 222–223.

Bendig, A. W. (1952). A preliminary study of the effect of academic level, sex, and course variables on student rating of psychology instructors. *Journal of Psychology, 34,* 2–126.

Bendig, A. W. (1953). Relation of level of course achievement of students, instructor and course ratings in introductory psychology. *Educational and Psychological Measurement, 13,* 437–488.

Borgatta, E. F. (1970). Student ratings of faculty. *American Association of University Professors, Bulletin, 56,* 6–7.

Braunstein, D. N., Klein, G. A., & Pachla, M. (1973). Feedback, expectancy and shifts in student ratings of college faculty. *Journal of Applied Psychology, 58,* 254–258.

Burdsal. C. A., & Bardo, J. W. (1986). Measuring students' perceptions of teaching: Dimensions of evaluation. *Educational and Psychological Measurement, 46,* 63–79.

Centra, J. A. (1973a). Effectiveness of student feedback in modifying college instruction. *Journal of Educational Psychology, 65,* 395–401.

Centra, J. A. (1973b). The student as godfather? The impact of student ratings on academia. In A.L. Sockloff (Ed.), *Proceedings of the First Invitational Conference on Faculty Effectiveness as Evaluated by Students.* Philadelphia: Temple University, Measurement and Research Center.

Clark, K. E., & Keller, R. J. (1954). Student ratings of college teaching. In R.A. Eckert (Ed.), *A university looks at its program.* Minneapolis: University of Minnesota Press.

Cohen, J., & Humphreys, L.G. (1960). Memorandum to faculty (unpublished manuscript). University of Illinois, Department of Psychology.

Costin, F., Greenough, W. T., & Menges, R. J. (1971). Student ratings of college teaching: Reliability, validity, and usefulness. *Review of Educational Research, 41,* 511–535.

Deming, W. E. (1972). Memorandum on teaching. *The American Statistician, 26,* 47.

Downie, N. W. (1952). Student evaluation of faculty. *Journal of Higher Education, 23,* 495–496, 503.

Doyle, K. O., & Whitely, S. E. (1974). Student ratings as criteria for effective teaching. *American Educational Research Journal, 11,* 259–274.

Drucker, A. J., & Remmers, H. H. (1951). Do alumni and students differ in their attitudes toward instructors? *Journal of Educational Psychology, 42,* 129–143.

Everly, J. C., & Aleamoni, L. M. (1972). The rise and fall of the advisor…students attempt to evaluate their instructors. *Journal of the National Association of Colleges and Teachers of Agriculture, 16(2),* 43–45.

Feldman, K. A. (1978). Course characteristics and college students' ratings of their teachers: What we know and what we don't. *Research in Higher Education, 9,* 199–242.

Frey, P. W. (1973). Student ratings of teaching: Validity of several rating factors. *Science, 182,* 83–85.

Frey, P. W. (1978). A two-dimensional analysis of student ratings of instruction. *Research in Higher Education, 9,* 69–91.

Gage, N. L. (1961). The appraisal of college teaching. *Journal of Higher Education. 32,* 17–22.

Gessner, P. K. (1973). Evaluation of instruction. *Science, 180,* 566–569.

Gillmore, G. M. (1973). *Estimates of Reliability Coefficients for Items and Subscales of the Illinois Course Evaluation Questionnaire* (Research Report No. 341). Urbana: University of Illinois, Office of Instructional Resources, Measurement and Research Division.

Gillmore, G. M., & Brandenburg, D. C. (1974). *Would the Proportion of Students Taking a Class as a Requirement Affect the Student Rating of the Course?* (Research Report No. 347). Urbana: University of Illinois, Office of Instructional Resources, Measurement and Research Division.

Goodhartz, A. S. (1948). Student attitudes and opinions relating to teaching at Brooklyn College. *School and Society, 68,* 345–349.

Grush, J. E., & Costin, F. (1975). The student as consumer of the teaching process. *American Educational Research Journal, 12,* 55–66.

Guthrie, E. R. (1949). The evaluation of teaching. *Educational Record, 30,* 109–115.

Guthrie, E. R. (1954). *The evaluation of teaching: A progress report.* Seattle: University of Washington.

Hayes, J. R. (1971). Research, teaching and faculty fate. *Science, 172,* 227–230.

Heilman, J. D., & Armentrout, W. D. (1936). The rating of college teachers on ten traits by their students. *Journal of Educational Psychology, 27,* 197–216.

Hildebrand, M., Wilson, R. C., & Dienst, E. R. (1971). *Evaluating university teaching.* Berkeley: University of California, Center for Research and Development in Higher Education.

Hogan, T. P. (1973). Similarity of student ratings across instructors, courses and time. *Research in Higher Education, I,* 149–154.

Isaacson, R. L., McKeachie, W. J., Milholland, J. E., Lin, Y. G., Hofeller, M., Baerwaldt, J. W., & Zinn, K. L. (1964). Dimensions of student evaluations of teaching. *Journal of Educational Psychology, 55,* 344–351.

Kohlan, R. G. (1973). A comparison of faculty evaluations early and late in the course. *Journal of Higher Education, 44,* 587–597.

Linsky, A. S., & Straus, M. A. (1975). Student evaluations, research productivity and eminence of college faculty. *Journal of Higher Education, 46,* 89–102.

Lovell, G. D., & Haner, C. F. (1955). Forced-choice applied to college faculty rating. *Educational and Psychological Measurement, 15,* 291–304.

Marsh, H. W. (1977). The validity of students' evaluations: Classroom evaluations of instructors independently nominated as best and worst teachers by graduating seniors. *American Educational Research Journal, 14,* 441–447.

Marsh, H. W. (1984). Students' evaluations of university teaching: Dimensionality, reliability, validity, potential biases, and utility. *Journal of Educational Psychology, 76,* 707–754.

Marsh, H. W., Fleiner, H., & Thomas, C. S. (1975). Validity and usefulness of student evaluations of instructional quality. *Journal of Educational Psychology, 67,* 883–889.

Marsh, H. W., & Overall, J. U. (1979). Long-term stability of students' evaluations: A note on Feldman's consistency and variability among college students in rating their teachers and courses. *Research in Higher Education, 10,* 139–147.

Marsh, H. W., Overall, J. U., & Kesler, S. P. (1979). Class size, students' evaluations, and instructional effectiveness. *American Educational Research Journal, 16,* 57–69.

Maslow, A. H., & Zimmerman, W. (1956). College teaching ability, scholarly activity and personality. *Journal of Educational Psychology, 47,* 185–189.

McDaniel, E. D., & Feldhusen, J. F. (1970). Relationships between faculty ratings and indexes of service and scholarship. *Proceedings of the 78th Annual Convention of the American Psychological Association, 5,* 619–620.

McGrath, E. J. (1962). Characteristics of outstanding college teachers. *Journal of Higher Education, 33,* 148.

McKeachie, W. J. (1979). Student ratings of faculty: A reprise. *Academe, 65,* 384–397.

McKeachie, W. J., Lin, Y. G., & Mendelson, C. N. (1978). A small study assessing teacher effectiveness: Does learning last? *Contemporary Educational Psychology, 3,* 352–357.

Menges, R. J. (1973). The new reporters: Students rate instruction. In C. R. Pace (Ed.), *New directions in higher education: Evaluating learning and teaching.* San Francisco: Jossey-Bass.

Miller, M. T. (1971). Instructor attitudes toward, and their use of, student ratings of teachers. *Journal of Educational Psychology, 62,* 235–239.

Null, E. J., & Nicholson, E. W. (1972). Personal variables of students and their perception of university instructors. *College Student Journal, 6,* 6–9.

Overall, J. U., & Marsh, H. W. (1979). Midterm feedback from students. Its relationship to instructional improvement and students' cognitive and affective outcomes. *Journal of Educational Psychology, 71,* 856–865.

Perry, R. P., Abrami, P. C., & Leventhal, L. (1979). Educational seduction: The effect of instructor expressiveness and lecture content on student ratings and achievement. *Journal of Educational Psychology, 71,* 107–116.

Pohlmann, J. T. (1975). A multivariate analysis of selected class characteristics and student ratings of instruction. *Multivariate Behavioral Research, 10*(1), 81–91.

Rayder, N. F. (1968). College student ratings of instructors. *Journal of Experimental Education, 37,* 76–81.

Riley, J. W., Ryan, B. F., & Lipschitz, M. (1950). *The student looks at his teacher.* New Brunswick, NJ: Rutgers University Press.

Rodin, M., Frey, P. W., & Gessner, P. K. (1975). Student evaluation. *Science, 187,* 555–559.

Rodin, M., & Rodin, B. (1972). Student evaluation of teachers. *Science, 177,* 1164–1166.

Seldin, P. (1993). How colleges evaluate professors 1983 v. 1993. *AAHE Bulletin,* October 1993, 6–12.

Sherman, T. M. (1978). The effects of student formative evaluation of instruction on teacher behavior. *Journal of Educational Technology Systems, 6,* 209–217.

Singhal, S. (1968). *Illinois Course Evaluation Questionnaire Items by Rank of Instructor, Sex of the Instructor, and Sex of the Student* (Research Report No. 282). Urbana: University of Illinois, Office of Instructional Resources, Measurement and Research Division.

Stallings, W. M., & Singhal, S. (1968). *Some Observations on the Relationships between Productivity and Student Evaluations of Courses and Teaching* (Research Report No. 274). Urbana: University of Illinois, Office of Instructional Resources, Measurement and Research Division.

Stevens, J. J., & Aleamoni, L. M. (1985). The use of evaluative feedback for instructional improvement: A longitudinal perspective. *Instructional Science, 13,* 285–304.

Sullivan, A. M., & Skanes, G. R. (1974). Validity of student evaluation of teaching and the characteristics of successful instructors. *Journal of Educational Psychology, 66,* 584–590.

Voeks, V. W. (1962). Publications and teaching effectiveness. *Journal of Higher Education, 33,* 212.

Walker, B. D. (1969). An investigation of selected variables relative to the manner in which a population of junior college students evaluate their teachers. *Dissertation Abstracts, 29(9–B),* 3474.

Ware, J. E., & Williams, R. G. (1977). Discriminate analysis of student ratings as a means of identifying lecturers who differ in enthusiasm or information giving. *Educational and Psychological Measurement, 37,* 627–639.

Wood, K., Linsky, A. S., & Straus, M. A. (1974). Class size and student evaluation of faculty. *Journal of Higher Education, 45,* 524–534.

Yongkittikul, C., Gillmore, G. M., & Brandenburg, D. C. (1974). *Does the Time of Course Meeting Affect Course Ratings by Students?* (Research Report No. 346). Urbana: University of Illinois, Office of Instructional Resources, Measurement and Research Division.

-----

* Portions of this chapter appeared in an article by Lawrence M. Aleamoni entitled Student Rating Myths Versus Research Facts published in the *Journal of Personnel Evaluation in Education, 1,* 1987, pp. 111–119. Used by permission.

15

Student Rating Form
Selection and Development Kit Part II:
Identifying and Selecting Published Forms

Student rating forms constitute a critical element of virtually every faculty evaluation system. Because the data generated by student rating forms can play a major role in the evaluation of faculty performance, it is important that the forms used be both reliable and valid and provide meaningful information that can be used for improvement purposes as well as personnel decision-making purposes. As has been noted earlier, the development of a valid and reliable student rating form is a process that requires the application of a host of professional measurement and statistical skills.

Because numerous student rating forms have been developed locally and may not possess the necessary psychometric qualities of reliability and validity, it is generally a good idea to consider adopting or adapting an existing form rather than developing one from scratch. This chapter provides guidelines for selecting from among a number of available student rating forms. Included here is a checklist for selecting forms and technical reviews of a number of well-known and commercially available forms including the Educational Testing Service's Student Instructor Rating forms, the Kansas State University's IDEA forms, the Purdue Cafeteria system, and the Aleamoni Course/Instructor Evaluation Questionnaire (CIEQ) system, as well as information on whom to contact to obtain samples of these and other forms. An example of a complete information packet for a recommended form, the Aleamoni CIEQ, is provided at the end of this chapter.

CHECKLIST FOR IDENTIFYING AND SELECTING PUBLISHED FORMS

In examining the field of published student rating forms for possible adoption or adaptation by your institution, it is best to follow a specific set of steps that give you the best possibility of identifying the better forms to consider. The following checklist is suggested as a guide for finding and testing such forms.

1. Use the *Mental Measurement Yearbook (MMY)* and *Tests in Print* to learn what forms are available. The *MMY* and the *Tests in Print* should be available in your library and provide critical reviews by experts concerning each form.

2. Write to the publishers, universities, or private corporations identified in the *MMY* as producing or reviewing such forms. Request any manuals and announcements for references to forms, services, and technical data from the publishers.

3. Review the literature on student ratings of instruction. Professional publications such as the American Educational Research Association's *Instructional Evaluation* or the National Council on Measurement in Education's *Measurement News* or *Journal of Educational Measurement* often contain announcements and/or reviews of new forms as well as general articles on the use and analysis of student rating forms. The bibliography at the end of this handbook provides an excellent starting point for reviewing the literature.

4. Send for a specimen set of the form or forms selected for consideration. Publishers will often provide such sets to institutions wishing to consider their purchase or use. Examine the specimen set to analyze in depth the questions used and material covered.

5. Try out the form. It is a good idea to simply try out the questionnaire or rating form in its original form.

Check with the form's publisher to determine policies concerning trial administrations.

6. After trying out a number of possible forms, have the individuals responsible for the courses or course sections in which such forms might be used critically review their appropriateness.

7. As part of the process in selecting a form for possible adoption or adaptation, determine whether the form publisher provides any of the following services and how much these services cost:

    a. Form scanning and processing.

    b. Rapid turn-around in providing computer analyses of form results.

    c. Comparative norms for appropriate groupings of faculty and courses.

    d. Willing to sell the system to your institution including debugged computer software and the rights to print modified forms.

In many instances, it may be more cost effective to buy the entire processing system. Buying a complete service or adapting an existing operating student rating system saves a good bit of time and effort in the overall development of your faculty evaluation system.

REVIEW OF SELECTED PUBLISHED OR COMMERCIALLY AVAILABLE STUDENT RATING FORMS

The following are descriptions of several selected systems for student rating of instruction in higher education. The systems reviewed are representative of the field and do not present an exhaustive listing of all commercially available student rating forms and systems. Rather, the information provided is intended to be used as a starting point for faculty and administrators who are may be interested in adopting a commercially available student rating system. The information contained in the reviews may also be helpful as an aid to those designing local systems to meet unique needs. However, potential users are urged to familiarize themselves with the relevant original reports and descriptions of a system and to obtain the most recent technical descriptions of products and services from the contact person listed. If none of the available forms meets the needs of your institution, you may wish to design and develop your own student rating form and computer analysis system. The following chapter outlines the recommended procedure for developing your own student rating form.

For each system review, the information is provided under the following headings:

Title. A complete title for the system with acronym.

Contact. Name, address, telephone number, and, when available, the fax number of the individual responsible for user inquiries about the rating system are provided.

Format. General description of the form(s) available with the system. This description typically includes information on type, number, and organization of evaluation items; response alternatives; answer sheet format; student background questions; optional items; and open-ended questions.

Results. Description of the organization and general format of the output, statistics provided (e.g., means, standard deviation, factor scores, frequency distributions, histograms), availability and type of comparative data.

Special Features. Description of unique or outstanding features of the system not described elsewhere. Examples of special features include the availability of interpretive manuals, newsletters, item bank catalogs, summary reports, special consultants, and processing services; and the existence of forms in foreign languages.

Development and Validation. A brief synopsis of published and unpublished research reports on the rating instruments used in each system. The studies surveyed may describe procedures for selecting and organizing rating items; reliability estimates; test-criterion relationships; and the impact of student, teacher, course, and administration factors on rating form results.

References. A list of the relevant articles particular to each system.

Purdue Cafeteria System (Cafeteria)

Contact: Marjorie Halsema
            Center for Instructional Services
            Purdue University
            West Lafayette, Indiana 47906
            (317) 494-5108
            (317) 494-5111 FAX

Format. The Cafeteria system allows instructors to select up to 40 items from an item catalog. It is also possible for instructors to include up to 3 items of their own design among the 40. These 40 items supplement a core set of 5 rating items which assess teacher-produced student motivation, instructor clarity, quality of assignments, overall course quality, and overall instructor quality. It is also possible for a department to make certain catalog items mandatory for its faculty as part of the 40 noncore items. There is also a core set of five student background questions: class level, sex, expected grade, major, and reason for taking the course. All items except student background questions are scored on a 5-point scale ranging from strongly agree to strongly disagree. Individualized rating forms are printed by computer and allow space for written student comments. Cafeteria answer sheets are machine scorable.

Results. The results are typically returned directly to the instructor and are reported on a computer output which lists the items, the number of students choosing each item response alternative, item medians, and percentile ranks for all catalog-selected and core items. Frequency counts from each student background question are also shown. Summary reports which provide normative data for each catalog item are also available. These list the number selecting the item, a frequency distribution of item medians, percentile equivalents, and a frequency histogram.

Special Features. Cafeteria was designed for installation at other institutions with computers having FORTRAN capabilities. The system includes four FORTRAN programs, a 200-page operations manual, a computer-managed catalog of 200 items, and a norm library. The Cafeteria item catalog is divided into 20 sections including Clarity and Effectiveness of Presentation, Student Interest/Involvement in Learning, and Broadening Student Outlook. As an option, institutions which adopt the Cafeteria system may elect to augment the 200 Cafeteria items with an additional 100 locally developed items. Institutions may also choose to contract evaluation services with Purdue's Center for Instructional Services.

Development and Validation. The Cafeteria system represents the original attempt to provide a flexible, efficient, computer-based student evaluation system. The item catalog was developed by first gathering a large number of items from other rating forms and editing them to conform to a single-response format. These items plus others written locally were then organized into content areas. After three semesters of pilot testing, the present Cafeteria system was designed. Derry (1977) reported that the average reliability of a Cafeteria rating form was .88. Derry, Seibert, Starry, Van Horn, and Wright (1974) suggested that the five core items appear to represent a unidimensional scale. Interitem correlations of item medians for 727 instructors ranged from .64 to .83.

References

Derry, J. O. (1977). *Strengths and Vulnerabilities of the Cafeteria Model.* Paper presented at the annual meeting of the American Educational Research Associations, New York, April, 1977. (Instructional Research Bulletin 77-1. West Lafayette, Indiana: Purdue University, Measurement and Research Center.)

Derry, J. O., Seibert, W. F., Starry, A. R., Van Horn, J. W., & Wright, G. L. (1974). *Purdue instructor and course appraisal: The Cafeteria system: Users manual.* Lafayette, Indiana: Purdue Research Foundation.

Derry, J. O., Seibert, W. F., Starry, A. R., Van Horn, J. W., & Wright, G. L. (1974). *The Cafeteria System: A New Approach to Course and Instructor Evaluation.* Instructional Research Bulletin 74-1. West Lafayette, Indiana: Purdue University, Measurement and Research Center.

University of Washington Instructional Assessment System (IAS)

Contact: Gerald M. Gillmore
Educational Assessment Center
University of Washington
1400 N. E. Campus Parkway
PB-30, Room 453
Seattle, Washington 98195
(206) 543-1170
(206) 543-3961 FAX

Format. The IAS consists of six rating forms, each tailored to one of six basic course types: Form A is designed for small lecture-discussion courses, Form B for large lecture courses, Form C for seminar courses, Form D for problem-solving courses, Form E for skills-oriented or practicum courses, and Form F for quiz sections which are offered by graduate teaching assistants in conjunction with a large lecture section. All forms are subdivided in five evaluative sections plus items assessing student background characteristics (e.g., student level, expected grade, program requirements). Except for responses to items in the final section, all student responses are marked on a computer-scorable answer sheet. All items in the first three sections are rated on a 6-point scale ranging from excellent to very poor. Section 1 is designed to provide general evaluative information. It consists of four items which ask for overall ratings of the course, content, instructor's contribution, and instructor's effectiveness. These items appear on all forms allowing comparisons to be made college-wide as well as department-wide. Section 2 is designed to provide diagnostic feedback to the instructor. It consists of 11 items which ask for ratings on specific instructor characteristics. Items are common within course type, allowing normative comparisons with other, similar courses. Examples of characteristics typically included are organization, voice explanations, use of examples, quality of issues raised, knowledge, enthusiasm, encouragement given to students, ability to answer questions, and availability for help outside of class. Section 3 is designed to provide information about the course and the instructor to students considering enrolling in the course. Advanced approval must be given by the instructor before Section 3 results are made public. It consists of seven items, common to all forms, dealing with use of class time, instructor's interest in students, amount learned, relevance of course content, grading, workload, and clarity of course requirements. Section 4 provides space for eight instructor-designed questions. Response alternatives provide for ratings on either the 6-point scale used in the previous sections or a 10-point scale. Section 5 is an optional, open-ended comment sheet which asks students to describe the aspects of the course which they felt were especially good and to indicate what changes could be made to improve the course.

Results. A one-page computer output summarizes the results of an instructor's evaluations, excluding student responses to the open-ended questions from Section 5 which are passed directly to the instructor. Frequency distributions of student responses to the background questions are listed. However, these items are not used to adjust rating scores or create separate norm groups. For all evaluation items, frequency distributions and mean ratings are provided. For Section 1 items, each mean item score and the mean of the four items are placed in a centile rank for the form used and for all forms combined. For each Section 2 and 3 item, the percentage of students who responded below good is listed. The relative rank of each item mean within a section and for the particular instructor is given. The reverse side of the output provides a brief guide to interpreting the results.

Special Features. The IAS is designed to provide three sets of information: general information on course rating for administrators, specific diagnostic information of instructor and course characteristics for instructors, and information to students who are considering taking the course. The different forms allow for the use of more specific or relevant items to suit different course types. IAS forms may be purchased at a fixed per-unit cost. Processing services are available separately and includes the provision of two copies of every class summary output. Additional copies are available at a slight additional cost.

Development and Validation. The IAS was developed at the University of Washington by Gerald Gillmore and his associates in 1974. In its original form, it consisted of five forms (each dealing with a different course type) and three basic sections (for administrator, instructor, and student information). The sixth form was added later for use with quiz sections and the forms were expanded to allow room for instructor-designed questions. Statistical analyses of the IAS are provided in Gillmore (1975) which is based on the system's first year of use. The analyses of all items from each form include means, standard deviations, interitem correlations, and interrater reliabilities for different class sizes (N=1, 10, and 40). Interitem correlations for items

common to all forms range from .54 to .95. Correlations between nonevaluative variables and ratings were also computed. These nonevaluative variables, including class size, expected grades, desire to take the course prior to enrolling, and the evaluation form used, were found to relate to ratings to a nontrivial extent. Reliabilities vary according to class size, from .15 to .34 for single raters to .88 and above for classes of 40 students.

References

Gillmore, G. M. (1974). *A Brief Description of the University of Washington Instructional Assessment System.* (EAC Report 276). Seattle: University of Washington, Educational Assessment Center.

Gillmore, G. M. (1976). *Statistical Analyses of the Data from the First Year of Use of the Student Rating Forms of the University of Washington Instructional Assessment System.* (EAC Report 503). Seattle: University of Washington, Educational Assessment Center.

Instructor and Course Evaluation (ICE)

Contact: Roberta Reeves, Director
             Instructional Evaluation Office
             Southern Illinois University at Carbondale
             Carbondale, Illinois 62901
             (618) 453-1626
             (618) 453-3440 FAX

Format. The rating form consists of five parts and a student biographical section used to develop appropriate norm groups. The form is designed to be scored by an optical scanning device for computer processing. Part I contains 19 items dealing with specific instructor characteristics such as preparation, grading, clarity, organization, enthusiasm, and availability for help. Also included is a general item assessing overall teaching effectiveness. Each item is scored on a 5-point scale ranging from exceptional to improvement definitely needed. Part II contains 20 items dealing with specific course characteristics such as organization, content, interesting material, texts, and examinations. This section also includes an overall rating of the course. Items are scored on a 5-point scale ranging from strongly agree to strongly disagree. Part III asks each student to rate the progress has made toward course objectives in the course compared to other courses. It consists of 10 items dealing with specific course objectives including gaining of factual knowledge, learning fundamental theories, developing creative capacities, and oral expression. Items are scored on a 5-point scale ranging from exceptional progress to no progress. The items in Part IV deal with the reasons behind the student's taking the course. These include interest level, expected grade, and motives in taking the course, as well as one item on the adequacy of the rating form for the course. These items are rated on a Yes-No basis. Part V allows space for optional, instructor-designed items which have up to five response alternatives.

Results. The results are presented to the instructor in a computer output divided into six parts plus an introductory section summarizing student responses to the background questions. Parts I–V of the output list the percentage of student responses to each item alternative and item means. Except for Parts IV and V (student self-ratings and optional items, respectively), decile rankings of each item mean are given in relation to each instructor's department, college, and university. Total score means for the four ICE factors are reported with the university-wide decile rankings adjusted for course level and the proportion of students taking the course as a requirement. Part I summarizes the results for the ICE factors related to instructor characteristics, personal-interpersonal skills, and course structure by instructor. Part II summarizes the course factors of quality and difficulty. Part III lists progress on objectives. Part IV indicates the five items on which the instructor scored best and the five items scored poorest for both instructor and course characteristics.

Special Features. Accompanying the ICE is an interpretive manual (Miller, 1978) which serves several functions. First, it explains the computer output summarizing the instructor's evaluations. Second, it briefly describes instructor, student, course, and curriculum characteristics related to instructional outcomes such as student achievement and attitudes. Third, it discusses instructor and course characteristics affecting ICE outcomes. Specific suggestions for teaching improvement are provided by describing teaching according to each of the items comprising the four factors of the ICE. A fourth section discusses aids to teaching and course improvement such as videotaped feedback, behavior modeling, speech training, and test construction. The appendices provide ICE factor loadings and summary statistics broken down by student biographical items.

Development and Validation. The ICE represents a revised version of the Instructional Improvement Questionnaire (IIQ). The revisions consist of items on course objectives (Part III) and student self-ratings (Part IV). Course objective items are intended to measure both cognitive and affective goals achievement. The 40 ICE items on instructor characteristics (Part II) are identical to IIQ items. The IIQ items were intended to have content validity for students, internal consistency, reliability of factor scores, test-

retest reliability, factor structure stability across instructors and within instructors across time, and the ability to discriminate among instructors. In addition, a positive relationship between student ratings and achievement was seen as desirable. Research on the IIQ is summarized in a series of published and unpublished reports.

Development of the IIQ began with a review of existing rating forms and the generation of an initial item pool. The pool was reviewed by a committee of students, faculty, and measurement specialists. Students and faculty reactions to the trial forms led to the final development of the 20 course and 20 instructor items.

Miller (1978) summarized a factor analysis of class means of the 40 IIQ items found on the ICE. The four factors accounted for 63.06% of total variance. Item factor loadings are moderate with correlations ranging from .25 to .79. Pohlman (1973) investigated the reliability of IIQ subscales. Internal consistency coefficients (Cronbach's alpha) ranged from .62 to .93. Three-month test-retest correlations ranged from .67 to .76.

The relationship between course characteristics and IIQ results was studied by Pohlman (1975). Two class characteristics, expected grade and percentage of students taking the course as an elective, were positively and moderately related to IIQ scores. Elmore and LaPointe (1974) found no significant relationship between IIQ ratings and faculty and student sex. However, teachers viewed by students as warm and interested in students received high IIQ ratings (Elmore & LaPointe, 1974).

References

Elmore, P. B., & LaPointe, K. A. (1974). Effects of teacher sex and student sex on the evaluation of college instructors. *Journal of Educational Psychology, 66,* 386–389.

Elmore, P. B., & LaPointe, K. A. (1975). Effect of teacher sex, student sex, and teacher warmth on the evaluation of college instructors. *Journal of Educational Psychology, 67,* 368–374.

Miller, W. G. (1978). *Guidelines for interpreting results of the instructor and course evaluation.* Carbondale, Illinois: Southern Illinois University, Instructional Evaluation Office.

Pohlmann, J. T. (1973). *Evaluating instructional effectiveness with the instructional improvement questionnaire.* Technical Report 72–73. Carbondale, Illinois: Southern Illinois University, Instructional Evaluation Office.

Pohlmann, J. T. (1975). A multivariate analysis of selected class characteristics and student ratings of instruction. *Multivariate Behavioral Research, 10,* 81–91.

Instructor and Course Evaluation System (ICES)

Contact: Richard Williams
               Instructional and Management Services/
                 Measurement and Evaluation Division
               307 Engineering Hall
               University of Illinois
               Urbana, Illinois 61801
               (217) 244-3842
               (217) 244-4431 FAX

Format. The rating form consists of three general core items dealing with course content, the instructor, and the course in general. These items are scored on a 6-point scale ranging from excellent to very poor. The form also provides space for up to 23 items which are chosen from a computer-stored item bank of over 600 items. The item bank lists the items according to general concept and specificity in six groups: course management, student outcomes of instruction, instructor characteristics and style, instructional environment, student preferences for instruction/learning style, and specific instructional setting. Tailor-made rating forms can be developed by departments (Option 1) or by individual instructors (Option 2). Alternatively, sets of complete forms for specific course types and specific course areas are available (Option 3). All noncore items are scored on a 5-point scale with only the endpoints labeled. These labels vary according to the item stem. Space is provided on the reverse side of the rating form for open-ended responses to four questions dealing with instructor strengths and weaknesses, the most beneficial aspect of the course, how the course might be improved, grading procedure and two optional instructor-designed questions. The form also requests certain other information from the students including (1) opinion of the instructor prior to taking the course, (2) sex of the student, (3) whether the course is required or an elective, (4)whether the course is in a student's major, (5) class level, and (6) expected grade.

Results. The computerized output varies somewhat, depending on the rating form options selected. However, two sections of results are reported regardless of the options selected. The first section summarizes student demographic data for students who completed ICES questionnaires. The second sections summarizes the global item results. These include means, standard deviations, and frequency distributions for the three core items. The instructor's mean score on each core item is compared to two groups. Group 1 is one of six university norm groups, where the groups were determined on the basis of course status (mostly required, mixed, mostly elective) and instructor status (teaching assistant, faculty member). Group 2 is the instructor's department. Comparisons are not made only in terms of relative placement of the instructor's mean rating: a range of scores is presented which takes into account the unreliability of the items. Department core item (Option 1) information parallels that presented for the core items except that only departmental comparisons are given. Option 2 item (instructor selected) results contain no normative information. Complete form (Option 3) results are reported with items first and subscales second. Summary statistics are provided along with normative comparisons for all other instructors using the form.

Special Features. The ICES item bank catalog is the first in a series of ICES newsletters which describe the rationale and uses of ICES. Because of the nature of the ICES system, detailed descriptions of teaching dimensions or specific suggestions for teaching improvement are not provided. Tailor-made and computer scorable rating forms can be easily generated by completing an evaluation request form. External users must order ICES questionnaires from the University of Illinois and return them for processing. Two copies of a faculty report are returned with local institutional norms provided for the three global items and any items selected as part of an institutional core. The cost per questionnaire depends on the number ordered.

Development and Evaluation. The ICES item bank is a set of items culled from other rating forms along with items generated by the authors. Validation of the item classification scheme for ICES is described in Brandenburg, Derry, and Hengstler (1978). Subsets of these items were initially classified in two ways: content categories (according to previous factor analytic studies) and item specificity (as global, general concept, or specific). Factor analyses showed that the items could be grouped into two large domains: influence (which consists of items related to student-perceived outcomes, instructor communication skills, and instructor/course stimulation) and security (which consists of items related to course management/structure and instructor warmth/concern). Brandenburg (1979) describes some other statistical properties of ICES items. Item reliabilities for global and general concept items typically range between .69 and .91 with a median of .80 for each subgroup, while reliabilities for specific items fluctuate more with a lower median of .70. Within-class variances among student responses to all items were between .67 and .87. Brandenburg, Slinde, and Batista (1977) provide a rationale for the required/elective and rank breakdown used in ICES.

References

Brandenburg, D. C. (1979). *Some Statistical Properties of Item Specificity*. Paper presented at the annual meeting of the National Council for Measurement in Education, San Francisco, California, April.

Brandenburg, D. C., Derry, S., & Hengstler, D. D. (1978). *Validation of an Item Classification Scheme for a Student Rating Item Catalog*. Paper presented at the annual meeting of the National Council on Measurement in Education, Toronto, Canada, March.

Brandenburg, D. C., Slinde, J. A., & Batista, E. E. (1977). Student ratings of instruction: Validity and normative interpretations. *Research in Higher Education, 1,* 67–78.

Braskamp, L. A., Ory, J. C., & Pieper, D. M. (1979). *Student Written Comments: Dimensions of Instructional Quality*. Research Report #368. Urbana, Illinois: University of Illinois, Office of Instructional Resources, July.

Ory, J. C., Brandenburg, D. C., & Pieper, D. C. (1979). *Selection of Course Evaluation Items by High and Low Rated Faculty of Varying Academic Rank*. Paper presented at the annual meeting of the National Council for Measurement in Education, San Francisco, April.

Ory, J. C., Braskamp, L. A., & Pieper, D. M. (1979). *The Congruence of Student Evaluative Information Collected by Three Methods*. Research Report #369. Urbana, Illinois: University of Illinois, Office of Instructional Resources, July.

———————

Instructional Development and Effectiveness Assessment System (IDEA)

Contact: William E. Cashin
Center for Faculty Evaluation and
   Development
Kansas State University
1627 Anderson Avenue
Box 3000
Manhattan, Kansas 66502
(800) 255-2757
(913) 532-5637 FAX

Format. The IDEA system requires instructors to describe their course objectives prior to administering the rating form. The instructor is asked to rate the importance, on a 3-point scale (essential, important, or minor importance), of each of 10 IDEA objectives which fall into three broad areas: subject matter master, general skills development, and students' personal development. The importance the instructor assigns to each objective is taken into account in tabulating results. The rating form is divided into seven parts, with student responses recorded on specially designed optical mark reader cards. The first section con-

sists of 20 items which deal with instructor characteristics. Students are asked to describe the frequency of each of 20 teaching procedures such as promotion of teacher-student discussion, instructor enthusiasm, expressiveness and variety of voice tone, and clarity of course objectives. Items are scored on a 5-point scale ranging from hardly ever to almost always. The second section deals with the students' evaluation of their progress on 10 course objectives, including gaining factual knowledge, learning fundamental principles, developing creative capacities, and discovering implications of the course material for understanding oneself. Students are asked to rate the progress made in the course on each objective as compared with the progress made in other courses. Each item is scored on a 5-point scale ranging from low (lowest 10% of courses taken) to high (highest 10% of courses taken). The third section deals with four course characteristics: amount of reading, amount of work in other assignments, difficulty of subject matter, and degree to which the various elements of the course seemed to be related. Characteristics are compared to other courses on a 5-point scale ranging from much less than most courses to much more than most. The next section includes a self-rating of student attitudes and behaviors in the course. Items assess the amount of work put into the course, desire to take the course, desire to take another course with the same instructor, feeling toward the field of study as a result of having taken the course, and consideration given to the questions on the course evaluation form. Each item is scored on a 5-point scale from definitely false to definitely true. The fifth section deals with demographic data such as student sex, age, and years at school, as well as questions on expected grade, number of courses evaluated using the IDEA form, and how well the form permitted the student to accurately describe the instructor and the course. The sixth section is for instructor-designed multiple choice questions. Finally, students may use the back of the response card for open-ended comments.

Results. The IDEA report consists of seven parts plus course identification data (e.g., number of students enrolled, class size, student motivation). The first three parts correspond to the second, third, and fourth sections of the rating form. The tabulation of results for each item includes the percentages responding at each level, mean rating, and a comparison of the mean with all courses rated and with courses of similar class size (four categories) and student motivation (five levels). These comparative data are based on the evaluations of approximately 100,00 courses from over 130 colleges and universities using the IDEA system. Part I (Evaluation) addresses the effectiveness of the instructor's teaching by presenting comparative rankings on a 5-point scale (low to high) only for those objectives which the instructor described as relatively important for that course. In addition, an overall evaluation is presented which represents progress on relevant objectives in comparison to national norms.

Part II (Course Description) provides information on how students described selective aspects of the course. Part III (Student Self-Ratings) describes certain characteristics of the students in the course. Part IV (Methods) summarizes responses to items dealing with instructor's teaching procedures. The 20 items are grouped under the four headings of Involving Students, Communicating Content and Purpose, Creating Enthusiasm, and Preparing Examinations. Percentages responding at each level and mean ratings are presented for each item along with a difference score which indicates how the mean score differs from classes of similar size and student motivation level. This difference score is translated into a rating of low, medium, or high to allow for easier interpretation. Part V (Additional Questions) provides a tabulation of responses to instructor-designed questions. Part VI (Diagnostic Summary) attempts to identify the modifications necessary to an instructor's teaching methods in order to improve teaching effectiveness. The summary lists the course objectives described as important or essential by the instructor. If student ratings of progress on each of these objectives is average or below, the teaching methods most needing attention are listed. The item numbers of the teaching methods which are related to progress on each objective are listed if the instructor received a low rating on those methods. Part VII (Summary Profile) provides a graphic representation of three teaching outcome measures and four measures of teaching methods in comparison to similar courses and all courses.

Special Features. The IDEA system is a commercial rating package. Charges for forms and processing vary depending upon the number of forms. If over 10,000 forms are ordered, the Center for Faculty Evaluation and Development will provide free, on-campus consultation. Forms must be ordered from the Center and returned to them for processing. Institutions receive three copies of IDEA computer reports plus one interpretive guide for each class evaluated. When 15 or more classes are evaluated at once, an institutional summary is also provided. In addition to the interpretation manual, the Center publishes *Exchange*, an occasional newsletter, and has available a series of technical and nontechnical publications on topics in faculty evaluation and development. Workshops and other services can also be arranged.

Development and Validation. The development and initial validation of the IDEA system is described by Hoyt and Cashin (1977). Items on instructor objectives were originally formed from earlier taxonomic classifications and factor analytic work. These items were subsequently critiqued and revised by award-winning teachers, faculty-student committees, and early users of IDEA. The 20 teaching method items now in use are based on an initial pool of items culled from existing questionnaires. This initial pool was reduced by examining item redundancy, item relationships with an overall effectiveness measure, responses of outstanding teachers and faculty-student committees, and item relationships with progress on objectives. Items on course management and student characteristics were also included, because it was felt that program objectives might be contingent on such factors. The reliability of individual method scales ranged from .81 to .94, averaging .87 for classes of 25 students. The reliability of progress items was similar, ranging from .84 to .90, also averaging .87. The validity of student ratings of progress, the relationships between teaching methods and objectives, and the influence of class size and student motivation were also explored. Student reports of progress on objectives were found to be positively related to instructor ratings of importance of objectives. Multiple regression analyses showed that each of the six teaching method scales contributed to the prediction of at least one progress-on-objectives rating. Item analyses also revealed that specific student ratings of instructor behaviors were related to progress, but that this varied with class size. Student motivation was also found to be strongly related to progress ratings. More recent technical reports (e.g., Cashin & Perrin, 1978) provide additional data on reliability and validity as well as describe the computational procedures and comparative data bases used in producing reports for the latest version of IDEA.

References

Cashin, W. E., & Perrin, B. M. (1978). *Description of the IDEA System Data Base—1978–79)* (IDEA Technical Report No. 4). Manhattan, Kansas: Kansas State University, Center for Faculty Evaluation and Development, December.

Cashin, W. E., & Slawson, H. M. (1978). *Description of the IDEA System Data Base—1976–77)* (IDEA Technical Report No. 2). Manhattan, Kansas: Kansas State University, Center for Faculty Evaluation and Development, April.

Cashin, W. E., & Slawson, H. M. (1977). *Description of the IDEA System Data Base—1977–78)* (IDEA Technical Report No. 3). Manhattan, Kansas: Kansas State University, Center for Faculty Evaluation and Development, December.

Hoyt, D. P., & Cashin, W. E. (1977). *Development of the IDEA System* (IDEA Technical Report No. 1). Manhattan, Kansas: Kansas State University, Center for Faculty Evaluation and Development, March.

Instructor Designed Questionnaire (IDQ)

Contact: James A. Kulik
Center for Research on Learning and Teaching
University of Michigan
109 E. Madison
Ann Arbor, Michigan 48109
(313) 763-2482
(313) 764-4221 FAX

Format. The IDQ rating form consists of five core items and up to 25 other items plus space for two essay questions. A computer-scorable answer sheet is available for student responses to multiple-choice items which must all be made on a 5-point scale ranging from strongly agree to strongly disagree. The core items deal with overall ratings of the course and the instructor, instructor's ability to motivate students, students' ratings of their performance in the course, and students' desire to take the course. The noncore items must be selected from an item catalog except for three items which may be original. The catalog describes a computerized bank which includes roughly 200 multiple-choice items organized under three major headings: Student development, instructor ratings, and course elements. In addition, the catalog lists 11 possible essay questions and a set of eight student counseling items which instructors may select if they wish some of their ratings to be made available for student use. A subset of required items for all instructors within a department may also be set.

Results. The single-page computer output returned to the instructor summarizes the results of the multiple-choice responses. Frequency distributions and medians are reported for each item. For every item except originals, normative data are provided based on other users of the item. Median scores are reported for three groups: lowest 25%, middle 50%, and upper 25%.

Special Features. If the instructor has chosen to include the student counseling items, a second report is prepared. This report summarizes the results of the university-wide and student counseling items only. It may be used to advise students on course selection.

Development and Validation. The IDQ is modeled after Purdue's Cafeteria system which also includes a core set of items and allows the instructor to select additional items from a catalog. The IDQ includes items covering various cognitive objectives of teaching as described in Bloom's taxonomy: knowledge, concepts, application, analysis, synthesis, and evaluation. Items reflecting affective objectives of instruction, as outlined by Krathwohl and others (1964), are also included. Items are listed which describe the six major areas of teaching behavior: teaching skill, rapport, interaction, feedback, organization, and difficulty. Other items were included to focus on specific course elements.

References

Bloom, Benjamin S. (Ed.) (1956). *Taxonomy of educational objectives, handbook 1, The cognitive domain.* New York: Mckay.

Krathwohl, David R., Bloom, Benjamin S., and Masia, Bert. (1964). *Taxonomy of educational objectives, handbook II, The affective domain.* New York: Mckay.

Kulik, J. A. (1976). Student reactions to instruction. *Memo to the Faculty* (No. 58), October. Ann Arbor, Michigan: University of Michigan, Center for Research on Learning and Teaching.

Kulik, J. A. (1978). *Using CRLT's Instructor-Designed Questionnaire to Improve Instruction.* Ann Arbor, Michigan: University of Michigan, Center for Research on Learning and Teaching.

Student Instructional Report (SIR)

Contact: Carol Owen
Student Instructional Report
Educational Testing Service
Mail Stop 31V
504 Carnegie Center
Princeton, New Jersey 08540
(609) 951-1505
(609) 951-1090 FAX

Format. The SIR rating form consists of 39 core items which are divided into three sections with space for up to 10 instructor-prepared supplementary questions. The form is printed on both sides of a scannable answer sheet. Section I, which focuses on instructor characteristics, has 20 items dealing with such factors as use of class time, stimulation of interest, and concern for students. Items are scored on a 4-point scale ranging from strongly disagree to strongly agree. Students have the option of choosing a fifth response choice, NA, if the question is not applicable or if they feel they are unable to give a knowledgeable response. Section II consists of 10 items, some of which deal with course characteristics such as level of difficulty, workload, and pace at which the material is presented. Other items deal with student characteristics such as expected grade, sex, and reasons for taking the course. Section III contains items on course variables such as texts, exams, and laboratories, as well as an overall course rating item and an item which assesses the instructor's overall effectiveness as compared to other instructors. All but this last item are scored on a 5-point scale ranging from poor to excellent with the students also having the option of responding NA if they choose. The optional instructor-designed questions in Section IV can use up to 10 response alternatives per question.

Results. The results are summarized in a two-page report which provides a frequency distribution of student responses for each item and the item mean, where appropriate. When class size is small and/or the percentage of students responding is low, responses may be flagged or not tabulated, reducing the probability of interpreting unreliable data. For 29 items, percentile equivalents are also provided. These ratings are based on a comparison of the instructor's average score on each item with national norms gathered from SIR administrations at either two-year colleges and technical institutions or four-year colleges and universities. Additional comparative data guides have been prepared separately for both institution types. Each guide contains data analyzed for specific institution types, class size, class level, class type, and subject area.

Special Features. SIR is a commercial rating system; the questionnaire must be purchased from the Educational Testing Service. However, institutions may score their own forms if they wish. Costs vary according to the number of rating forms ordered. Three copies of each class report are returned within 3 weeks of receipt of the answer sheets by ETS. Summary reports are available in combinations requested by the institution (e.g., departmental or institution). The SIR package also includes an instructor self-evaluation form. Special student rating forms are available in Spanish and in English and French for Canadian institutions.

Development and Validation. The preliminary SIR form contained 112 items divided into five groups: course organization and content, instructor-student relations, communication, assignments and evaluation, and student's involvement in the course (Centra, 1972a & b). This form was revised twice on the basis of factor analytic studies and faculty opinions of the items until 39 items remained. Centra (1973) found item reliabilities to be generally above .70 when comparing within-class variances to between-class variances for 20 or more students per class. The test-retest reliabilities of the majority of the items was also found to be above .70. Principal axis factor analysis employing oblique promax rotation identified six factors among 31 relevant SIR items (Centra, 1973). These factors were labeled Teacher-Student Relationship, Course Objectives and Organization, Reading Assignments, Course Difficulty and Workload, Lectures, and Examinations. Intercorrelations among the six factors suggested that the factors are reasonably interrelated. Centra (1973) also found that the rank order correlations of student and alumni SIR ratings of the same teachers were significantly positive. Mean SIR ratings were correlated with exam scores in 72 sections of seven courses (Centra, 1976). In two of the courses, students were randomly assigned. Global ratings of teaching effectiveness and course value were the most highly related to exam scores. Ratings of Course Difficulty and Workload

and Teacher-Student Relationship were not highly related to exam scores. Centra (1976) investigated possible bias in student ratings by considering a number of student, teacher, and course characteristics. The findings revealed that many of the variables have relatively weak relationships to ratings.

Presently ETS has a new version of the SIR under development. Potential users may wish to contact ETS to inquire as to its status and availability.

References

Centra, J. A. (1972a). *The Student Instructional Report: Its Development and Uses* (SIR Report No. 1). Princeton, New Jersey: Educational Testing Service.

Centra, J. A. (1972b). *Two Studies on the Utility of Student Ratings for Instructional Improvement. I. The Effectiveness of Student Feedback in Modifying College Instruction. II. Self-Ratings of College Teachers: A Comparison with Student Ratings* (SIR Report No. 2). Princeton, New Jersey: Educational Testing Service.

Centra, J. A. (1973). *Comparisons with Alumni Ratings, Reliability of Items, and Factor Structure* (SIR Report No. 3). Princeton, New Jersey: Educational Testing Service.

Centra, J. A. (1976). *Two Studies on the Validity of the Student Instructional Report: I. Student Ratings of Instruction and Their Relationship to Student Learning. II. The Relationship Between Student, Teacher, and Course Characteristics and Student Ratings of Teacher Effectiveness* (SIR Report No. 4). Princeton, New Jersey: Educational Testing Service.

Student Instructional Rating System (SIRS)

Contact: LeRoy A. Olson
          Scoring Office
          408B Computer Center
          Michigan State University
          East Lansing, Michigan 48824-1024
          (517) 353-5296
          (517) 353-9487 FAX

Format. The SIRS rating form is a machine-scorable answer sheet which consists of 25 standard multiple-choice items, space for eight additional multiple-choice items, and an open-ended comment area on the back of the form. Except for two items, student responses must be made on a 5-point scale ranging from superior to inferior. The multiple choice questions are divided into two sections: Instruction and Student Background. The Instruction section is made up of 21 items assessing five composite profile factors: Instructor Involvement, Student Interest, Student-Instructor Interaction, Course Demands and,

Course Organization. Space is provided for eight additional items which the instructor may select from the SIRS Supplementary & Diagnostic Item Catalog. The Student Background sections consists of four items dealing with whether the course is required, gender, GPA, and class level.

Results. The SIRS report is a two-page computer output divided into four sections: Report Identification, Instruction, Composite Profile Factors, and, Student Background. The report lists the percentage of student responses to each item alternative, item means, and standard deviations. The composite profile lists means, standard deviations, and percentile ranks on the following five profile factors: instructor involvement, student interest, student-instructor interaction, course demands, and course organization.

Special Features. SIRS is not a commercial rating package, although the materials are available to other institutions, and arrangements for processing forms can be made on an individual basis with MSU Scoring Office. The SIRS Manual briefly describes the rating form and administration and scoring practices. It contains a guide to interpreting the computer output and student ratings generally. Appendices include more than 200 supplementary and diagnostic items for use as SIRS optional items and 20 suggestions for open-ended questions.

Development and Validation. The development of the 21 standard instructor rating items of the SIRS form is described in the *Technical Bulletin* (Davis, 1969). Initially, 250 items were constructed based on interviews with students and instructors in a wide range of courses. A sample of faculty and students was then asked to rate the items by responding to four questions about each item, such as whether they would include the item on a rating form. This led to selecting 52 items for the preliminary form. Factor analyses using a varimax solution revealed a five-factor solution from which the highest loading items were selected per factor (see also Research Report #2, 1971). These 20 items plus a general affect item made up the final form. SIRS Research Report #4 (1972) describes the relationship between student SIRS responses and both student characteristics and student achievement. Multivariate multiple regression analyses showed that three student characteristics (previous GPA, sex, and expected grade) were significantly related to SIRS composite profile scores. However, the correlations between profile scores and student characteristics were low, and the proportion of variance accounted for was small. SIRS composite profile scores were also found to be significantly related to student achievement variables. However, the proportion of variance accounted for was small. SIRS item reliabilities are reported by Showers (1974). Individualized item corrected split-half reliabilities for class sizes of 20 students averaged .75, ranging from .53 to .90.

References

Analysis of Responses for Winter Term, 1970 (SIR Research Report #1). East Lansing, Michigan: Michigan State University, The Office of Evaluation Services, 1971.

Davis, R. H. (1969). *Student Instructional Rating System (SIRS) Technical Bulletin,* East Lansing, Michigan: Michigan State University, The Office of Evaluation Services.

Showers, B. (1974). *SIRS Research Report #5: The Effects of Three Kinds of Response Options on Student Ratings of Instruction.* East Lansing, Michigan: Michigan State University, The Office of Evaluation Services.

Stability of Factor Structure (SIR Research Report #2). East Lansing, Michigan: Michigan State University, The Office of Evaluation Services, 1974.

Student Characteristics (SIR Research Report #4). East Lansing, Michigan: Michigan State University, The Office of Evaluation Services, 1972.

Student Instructional Rating System (SIRS). (Testing and Evaluation Bulletin No 9). East Lansing, Michigan: Michigan State University, The Office of Evaluation Services, 1970.

Student Instructional Rating System Manual. East Lansing, Michigan: Michigan State University, The Office of Evaluation Services, 1970.

Using the Student Instructional Rating System Report in the Decision-Making Process. East Lansing, Michigan: Michigan State University, The Office of Evaluation Services, 1972.

Student Perceptions of Teaching (SPOT)

Contact: Joyce Moore
        Evaluation and Examination Service
        University of Iowa
        300 Jefferson Building
        Iowa City, Iowa 52242
        (319) 335-0356

Format. The SPOT system allows the instructor to select up to 20 items from the SPOT item catalog. These items are printed on one side of a computer scorable answer sheet. All items must be marked on a 6-point scale ranging from strongly agree to strongly disagree. The reverse side of the answer sheet may be used for up to eight instructor-designed questions. Students responses to these items may be on any scale with six alternatives or less. Space is also provided for student written comments.

Results. SPOT results are reported on a computer summary which lists for each item the number of students responding, the percentage of students choosing each response alternative, and the item mean. In addition, for items selected from the SPOT catalog for which sufficient normative data exist, item means are translated into one of three percentile ranks. The three groups used for comparisons are "Base," representing data from a 1974 SPOT administration, "Dept." representing data from all classes in the instructor's department, and "User," representing data from all users at the university. Below each percentile rank, a confidence interval is printed.

Special Features. The SPOT item catalog lists in excess of 100 items organized into seven sections. The first four sections (course content, structure, and organization; instructor's behavior; instructional methods and materials; and outcomes of instruction) include items particularly useful for traditional style courses. The supplementary items in the remaining sections (laboratory courses and sections; clinical courses; and production courses) are for more specialized teaching situations. There is a uniform price for SPOT forms and computer scoring, regardless of the number ordered.

Development and Validation. An initial pool of more than 800 items was gathered from other rating forms and subdivided into four categories. The pool was reduced to 139 items by excluding redundant items, unclear items, over specific items, etc. These items were submitted to the faculty and a sample of students at the University of Iowa in March 1974. They were asked to rate each item for importance to learning and student ability to evaluate the characteristic studied. The results of this survey yielded an 80-item SPOT pool. Other items have been added to meet needs for courses and instructional situations.

Weerts and Whitney (1975) investigated the relationship between average student responses to the 80 items and selected student and instructor characteristics. In general, they found small and inconsistent relationships between SPOT item scores and class size, class rank, required versus elective course, percentage of class responding, instructor rank, instructor sex, instructor age, and instructor graduate preparation. Average expected grade was substantially related (.30 or higher) to 31 of 80 SPOT items.

References

Student Perceptions of Teaching (SPOT): II. Asking the Right Questions. (Research Report No. 76). Iowa City, Iowa: University of Iowa, Evaluation and Examination Services, August 1974.

Student Perceptions of Teaching (SPOT): III. The 1978–79 Item Pool. (Memo No. 26). Iowa City, Iowa: University of Iowa, Evaluation and Examination Services, August 1978 (revised).

Student Perceptions of Teaching (SPOT): IV. Baseline Data for a Representative Sample of Classes. (Summary Report No. 44). Iowa City, Iowa: University of Iowa, Evaluation and Examination Services, December 1976 (revised).

Weerts, R. R. & Whitney, D. R. (1975). *Student Perceptions of Teaching (SPOT): V. Relationships Between Averaged Student Responses and Selected Course Characteristics.* (Research Report No. 78). Iowa City, Iowa: University of Iowa, Evaluation and Examination Services, June (revised).

Aleamoni Course/Instructor Evaluation Questionnaire (CIEQ)

Contact: Lawrence M. Aleamoni
Comprehensive Data Evaluation Services, Inc.
6730 N. Camino Padre Isidoro
Tucson, AZ 85718
(602) 297-5110

Format. The CIEQ rating form is available on a computer scorable answer sheet which is divided into five sections. The first section elicits student background information including student level, whether the student is taking the course as an elective, student gender, expected grade, the proportion of students taking the course as a part of their major, and the semester in which the evaluation takes place. The second section consists of three general items which elicit student responses to the course content, the instructor, and the course in general. Ratings in this section are made on a 6-point scale ranging from excellent to very poor. Section three includes 21 statements which represent five subscales or factors labeled General Course Attitude, Method of Instruction, Course Content, Interest and Attention, and Instructor. A sixth scale, Total, provides scores for all items combined. Items are rated on a 4-point scale ranging from agree strongly to disagree strongly. The forth section provides space for 42 optional items if the instructor wishes to include any additional items. These items may either be selected from an item catalog which is part of the CIEQ system or written by the instructor. The final section allows for open-ended responses to questions on course content, the instructor, course objectives, papers and homework, examinations, suggested improvements, and an evaluation of the course based upon student satisfaction with the course and student perceptions of its value as an educational experience.

Results. The results of the CIEQ are presented on computer output in four parts. The first part presents course and instructor identification. The second part presents student background information and results for the three general items. Given are the proportion and number responding to each item alternative (and the proportion *not* responding). The mean and the standard deviation are also presented for each of the general items. The third part lists the responses to the five subscales. Included are the percentage responding, the mean response, the standard deviation, the reliability coefficient (based upon an internal consistency calculation), and a variety of normative comparisons. These comparisons include the rank norm (a comparison of the course with all courses given by instructors at the same rank), the level norm (a comparison of the course with all courses at the same course level), the institution norm (a comparison of the course with all courses at the university), the college norm (a comparison of the course with all other courses in the appropriate college within the university), the nationwide norm (a comparison of the course to all the courses throughout the US which have used the CIEQ), and the department norm (a comparison of the course with all other courses in a particular department). The final part lists each of 21 standard items and gives the proportion and number responding to each alternative, the most favorable response, the mean response, the standard deviation, and the college-wide norm decile (a comparison of the mean response with those obtained throughout the college or university) for each item.

Special Features. The optional item catalog (Aleamoni & Carynnk, 1977) contains 350 items divided into 20 categories. The Results Interpretation Manual (Aleamoni, undated) provides information on scale development and validation, recommended uses and administrative procedures, description and interpretation of results, and decile norm cutoff scores for seven data bases.

Institutions wishing to use the CIEQ may select one of two options: (1) CIEQ forms may be purchased individually from Comprehensive Data Evaluation Services, Inc. (CODES) and returned for processing, or (2) an institution may choose to purchase the computer analysis program and rights to print and use the CIEQ under a royalty arrangement. Institutions purchasing the program receive annual updates of the normative data base derived from the hundreds of institutions presently using the CIEQ. The computer program is written for the Apple Macintosh computer and is designed to be used as a simple, desk-top system.

Development and Validation. The CIEQ was developed in 1975 through an analysis of the Illinois Course Evaluation Questionnaire (CEQ). The original CEQ was based on an initial pool of over 1000 items collected in the early 1960s, reduced and refined by a variety of techniques, including factor analysis, to a form containing 50 items (Aleamoni & Spencer, 1973). The current version (Form 76) uses normative data from roughly 1600 course sections at the University of Arizona and the University of Illinois at Urbana-Champaign and 6800 sections from other US institutions gathered from 1972 through 1978. Internal consistency reliability coefficients for the five subscales range from .81 to .94 (Aleamoni, undated). Test-retest reliability ranges from .92 to .98 for the subscales and the total and from .81 to .94 for individual items (Gillmore, 1973). Aleamoni (1978) reviews several studies of the CEQ which he claims are generalizable to the CIEQ. He reports that the CIEQ is not affected by gender, term, curriculum, class size, instructor rank, required/elective, major/minor, student status, pass/fail, expected grade, and final grade. In addition, the ratings of colleagues and trained judges appear to correlate with CIEQ student ratings (Aleamoni, 1978).

Research on the CIEQ has shown it to be a valid, reliable measure of student reactions to the course and instructor. The CIEQ provides meaningful information that may be successfully used in a program of instructional improvement or as part of a comprehensive faculty evaluation system designed to provide data for faculty personnel decisions. Figure 29 shows a copy of the CIEQ form (front side) and Figure 29 (continued) shows the back side which contains the free response section. Figure 30 presents an example of the analysis printout for the CIEQ followed by a copy of the interpretation guide provided each faculty member.

Figure 29   CIEQ Form (front side)

ALEAMONI COURSE/INSTRUCTOR EVALUATION QUESTIONNAIRE (CIEQ) (FORM 76)
COMPREHENSIVE DATA EVALUATION SERVICES, INC. © LAWRENCE M. ALEAMONI, 1975

MARKING INSTRUCTIONS	STUDENT INFORMATION	COURSE INFORMATION	CODING INFORMATION

MARKING INSTRUCTIONS

MARK:

AS — IF YOU AGREE STRONGLY WITH THE ITEM

A — IF YOU AGREE MODERATELY WITH THE ITEM

D — IF YOU DISAGREE MODERATELY WITH THE ITEM

DS — IF YOU DISAGREE STRONGLY WITH THE ITEM

MARK ONLY ONE RESPONSE PER ITEM USING PENCIL ONLY

ERASE CHANGED ANSWERS CLEANLY AND COMPLETELY.

SAMPLE MARK

STUDENT INFORMATION

ARE YOU A: FRESHMAN, SOPHOMORE, JUNIOR, SENIOR, GRADUATE, OTHER

ARE YOU TAKING THIS COURSE FOR PASS/FAIL: YES, NO

ARE YOU TAKING THIS COURSE AS A: REQUIRED, ELECTIVE, BOTH

ARE YOU A: MALE, FEMALE

YOUR EXPECTED GRADE IN THIS COURSE IS: A B C D E

THIS COURSE IS WITHIN YOUR: MAJOR, MINOR, OTHER

SEMESTER: FALL, SPRING, SUMMER, OTHER

COURSE INFORMATION

RATE EACH OF THE FOLLOWING

COURSE CONTENT: EXCELLENT, VERY GOOD, GOOD, FAIR, POOR, VERY POOR

MAJOR INSTRUCTOR: EXCELLENT, VERY GOOD, GOOD, FAIR, POOR, VERY POOR

COURSE IN GENERAL: EXCELLENT, VERY GOOD, GOOD, FAIR, POOR, VERY POOR

CODING INFORMATION

COURSE CODE

SPECIAL CODE

TECHNI-FORMS 0613

THE MAJOR INSTRUCTOR OF THIS COURSE IS (Number)

THE NAME AND NUMBER OF THIS COURSE IS (Name)

PLEASE PRINT.

STANDARD ITEM SECTION

#	Item		Sec I		Sec II
1	It was a very worthwhile course.	AS A D DS	22	43	
2	I would take another course that was taught this way.		23	44	
3	The instructor seemed to be interested in students as individuals.		24	45	
4	The course material was too difficult.		25	46	
5	It was easy to remain attentive.		26	47	
6	NOT much was gained by taking this course.		27	48	
7	I would have preferred another method of teaching in this course.		28	49	
8	The course material seemed worthwhile.		29	50	
9	The instructor did NOT synthesize, integrate or summarize effectively.		30	51	
10	The course was quite interesting.		31	52	
11	The instructor encouraged development of new viewpoints and appreciations.		32	53	
12	I learn more when other teaching methods are used.		33	54	
13	Some things were NOT explained very well.		34	55	
14	The instructor demonstrated a thorough knowledge of the subject matter.		35	56	
15	This was one of my poorest courses.		36	57	
16	The course content was excellent.		37	58	
17	Some days I was NOT very interested in this course.		38	59	
18	I think that the course was taught quite well.		39	60	
19	The course was quite boring.		40	61	
20	The instructor seemed to consider teaching as a chore or routine activity.		41	62	
21	Overall, the course was good.		42	63	

OPTIONAL ITEMS — SECTION I — SECTION II

PLEASE FILL OUT THE OTHER SIDE

Arreola, R.A. (1995). *Developing a Comprehensive Faculty Evaluation System.* Bolton, MA: Anker Publishing Co., Inc.

Figure 29 (continued)   CIEQ Form (back side)

CIEQ

PLEASE USE THIS SIDE OF THE FORM FOR YOUR PERSONAL COMMENTS ON TEACHER EFFECTIVENESS AND GENERAL COURSE VALUE. YOUR INSTRUCTOR WILL NOT SEE YOUR COMPLETED EVALUATION UNTIL AFTER FINAL GRADES ARE IN FOR YOUR COURSE.

COURSE CONTENT

PLEASE GIVE YOUR COMMENTS ON THE COURSE CONTENT, SUBJECT MATTER AND ANY PARTICULAR RELEVANCE THIS COURSE HAS HAD TO YOUR AREA OF STUDY.

INSTRUCTORS

WRITE THE NAME OF YOUR PRINCIPAL INSTRUCTOR_____T.A._____
WHAT ARE YOUR GENERAL COMMENTS ABOUT THE INSTRUCTOR(S) IN THIS COURSE?

COURSE/INSTRUCTIONAL OBJECTIVES

WERE THE OBJECTIVES CLEARLY STATED FOR THIS COURSE?   YES_____NO_____   COMMENT:

PAPERS AND HOMEWORK

COMMENT ON THE VALUE OF THE BOOKS, HOMEWORK AND PAPERS (IF ANY) IN THIS COURSE.

EXAMINATIONS

COMMENT ON THE EXAMINATIONS AS TO DIFFICULTY, FAIRNESS, ETS.

GENERAL

1. WHAT IMPROVEMENTS WOULD YOU SUGGEST FOR THIS COURSE?

2. WHAT IS YOUR EVALUATION OF THIS COURSE BASED UPON (A) YOUR SATISFACTION WITH WHAT YOU GOT OUT OF THIS COURSE AND (B) WHETHER IT WAS A VALUABLE EDUCATIONAL EXPERIENCE OR A DISAPPOINTMENT? PLEASE COMMENT.

PLEASE FILL OUT OTHER SIDE

Arreola, R.A. (1995). *Developing a Comprehensive Faculty Evaluation System.* Bolton, MA: Anker Publishing Co., Inc.

Figure 30 **Example of CIEQ analysis printout.**

CIEQ Analysis   University of Arizona   Fall 1994

ALEAMONI COURSE/INSTRUCTOR EVALUATION QUESTIONNAIRE

Instructor: ALEAMONI   **Class: EDP 646**   **Sample size: 10**
Process Date: 12/7/94   **College Code: 78933**

Class Description Results

Class Information

	Fr	So	Jr	Sr	Grad	Oth	OMIT
%	0.00	0.30	0.10	0.40	0.20	0.00	0.00
#	0	3	1	4	2	0	0

Gender

	M	F	OMIT
%	0.20	0.80	0.00
#	2	8	0

Course Option

	Req	Elec	OMIT
%	0.70	0.30	0.00
#	7	3	0

Pass-Fail Option

	Yes	No	OMIT
%	0.10	0.90	0.00
#	1	9	0

Major-Minor

	Maj	Min	Oth	OMIT
%	0.90	0.10	1.00	0.00
#	9	1	0	0

Expected Grade

	A	B	C	D	E	OMIT
%	0.30	0.30	0.30	0.00	0.00	0.10
#	3	3	3	0	0	1

Content Rating

	V.P.	Poor	Fair	Good	V.G.	Ex	OMIT			
%	0.00	0.10	0.00	0.20	0.20	0.50	0.00	Mean	=	5.00
#	0	1	0	2	2	5	0	S.D.	=	1.33

Instructor Rating

	V.P.	Poor	Fair	Good	V.G.	Ex	OMIT			
%	0.00	0.10	0.10	0.10	0.20	0.50	0.00	Mean	=	4.90
#	0	1	1	1	2	5	0	S.D.	=	1.29

Course Rating

	V.P.	Poor	Fair	Good	V.G.	Ex	OMIT			
%	0.00	0.10	0.10	0.10	0.20	0.50	0.00	Mean	=	4.80
#	0	1	1	1	2	5	0	S.D.	=	1.69

Subscale Results

Subscale	Items	% Res	Mean	S.D.	Rel.	IR	CL	D	C	UA	N
Attitude	4	1.00	3.28	1.06	0.98	4	5	3	4	5	6
Method	4	1.00	3.13	1.09	0.94	6	7	6	6	6	7
Content	4	1.00	3.30	0.91	0.68	8	8	8	8	8	9
Interest	4	1.00	3.08	1.07	0.88	7	7	5	6	7	7
Instructor	5	0.98	3.27	0.93	0.91	4	5	2	4	5	5
Total	21	1.00	3.21	1.01	0.98	6	7	5	6	6	7

IR=Instructor Rank; CL=Class Level; D=Department; C=College; UA=University of Arizona; N=Nationwide. NA in a normative decile category indicates that normative data is not available for this category or that this category is not applicable to the current data.

Arreola, R.A. (1995). *Developing a Comprehensive Faculty Evaluation System.* Bolton, MA: Anker Publishing Co., Inc.

Figure 30 (continued)   **Example of CIEQ analysis printout**

Instructor: ALEAMONI   **Class: EDP 646**   **Sample size: 10**
Process Date: 12/7/94   **College Code: 78933**

Individual Item Results

1. It was a very worthwhile course.

	AS	A	D	DS	OMIT	BEST	MEAN	S.D.	DEC
%	0.70	0.00	0.20	0.10	0.00	AS	3.30	1.16	5
#	7	0	2	1	0				

2. I would take another course that was taught this way.

	AS	A	D	DS	OMIT	BEST	MEAN	S.D.	DEC
%	0.70	0.00	0.20	0.10	0.00	AS	3.00	1.16	7
#	7	0	2	1	0				

3. The instructor seemed to be interested in students as individuals.

	AS	A	D	DS	OMIT	BEST	MEAN	S.D.	DEC
%	0.50	0.20	0.20	0.00	0.10	AS	3.33	0.87	4
#	5	2	2	0	1				

4. The course material was too difficult.

	AS	A	D	DS	OMIT	BEST	MEAN	S.D.	DEC
%	0.00	0.00	0.30	0.70	0.00	DS	3.70	0.48	10
#	0	0	3	7	0				

5. It was easy to remain attentive.

	AS	A	D	DS	OMIT	BEST	MEAN	S.D.	DEC
%	0.50	0.30	0.20	0.00	0.00	AS	3.30	0.82	8
#	5	3	2	0	0				

6. NOT much was gained by taking this course.

	AS	A	D	DS	OMIT	BEST	MEAN	S.D.	DEC
%	0.00	0.30	0.00	0.70	0.00	DS	3.40	0.97	5
#	0	3	0	7	0				

7. I would have preferred another method of teaching this course.

	AS	A	D	DS	OMIT	BEST	MEAN	S.D.	DEC
%	0.20	0.10	0.20	0.50	0.00	DS	3.00	1.25	6
#	2	1	2	5	0				

8. The course material seemed worthwhile.

	AS	A	D	DS	OMIT	BEST	MEAN	S.D.	DEC
%	0.50	0.30	0.20	0.00	0.00	AS	3.30	0.82	6
#	5	3	2	0	0				

9. The instructor did NOT synthesize, integrate or summarize effectively.

	AS	A	D	DS	OMIT	BEST	MEAN	S.D.	DEC
%	0.00	0.10	0.30	0.60	0.00	DS	3.50	0.71	8
#	0	1	3	6	0				

10. The course was quite interesting.

	AS	A	D	DS	OMIT	BEST	MEAN	S.D.	DEC
%	0.50	0.20	0.20	0.10	0.00	AS	3.10	1.10	5
#	5	2	2	1	0				

Arreola, R.A. (1995). *Developing a Comprehensive Faculty Evaluation System*. Bolton, MA: Anker Publishing Co., Inc.

Figure 30 (continued)   Example of CIEQ analysis printout.

11. The instructor encouraged development of new viewpoints and appreciations.

	AS	A	D	DS	OMIT	BEST	MEAN	S.D.	DEC
%	0.50	0.10	0.30	0.10	0.00	AS	3.00	1.15	4
#	5	1	3	1	0				

12. I learn more when other teaching methods are used.

	AS	A	D	DS	OMIT	BEST	MEAN	S.D.	DEC
%	0.00	0.20	0.40	0.40	0.00	DS	3.20	0.79	9
#	0	2	4	4	0				

13. Some things were not explained very well.

	AS	A	D	DS	OMIT	BEST	MEAN	S.D.	DEC
%	0.10	0.00	0.60	0.30	0.00	DS	3.10	0.88	8
#	1	0	6	3	0				

14. The instructor demonstrated a thorough knowledge of the subject matter.

	AS	A	D	DS	OMIT	BEST	MEAN	S.D.	DEC
%	0.60	0.30	0.10	0.00	0.00	AS	3.50	0.71	4
#	6	3	1	0	0				

15. This was one of my poorest courses.

	AS	A	D	DS	OMIT	BEST	MEAN	S.D.	DEC
%	0.10	0.20	0.10	0.60	0.00	DS	3.20	1.14	3
#	1	2	1	6	0				

16. The course content was excellent.

	AS	A	D	DS	OMIT	BEST	MEAN	S.D.	DEC
%	0.60	0.10	0.10	0.20	0.00	AS	3.10	1.29	6
#	6	1	1	2	0				

17. Some days I was NOT very interested in this course.

	AS	A	D	DS	OMIT	BEST	MEAN	S.D.	DEC
%	0.40	0.10	0.20	0.30	0.00	DS	2.40	1.35	5
#	4	1	2	3	0				

18. I think that the course was taught quite well.

	AS	A	D	DS	OMIT	BEST	MEAN	S.D.	DEC
%	0.50	0.20	0.10	0.20	0.00	AS	3.00	1.25	4
#	5	2	1	2	0				

19. The course was quite boring.

	AS	A	D	DS	OMIT	BEST	MEAN	S.D.	DEC
%	0.00	0.10	0.30	0.60	0.00	DS	3.50	0.71	8
#	0	1	3	6	0				

20. The instructor seemed to consider teaching as a chore or routine activity.

	AS	A	D	DS	OMIT	BEST	MEAN	S.D.	DEC
%	0.20	0.00	0.40	0.40	0.00	DS	3.00	1.15	2
#	2	0	4	4	0				

21. Overall, the course was good.

	AS	A	D	DS	OMIT	BEST	MEAN	S.D.	DEC
%	0.60	0.10	0.20	0.10	0.00	AS	3.20	1.14	4
#	6	1	2	1	0				

Arreola, R.A. (1995). *Developing a Comprehensive Faculty Evaluation System.* Bolton, MA: Anker Publishing Co., Inc.

A Brief CIEQ Interpretation Guide

The following outline is provided as an aid to the rapid interpretation of CIEQ results. This guide can be used as a checklist when examining the computerized analysis output of the CIEQ. CIEQ interpretation is discussed in complete detail in the *Manual*.

STEP 1. ADEQUACY OF RESULTS

A. Refer to the top of the first page of the CIEQ output. Check the SAMPLE SIZE. If it or number of the students responding is less than one-half of the course enrollment, results may be biased and should be interpreted with caution.

B. At the bottom of the first page is the section entitled SUBSCALE RESULTS that contains a column of figures labeled REL. This column contains the obtained reliabilities for the six subscales of the CIEQ. Any subscale with a REL below .65 should be interpreted with caution. Consult the *Manual* for further details.

STEP 2. COMPARATIVE INFORMATION

A. In all cases, comparative information is provided by decile rank (DEC). The decile rank describes the current course MEAN in relation to other courses that have administered the CIEQ. Decile ranks are always interpreted as follows:

    1 – 3   Substantial improvement needed

    4 – 7   Some improvement needed

    8 – 10   No improvement needed

Differences between adjacent pairs of decile ranks within each interval (e.g., 1 vs. 2, or 4 vs. 5) are not considered to be significantly different.

B. First refer to the SUBSCALE listing at the bottom of output on page 1. Each subscale represents a different aspect of the course as indicated by its title. Decile ranks for the current course/instructor are listed for each subscale in comparison to six normative groups:

    1. IR   all instructors of the same faculty rank

    2. CL   all courses at the same grade level (e.g., freshman, sophomore., etc.)

    3. D   all courses within the same department

    4. C   all courses within the same college

    5. UA all course at the University of Arizona

    6. N   all courses that have used the CIEQ in the United States

C. On the following two pages under INDIVIDUAL ITEM RESULTS are listed each of the 21 individual items of the CIEQ along with the proportion (%), frequency (#), mean, and standard deviation (SD) of responses to each individual item of the CIEQ. Also listed are the text of each item and the most favorable response or BEST answer for each item. All means have been scaled such that 4.00 is the most favorable response and 1.00 is the least favorable response, regardless of the initial wording of the item. To the far right of each individual item are listed decile ranks that compare each item mean to the item means obtained in all courses within the same college.

D. In interpreting results, refer first to the decile ranks for subscales. Low deciles for a subscale identify potential problem areas. Individual items can then be examined for more specific information. The subscales are composed of the following individual items:

Attitude	items 1, 6, 15, 21
Method	items 2, 7, 12, 18
Content	items 4, 8, 13, 16
Interest	items 5, 10, 17, 19
Instructor	items 3, 9, 11, 14, 20
Total	items 1–21

STEP 3. DESCRIPTIVE INFORMATION

A. Refer to the top of the first page of CIEQ output. Following the initial titles, information is listed on the composition of the responding sample under the heading Class Description Results. Both the proportion and frequency of responses are listed for each alternative of the following items: Class Information, Gender, Course Option, Pass-Fail Option, Major-Minor, and Expected Grade.

B. The next portion of the output lists the proportion (%), frequency (#), mean, and and standard deviation (SD) of responses to three global ratings: Course Content, Instructor Rating, and the Course Rating. A mean value of 6.00 is the most favorable rating. *These three items have NOT been validated and should therefore be used only for the purpose of feedback to the instructor.*

References

Aleamoni, L. M. (1978). Development and factorial validation of the Arizona course/instructor evaluation questionnaire. *Educational and Psychological Measurement, 38,* 1063–1067.

Aleamoni, L. M. *Arizona Course/instructor Evaluation Questionnaire: Results Interpretation Manual.* Tucson, Arizona: University of Arizona, Office of Instructional Research and Development, undated.

Aleamoni, L. M., & Carynnk, D. B. (1977). *Optional item catalog (revised).* (Information Memorandum No. 6) Tucson, Arizona: University of Arizona, Office of Instructional Research and Development.

Aleamoni, L. M., & Spencer, R. E. (1973). The Illinois course evaluation questionnaire: A description of its development and a report of some of its results. *Educational and Psychological Measurement, 33,* 669–684.

Gillmore, G. M. (1973). *Estimates of Reliability Coefficients for Items and Subscales of the Illinois Course Evaluation Questionnaire (RR 341).* Urbana, Illinois: University of Illinois, Measurement and Research Division, Office of Instructional Resources.

Using the CIEQ for Long-Term Instructional Improvement: A Case Study

As part of a larger faculty evaluation system which includes information from a variety of sources, student ratings have been found to be an important tool in efforts to improve the instructional effectiveness of the instructor. Reviews of the validity of student ratings have established the usefulness of well-designed student rating forms as a measure of instructional effectiveness (Aleamoni, 1980; Centra, 1979; Cohen, 1981; Kulik & Kulik, 1974; Marsh, 1980; McKeachie, 1979; Millman, 1981). Information derived from student ratings can serve a number of purposes. Cohen (1980) defined three such purposes: (1) to aid in administrative decisions, (2) to aid students in course/instructor selection, and (3) to provide feedback to instructors for instructional improvement.

Some disagreement exists in recent reviews regarding the effectiveness of student evaluations for improving instruction. A review by Rotem and Glasman (1979) concluded that "feedback from student ratings does not seem to be effective for the purpose of improving performance of university teachers" (p. 507). Similarly, Kulik and McKeachie (1975) concluded that the improvement of instruction through written feedback was not supported by the available research.

Two recent reviews were more supportive of the effect of feedback on instructional improvement. Cohen (1980) conducted a meta-analysis of 22 instructional feedback studies. From the analysis, he concluded that feedback had a modest but significant effect (15 percentile points) in improving instruction. Cohen also found that this effect was accentuated when consultation accompanied feedback. In the most extensive review to date, Levinson-Rose and Menges (1981) reviewed 71 studies of instructional improvement interventions. Studies were categorized by the type of intervention used and the author's degree of confidence in the methodology of the study. Within the intervention category of student ratings feedback (38 studies), 66% of the studies reported successful interventions. Levinson-Rose and Menges concluded that student ratings feedback "can positively affect subsequent teaching, particularly if ratings are accompanied by consultation" (p. 419).

Thus, both the available body of research and the conclusions of the reviews are at odds. While a number of studies have reported no apparent effect of feedback on instructional improvement, others have reported substantial effects. For example, Overall and Marsh (1979) found that student ratings, achievement, and motivation all increased following feedback to the instructor. At this point in time, therefore, it seems most reasonable to conclude that instructional improvement occurs as a function of feedback only with certain experimental settings and interventions and, perhaps, only with certain instructors or courses. There does seem to be agreement that consultation augments the effects of feedback. Isolation and definition of variables responsible for differences in reported results has not yet been demonstrated empirically.

A number of authors have specified constraints that may minimize the benefits of student-ratings feedback (Cohen, 1980; Kulik & Kulik, 1974; McKeachie, 1979). First of these is the novelty of the feedback information provided by student ratings. If ratings do not result in new information or information that is perceived as worthwhile, the instructor may not be motivated to change. A second potential constraint involves the consistency of student ratings with the instructor's self-rating or self-perception of instructional effectiveness. Some discrepancy between instructor self-rating and student ratings may be necessary to motivate instructor change. The third, and perhaps most important, constraint is that the instructor may not know *how* to change. That is, providing critical feedback does not ensure that implementation of effective strategies for improvement will occur.

One important aspect of the study of instructional improvement has been neglected in the literature, that of the long-term effects of intervention. Of the 71 studies reviewed by Levinson-Rose and Menges (1981), only two were of a longer duration than 2 years. No study has been reported that assessed the effects of feedback over a period longer than 4 years. Yet the long-term development of the instructor is obviously a crucial aspect of instructional improvement. For purposes of instructional improvement and development, the greatest import attaches to those interventions that result in lasting gain for the instructor. Interventions that produce only short-term improvement must be accorded lesser importance. Surprisingly, however, the design of most studies of instructional intervention is of such short duration that the identification of long-term effects is impossible. It is unknown whether reported short-term effects continue over time or are limited to the one- or two-semester duration of most studies. Levinson-Rose and Menges appropriately caution that instructional improvement interventions are unlikely to produce lasting changes "unless participants continue skill practice and receive critical feedback on their efforts" (p. 419).

The purpose of this study was to investigate some aspects of the longitudinal study of instructional improvement. The study reports the long-term follow-up of an instructional intervention conducted during academic year 1971-72 by Aleamoni (1978). In this study, a significant increase in student ratings was reported after both feedback and consultation were provided to instructors. As part of a 3-day workshop held at the University of Arizona, 33 instructors administered the third generation of the Course/Instructor Evaluation Questionnaire. The student ratings obtained on the CIEQ were provided to all instructors as feedback. In addition, 20 of the 33 instructors participating in the study engaged in individual diagnostic consultations with the author. After a 1-semester delay, CIEQ student ratings were found to be significantly higher for those instructors who had received feedback and consultation in comparison to instructors receiving feedback (CIEQ results) only.

In 1975, three years after the original study, the University of Arizona established the Office of Instructional Research and Development (IRAD). Among other services, the office provided student evaluations of instruction using the CIEQ. As a result, instructors who had participated in the original study had the opportunity to continue use of the CIEQ and seek other instructional support services (e.g., consultation, teaching workshops) on a voluntary basis from 1975 to the present. The availability of the same evaluation instrument over a 10-year interval resulted in a unique but unplanned opportunity to examine the long-term effects of instructional intervention. The purpose of the present study was to examine the use and results of student ratings evaluation for the instructors who had participated in the original study.

Method
Sample. In the original study (Aleamoni, 1978), 33 instructors at the University of Arizona during the fall 1971 and spring 1972 semesters served as subjects. All instructors were teaching courses in the College of Agriculture. The courses ranged from freshman to graduate level and represented a wide range of course material (e.g., agricultural engineering, plant pathology, entomology). The 33 instructors taught 52 courses with a total enrollment of 3358 students. The instructors participating in the study held faculty positions ranging from instructor to full professor (mean rank was between assistant and associate professor). At the time of the original study, 27 of the instructors held a doctoral degree and the remaining 6 instructors held a master's degree. The mean number of years since degree completion was 10 and ranged from 1 to 38 years.

Instrumentation. In both the original and the follow-up studies, student ratings were obtained on the CIEQ. The CIEQ is the fourth generation of an evaluation instrument originally developed at the University of Illinois. The instrument was designed to elicit student opinions about a standardized set of statements that reflect particular aspects of an instructional program. The CIEQ is composed of 21 statements. The students respond to each statement on a 4-point scale ranging from agree strongly to disagree strongly. Previous factor-analytic studies established five subscales that were labeled General Course Attitude, Method of Instruction, Course Content, Interest and Attention, and Instructor. The label of the subscale accurately reflects the content of items composing the subscale. For example, instructor items elicit evaluations of actual instructor performance as opposed to course content items which reflect course materials or information presented. The subscales were designed to identify general areas of instructional excellence or difficulty. No changes in the instrument occurred between the original and follow-up studies. Further information on the CIEQ, its subscales, and reliability and validity is available in Aleamoni (1979), Aleamoni and Spencer (1973), and Brandenburg and Aleamoni (1976).

Procedure. For each instructor who had participated in the original study, data were collated for all uses of the CIEQ following termination of the original study (December 1972). The CIEQ was not available to instructors from the spring term of 1973 through the spring term of 1975. The follow-up period, therefore, encompassed 14 semester from fall 1975 to spring 1982. During this time the CIEQ was available for voluntary use by all University of Arizona teaching faculty. Records were also searched to determine the number of times instructors had used instructional resources during the follow-up period. The primary resources available to instructors were individual consultations on the CIEQ and its interpretation and intensive workshops on instructional effectiveness.

In the original study, two experimental groups were defined: An experimental group (feedback with consultation) and a control group (feedback only). Feedback was provided to all instructors in the form of computerized

CIEQ results. These results included the distribution of student ratings for each item, item means and standard deviations, subscale means, standard deviations and reliabilities, and comparisons of the obtained items and subscale means with a norm group. In addition to this feedback information, 20 instructors engaged in a diagnostic interpretation interview with the consultant (the minor author). The consultant had made arrangements to interview all 33 instructors. Because of time constraints, however, not all of the instructors met with the consultant. Instructors had submitted their available times to the dean of resident instruction. The dean then matched the instructor's available time to the schedule of the consultant. Determination of which instructors met with the consultant was then decided by the dean as a function of concordance in the schedules. This resulted in two *ex post facto* experimental groups, one of whom received only CIEQ results with no consultative follow-up.

Each consultation interview consisted of the inspection of CIEQ results by the instructor and the consultant. When student ratings on a particular subscale were poor, results for specific items composing that subscale were examined. On the basis of this examination and further discussion, potential difficulties and strategies for improvement were considered. This procedure was followed for 17 of the 20 scheduled instructors. The obtained CIEQ results for the three remaining instructors exhibited no deficiencies (mean ratings above 80% of the norm group). No further consultation occurred with these three instructors.

Thus, the 33 instructors participating in the original study encountered three distinct forms of informational feedback. Thirteen instructors received student ratings results only. Seventeen instructors received student rating results, interpretation of rating results, and consultation for improvement. Three instructors received ratings results and results interpretation with no additional consultation. These last three instructors were excluded from the report of the original study on the rationale that they were not properly part of the experimental consultation group. These three groups of instructors are hereafter referred to as the feedback only (FO) group, the feedback with consultation (FC) group, and the feedback-excluded from consultation (FEC) group, respectively. In summary, three *ex post facto* experimental groups were defined as a function of the type of feedback information delivered. Two groups (FO and FC) were defined by the instructors' dean of resident instruction on the basis of scheduling constraints. The third group (FEC) was determined by the consultant's interpretation of obtained student ratings.

Results

Seventeen of the original 33 instructors (52%) were identified as using the CIEQ during the following period. Table 2 details instructor and course information during both the original and follow-up studies. A total of 7095 students were enrolled in 132 courses in which the CIEQ was administered during the follow-up period. This represented a decrease in average class size from the original study (X=64.6 students per class) to the follow-up study (X=53.8 students per class). The level of the course also increased from the original study (X=2.1) to follow-up study (X=2.6). As would be expected, instructor rank increased over time. Univariate analyses of variance were computed to test the comparability of the three groups on these three course/instructor variables. The 3X(2) analyses (groups by time) indicated that no significant differences were present between groups or from the original to the follow-up study in terms of class size, course level, or instructor rank (all Fs<1.0).

Use of Instructional Resources. Although CIEQ data were available for only 17 of the original instructors during the follow-up period, attrition of instructors was related to group membership. Inspection of records revealed that the majority of the instructors (70%) were present at the institution during the follow-up period (Table 3). Of the 10 instructors no longer present, 3 FO group instructors, 3 FC group instructors, and 1 FEC group instructor had left the institution. Three other FC group instructors achieved emeritus status in the interim between the original and follow-up studies and were no longer teaching.

All but one of the remaining FC and FEC group instructors used the CIEQ during the follow-up period. However, only 50% of the remaining FO group instructors used the CIEQ. A z-test of proportions was computed to determine whether the obtained distribution of CIEQ users from the three groups was probable by chance. A significantly greater proportion of the FC group instructors used the CIEQ in comparison to FO group instructors (z=2.07, p<0.05). The two remaining comparisons of proportional differences (FC vs. FEC, FEC v. FO) were not significant.

It was also apparent that the frequency of CIEQ used was different among those instructors using the CIEQ during the 14 semester follow-up period. The mean frequency of use by the three groups was 9.2, 6.5, and 5.4 by the FC, FEC, and FO instructors, respectively. A one-way analysis of variance of frequency of use by groups was significant (F(2,25)=4.24, MS=4.28, p<0.05). Post hoc comparison of the three group means using the Newman-Keuls method indicated that the frequency of use by the FC group was significantly greater (p<0.05) than the frequency of use by either the FO or FEC groups.

Visual inspection of the CIEQ ratings obtained in the original study by individual FO group instructors revealed an apparent association between continued use of the CIEQ and pre- to postchanges in student ratings. FO group data were cast into a 2X2 classification composed of pre-post gain vs. decline in original study ratings crossed with later CIEQ use vs. nonuse (Table 4). As previously reported, 5 of the 10 FO group instructors remaining at the institution did not use the CIEQ during the follow-up period. All five of these instructors experienced a decline in student ratings during the original study. Fisher's exact test was applied to the classification in Table 4. The test yielded an estimate of the chance probability of this distribution of instructors equal to 0.04. During the original study, student ratings declined from pre to post for three of the FC instructors and both of the FEC instructors who were present during the follow-up. In contrast with the FO group, however, all other instructors who experience a pre-post decline in student ratings in the original study used the CIEQ during the follow-up period.

Table 2   Instructor and Course Data

Original Study (2 semesters)

Group	No. of instructors	No. of courses	Mean courses per instructor	Mean course level*	Mean instructor rank**	Mean years since last degree
Feedback Only	13	18	1.4	2.5	2.5	9.0
Feedback with Consultation	17	30	1.8	1.9	2.9	11.1
Excluded from Consultation	3	4	1.3	2.5	3.0	8.3
Total	33	52	1.6	2.1	2.8	10.0

Follow-up Study (14 semesters)

Group	No. of instructors	No. of courses	Mean courses per instructor	Mean course level*	Mean instructor rank**	Mean years since last degree
Feedback Only	5	27	0.8	2.8	3.4	
Feedback with Consultation)	10	92	1.3	2.2	3.9	
Excluded from Consultation	2	13	0.9	3.3	3.5	
Total	17	132	1.1	2.6	3.7	

* Course level coded as follows: 1 = freshman, 2 = sophomore, 3 = junior, 4 = senior, 5 = graduate.
** Instructor rank coded as follows: 1 = instructor, 2 = assistant professor, 3 = associate professor, 4 = full professor.

Table 3   Group Composition and Use of CIEQ by Group

Group	Original Study	Follow-up period		
	No. of instructors	No. of Instructors present at follow-up*	No. of Instructors using CIEQ*	Mean no. of uses of CIEQ
FO	13	10 (77%)	5 (50%)	5.4
FC	17	11 (65%)	10 (91%)	9.2
FEC	3	2 (67%)	2 (100%)	6.5
Total	33	23 (70%)	17 (52%)	7.8

* Percentage of original group.
** Percentage of instructors at the institution during follow-up.

Arreola, R.A. (1995). *Developing a Comprehensive Faculty Evaluation System.* Bolton, MA: Anker Publishing Co., Inc.

Table 4   Original Study, Pre- to Post-rating Differences for FO Group Instructors as a Function of Later Use of the CIEQ

CIEQ used during follow-up?	Increase	Decrease	Total
Yes	3	2	5
No	0	5	5
Total	3	7	10

Figure 31 illustrates the use of the CIEQ and other instructional resources during the follow-up period. After the termination of the original study, no FEC group instructors and only one FO group instructor used resources other than the CIEQ. This instructor attended one instructional workshop and engaged in one individual consultation during the follow-up. However, 6 of the 10 FC group instructors used resources. Five of these instructors attended workshops and four instructors engaged in a total of seven individual consultations. This difference among groups in the proportion of instructors using instructional resources was significant $[X^2(2)=6.8, p<0.05]$.

Thus, a clear pattern of discrepancy among the groups was evidenced during the follow-up period on all available measures of the use of instructional resources. Almost all FC and FEC instructors used the CIEQ as compared to 50% of the FO instructors. Of those instructors who used the CIEQ during the follow-up period, the most frequent use was evidenced by the FC group instructors who aver-

aged approximately 1.3 uses per year. The CIEQ was used least frequently by FO group instructors at an average of less than once per year. Because the CIEQ was used by nearly all FC and FEC instructors, there was no association between pre-post differences during the original study and use of CIEQ during the follow-up study. However, there was an association between original study ratings decline and later nonuse of the CIEQ for the FO group instructors. Additionally, instructional resources were used by more FC group instructors than by instructors from the other two groups.

In summary, FC group instructors used student ratings and related resources much more frequently than instructors from the other groups. FEC group instructors used the CIEQ, but used the instrument less frequently and did not use instructional resources. Only half of the FO group instructors used the CIEQ. Of the five FO instructors who did not use the CIEQ during the follow-up, all experienced a pre-post decline in student ratings during the original study. And only one FO instructor used related resources during the follow-up period.

Student Ratings of Instruction. The individual course was the unit of analysis in the original study. The focus of the present study, however, was instructor change over time. Therefore, the instructor was the unit of analysis in the present study. To accomplish this change in unit of analysis, the student ratings for all multiple courses within a semester were averaged for each instructor. This was done for student ratings from both the original study and the follow-up study. The resulting number of instructors using the CIEQ in each cell of the three-groups-by-14-semesters matrix varied greatly and included a number of empty cells. Because CIEQ use differed by group, the occurrence of

Figure 31   Use of Instructional Resources During the Follow-Up Period of Three Groups

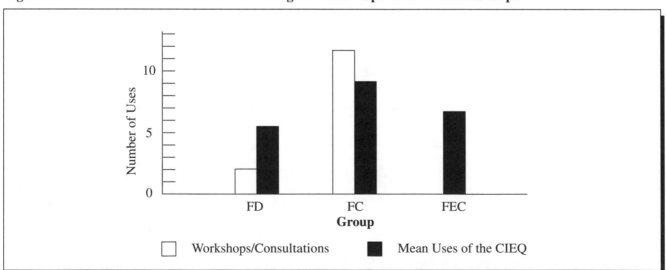

Arreola, R.A. (1995). *Developing a Comprehensive Faculty Evaluation System.* Bolton, MA: Anker Publishing Co., Inc.

empty cells was related to group membership. The 14 semesters of ratings data were, therefore, collapsed for each instructor to form two follow-up ratings means on each CIEQ subscale. These means represented two equal follow-up intervals. The first interval represented ratings obtained from fall 1975 to fall 1978 (7 semesters). An average of 4.8 years elapsed between the termination of the original study and this first follow-up period. The second follow-up interval consisted of averaged student ratings from spring 1979 to spring 1982 (7 semesters). The average elapsed time for this interval was 8.6 years. This resulted in a three-groups-by-four-time-intervals (original study pre and post, follow-up one and two) matrix with no empty cells. The means of the five subscales are presented in Table 5.

The five subscales of the obtained CIEQ ratings were then analyzed using a 3x(4), groups by time interval, mixed-design multiple analysis of variance. Three effects were tested, the main effects of group and of time and the interaction of groups and time. None of the multivariate tests was significant (all Fs<2). However, small but significant interaction effects were obtained in the univariate tests of two of the five subscales. In the test of the Method subscale, $F_{(3,39)} - 2.98$, MSe=0.03, p<0.05. The group by time interaction was also significant on the Instructor subscale, for which $F_{(3,39)}-3.58$, MSe=0.02, p<0.05. Newman-Keuls comparisons among the Method subscale interaction means resulted in two significant comparisons (p<0.05). These two differences were between the FEC second follow-up and the FO original study posttest means (both Xs=2.91) against the FEC group pretest means (3.32). Newman-Keuls comparisons among the Instructor subscale interaction means yielded four significant mean differences (p<0.05). The FEC group pretest mean was greater than both of the FEC group follow-up means. The FEC group pretest and posttest means were significantly greater than the FO group posttest mean. No other comparisons were significant.

The group-by-time-interval interaction on the method and instructor subscales is presented in Figure 32. Student ratings for the three other subscales showed smaller overall differences between groups but otherwise resembled the ratings obtained on the method subscale. The change in analysis unit from courses to instructors did not alter the pattern of results reported in the original study. On all subscales, averaged FC group ratings increased from pre to post and relative to the FO group ratings. The FEC group

Table 5 Obtained CIEQ Subscale Means by Group and Time Period

Condition	Original study		Follow-up study	
	Pre	Post	First interval	Second interval
Feedback Only (FO)				
Attitude	3.37	3.25	3.36	3.39
Method	2.98	2.91	2.98	3.01
Content	3.08	3.06	3.07	3.17
Attention	3.08	2.96	2.94	2.93
Instructor	3.30	3.19	3.35	3.46
Feedback with Consultation (FC)				
Attitude	3.30	3.34	3.45	3.5
Method	2.96	3.07	3.2	3.24
Content	3.04	3.14	3.2	3.25
Attention	3.02	2.99	3.05	3.06
Instructor	3.25	3.32	3.37	3.46
Feedback-Excluded Consultation (FEC)				
Attitude	3.55	3.45	3.32	3.47
Method	3.32	3.07	2.97	2.91
Content	3.26	3.19	3.03	3.05
Attention	3.32	3.04	2.92	3.01
Instructor	3.55	3.50	3.23	3.23

Arreola, R.A. (1995). *Developing a Comprehensive Faculty Evaluation System.* Bolton, MA: Anker Publishing Co., Inc.

instructors, who had been excluded from the original study, showed a marked decline in student ratings from pre to post.

During the follow-up period, FC group ratings increased from the first to the second interval and were higher than ratings for the other two groups on four of the five subscales. On the Instructor subscale, ratings for the FC group were quite similar to FO group ratings at both follow-up occasions. FO group ratings increased on two subscales (Instructor and Course Content) over the two follow-up intervals. On the other three subscales, FO group ratings showed little change over follow-up intervals. On all five subscales, FEC group ratings showed little change over follow-up intervals and were consistently low relative to FO group ratings. As reported previously, however, only the most extreme mean differences on the Method and Instructor subscales were supported by Newman-Keuls tests.

Discussion

In general, the obtained results support the conclusion that the original intervention produced instructor change. Significant differences were found between groups on all measures of the use of instructional resources and on student ratings of instructor performance. Two interpretative considerations add strength to this conclusion. First, though the obtained effects are statistically small, the power of tests was low. In the 3x4 matrix of student ratings reported earlier, the harmonic mean of cell n-size was 4.75. Post hoc estimation of the power of the MANOVA of student ratings indicated that even with a sample size of 10, the power of test would have been less than 0.48 (Stevens, 1980).

Figure 32   Mean Student Ratings by Group in Two CIEQ Subscales at Four Occasions

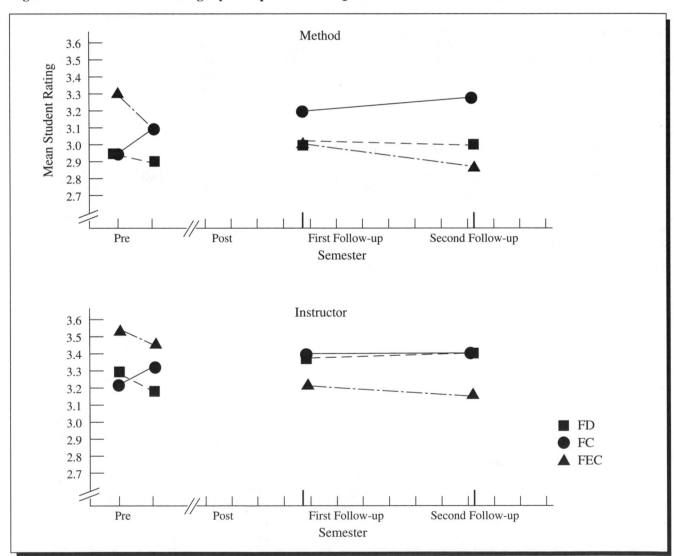

Arreola, R.A. (1995). *Developing a Comprehensive Faculty Evaluation System.* Bolton, MA: Anker Publishing Co., Inc.

Given larger cell size and the concomitant increase in statistical power, the chance likelihood of the reported results decreases substantially. It was possible to enhance power estimation in the present study by using normative CIEQ information. The CIEQ norms were based on 8335 courses in which the CIEQ was administered at the University of Arizona. Normative statistics can be used as stable estimators of the population parameters u and δ. For the Method subscale, these estimates are u = 2.98 and δ = 0.43, and u = 3.29, δ = 0.34 on the Instructor subscale. Using these values, estimated power in the present study was also estimated to be no greater than 0.50, dependent on the assumed effect size.

The second interpretative consideration was also provided from normative information. The reported discrepancies between groups represent substantive differences in comparison to the norm distribution. For example, on the Method subscale, the mean normative percentile rank of the FC group during follow-up was approximately 65. The mean FO group percentile rank during follow-up was approximately 44. Thus, a difference of more than two deciles existed in the norm distribution between the FC and FO groups during the follow-up period. In comparison to normative standards, this discrepancy was larger and substantive.

The instructional behavior of the FC group instructors was quite different from that of other instructors throughout the follow-up period. These instructors were characterized by moderate to high student ratings on all CIEQ subscales that tended to improve modestly over time. These instructors were, as a group, relatively frequent users of available instructional resources. They used the CIEQ regularly for course evaluation, attended instructional workshops, and initiated individual consultation on instruction.

The feedback-only group of instructors was represented by half of the remaining instructors who had participated in the original study. The five nonparticipating instructors used no instructional resources and did not use the CIEQ for course evaluation at any time during the 14 semester follow-up period. It was not possible to determine whether these instructors had used alternative forms of course evaluation. However, the CIEQ was the only norm-based, standardized instrument available at the institution during the reported interval. These five nonparticipating instructors had all experienced a decline in student ratings during the original study.

The five participating instructors in the FO group were characterized by moderate student ratings. Average FO group ratings were lower than FC group ratings on all five subscales at both follow-up intervals. On the Instructor subscale, FO group ratings closely mirrored FC group ratings. The participating FO group instructors used the CIEQ regularly but much less frequently than FC group instructors. And four of the five FO group instructors did not use instructional resources at any time during the follow-up.

The FEC group instructors were characterized by moderate to low student ratings that were quite disparate in comparison to FC group ratings. While the FEC instructors used the CIEQ, they did not use instructional resources. Furthermore, their use of the CIEQ continued despite a marked decline of student ratings in the original study.

These characterizations of instructor behavior during the follow-up appear to be substantive given considerations of power and normative information. Interpretation of these results, however, was complex. A number of methodological issues were considered that are germane to both the present study and the longitudinal study of instructional intervention in general.

The first of these concerns was sample size. The majority or reported instructional intervention studies have used small samples. A common misconception is that low confidence automatically attaches to small sample studies (Rosenthal & Gaito, 1963). Actually, all other things being equal, rejection of the null hypothesis when N is small increases confidence that differences are reliable. A more relevant concern regarding sample size in instructional intervention studies is the ability to generalize from limited samples. In the present study, the sample was not drawn randomly and was quite small. Therefore, to the extent that these instructors were not representative of university instructors in general, the reported results are limited. The possible interaction of nonrepresentative instructor characteristics with characteristics of the consultant or the methods of intervention should also be considered.

A second interpretative concern was the quasi-experimental nature of the present study. The definition of groups in the original study was beyond experimental control and was, therefore, nonsystematic. It is unknown whether the resultant instructor groups were comparable. Analysis of the available course and instructor variables did not reveal significant differences between groups. This result, however, may also have been a function of low statistical power. Furthermore, potentially relevant concomitant variables can be postulated for which no test of comparability of groups was available (e.g., instructor motivation).

A common criticism of some instructional intervention studies is the failure to use random assignment procedures. The automatic application of this criticism obscures several important considerations of design and interpretation. First, the majority of instructional intervention studies use small samples. Though the number of students may be large, assignment is usually performed using instructors or intact classes. The total number of sampling units, therefore, is seldom as large as 50, and assignment is usually made to two or more groups. This poses a serious difficulty in that random assignment is relatively ineffective as a tactic of control when samples are small. However, critical reviews of instructional intervention studies have placed high confidence in small sample studies using random assignment and low confidence in studies that exert less control over group composition. It is important to realize that few studies have adequately addressed the composition of experimental groups, and low confidence in experimental control therefore accrues to many studies, including some using random assignment. While the use of random assignment is advisable even if sample size is small, other tactics of blocking, matching, or statistical control should augment random assignment (cf. Cook & Campbell, 1979). And, as Weisberg (1979) has pointed out, "until we have tried to develop alternatives not based on 'approximations' to randomization" (p. 1163), we may need to proceed with the cautious interpretation of uncontrolled studies. That is, we must apply the same interpretative caution to "weak" randomization studies that is accorded to quasi-experimental studies. Strong interpretations are not warranted in either case.

A second outcome of automatic allegiance to random assignment is the neglect of the identification and description of relevant extraneous or concomitant variables. A number of studies are available that describe the interrelationship of student ratings and several concomitant variables (e.g., faculty rank, class size, required vs. elective courses). These studies serve as useful guidelines. However, identifying variables that interact with the effects of instructional intervention *over time* has yet to occur. Identifying such variables will certainly aid researchers in interpreting results and in devising more precise methods of experimental and statistical control.

In the present study, several sources of uncontrolled variation hamper a direct interpretation of results. The difficulty of interpretation can be illustrated through the presentation of ratings from three individual instructors. Figure 33 displays student ratings obtained over time on the Method subscale for two of the FC group instructors and one FO group instructor.

The two FC group instructors were the most frequent users of the CIEQ and had attended at least one workshop. The third instructor was the most frequent user of the CIEQ from the FO group. Inspection of Figure 33 reveals that all three instructors experienced a pre-post increase in student ratings during the original study. In comparison to norms, Instructor 1 received high student ratings throughout the follow-up period. A marked declined in ratings occurred at

Figure 33 **Student Ratings on the Method Subscale for Three Individual Instructors over 11 Years. Inset contains the percentage of studies reported using four duration categories: A=<1/2 year, Avg. = 0.25; B = 0.5 - 0.9 year, Avg. = .51; C = 1 year, Avg. = 1.0; D = 1.1 - 4 years, Avg. = 2.75.**

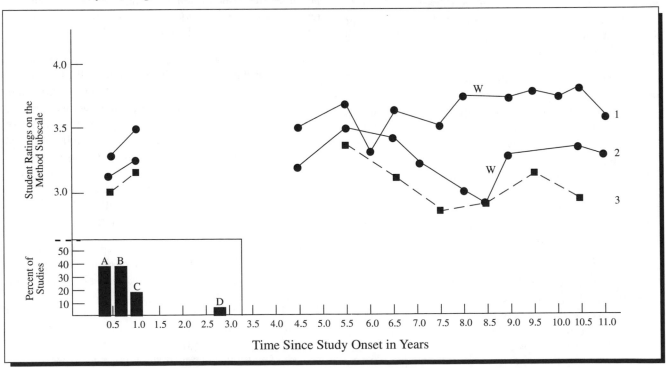

Arreola, R.A. (1995). *Developing a Comprehensive Faculty Evaluation System.* Bolton, MA: Anker Publishing Co., Inc.

year 6 when instructor 1 was appointed director of a research laboratory. The "w" preceding year 8 denotes the time at which instructor 1 participated in an instructional workshop. A slight increase in ratings occurred following the workshop. Instructor 2 demonstrated greater variability in obtained student ratings over time. As with instructor 1, instructor 2 received higher student ratings directly following participation in an instructional workshop. Instructor 3's student ratings are lower than the ratings of the other two instructors and also display substantial variability over time. As with the other two instructors, high frequency of CIEQ use during follow-up was associated with a pre-post gain in the original study.

In the present study, interpretation of the obtained results was aided by the availability of repeated follow-up measurement. Several competing interpretations that were tenable as explanations of the original study results are unlikely given the results obtained in the follow-up study. For example, it could have been hypothesized that group differences in the original study were an artifact arising from a regression effect. Continued separation of the groups throughout the follow-up period, however, negates the acceptance of this and several other competing interpretations.

The initial composition of groups remains a difficulty in interpretation. The obtained results can be ascribed either to initial differences in instructor groupings or to the effects of feedback and consultation. In either case, several conclusions can be drawn from the present study. First, the reported results are indicative of a phenomenon that is relatively stable over time. If group differences are a function of an uncontrolled artifact influence, then the effect of the hypothesized influence is long-lived. One such influence that can be hypothesized is differential instructor motivation. We can speculate that the original groups were composed in such a way that highly motivated instructors were assigned to the feedback with consultation group and less motivated instructors were assigned to the feedback only group. If so, then the artifact motivational differences responsible for the results of the original study continue over time or, at least, initiate an effect that was long-lived. A similar conclusion applies if it is assumed that the original groups were comparable prior to intervention. In this case, the obtained results indicate that the effects of the intervention are long-lived or that intervention can initiate an effect that is long-lived.

It can also be concluded that high student ratings are associated with the use and greater frequency of use of instructional resources. There was a marked difference in resource utilization between the feedback with consultation instructors and the other two instructor groups. This association obtains regardless of the mechanism hypothesized to account for intergroup differences in student ratings.

A third conclusion drawn from the present study was that group membership interacts with the relationship between the initial results of feedback and future use of student ratings. All but one of the FC and FEC instructors continued to use the CIEQ during the follow-up period. However, use of the CIEQ during follow-up by the feedback-only instructors was related to pre-post changes in ratings in the original study.

Figure 33 also illustrates a number of concerns in the study of instructional improvement. First, the focus of improvement studies is too often on aggregate differences to the neglect of the individual instructor. Our true interest is in the development of *individuals* as effective instructors. This interest can be served through more frequent consideration of alternative research strategies including single subject and time series methods, often advocated for other areas of research (Bergin & Strupp, 1972; Hersen & Barlow, 1976; Kratochwill, 1978). Second, an emphasis on aggregate differences often obscures particularly useful information. In Figure 33, what changes may have occurred that interacted with instructors or raters to influence the obtained ratings? The change in professional responsibilities experienced by instructor 1 at year 6 suggests such an influence. Numerous extraneous factors are present in the instructional milieu that may threaten the evaluation of the success of an instructional intervention. Such variables are often neglected to the detriment of our understanding of the processes governing instructional improvement. Greater experimental and statistical control of these variables will increase confidence in studies of instructional intervention. Furthermore, these variables may interact with the effectiveness of instructional interventions. To the extent such interactions occur, these variables must be identified to further the effectiveness of intervention. In the present study, no strong conclusions regarding the effects of intervention on individuals were attempted. Such conclusions are precluded by the lack of experimental control over the presentation of treatments and the influence of extraneous variables. Figure 33 does suggest, however, the complexity of the study of the individual in the demonstration of effective instructional intervention.

Last, Figure 33 illustrates the failure of instructional intervention studies to address the longitudinal nature of instructional improvement and development. Levinson-Rose and Menges (1981) reported the approximate duration of the 71 studies they reviewed. These durations were collated in the present study to form four length-of-study categories. This information is presented in histogram form in the inset in Figure 33. The distance from the ordinate represents the mean study duration in each category. The height of histogram bars represents the percentage of all studies reported that are contained in the particular duration category. Eighty percent of all studies encompassed an interval of less than 1 year. Forty percent of the studies lasted less than 1 semester. In general, it may be concluded that the longitudinal study of instructional improvement has not yet occurred. The short duration of studies reported in the literature also raises questions regarding the adequacy of experimental control. Several threats to validity are unlikely to be controlled in the typical short-term design. For example, Hawthorne or instrument sensitization effects are likely to be problematic in studies that encompass less than 1 semester. In studies conducted over 2 terms, changes in rater group composition, regression effects, changes from fall to spring in composition or course conduct, changes in rating scale use (rating inflation or deflation), as well as other potential changes are possible. Figure 33 should, therefore, serve not only to underscore both the complexity of longitudinal study and the concomitant need for experimental control, but also the inadequacy of the available literature in describing the longitudinal development of the instructor.

The results obtained were consistent with the conclusions of the reviewers. Providing feedback information alone did not result in consistent gains for the instructor. Providing consultation in addition to student rating feedback resulted in an increase in student ratings that was maintained over time and in greater use of instructional resources. This result was similar to Cohen's (1980) finding that providing normative comparisons of feedback results was not related to instructional improvement.

In summary, alternative tactics of experimental design should be considered in the study of the effects of intervention on instructional improvement. Longer durations of study; the identification, measurement, and control of concomitant variation; and greater concern for the individual instructor are indicated. While the present study must be interpreted with caution, the results obtained are consistent with the preponderance of reported evidence. Rotem and Glasman (1979) point out that the effectiveness of student evaluations depend on their use and intended purpose. When the purpose of evaluation is instructional improvement, it is unlikely that providing feedback alone will suffice. Rather, feedback must be integrated with a system of instructor training and available instructional support services.

References

Aleamoni, L. M. (1978). The usefulness of student evaluation in improving college teaching, *Instructional Science 7*, 95–105.

Aleamoni, L. M. (1979). *Arizona course/instructor evaluation questionnaire (CIEQ): Results interpretation manual, form 76*, Tucson Arizona: University of Arizona, Office of Instructional Research and Development.

Aleamoni, L. M. (1980). The use of student evaluations in the improvement of instruction, *National Association of Colleges and Teachers of Agriculture 24*(3), 18–21.

Aleamoni, L. M., & Spencer, R. E. (1973). The Illinois course evaluation questionnaire: A description of its development and a report of some of its results, *Educational and Psychological Measurement 33*, 669–684.

Bergin, A. E., & Strupp, H. H. (1972). *Changing frontiers in the science of psychotherapy.* Chicago: Aldine-Atherton.

Brandenburg, D. C., & Aleamoni, L. M. (1976). *Illinois course evaluation questionnaire: Results interpretation manual, form 73,* Urbana, Illinois: University of Illinois, Measurement and Research Division, Office of Instructional Resources.

Centra, J. A. (1979). *Determining faculty effectiveness.* San Francisco: Jossey-Bass.

Cohen, P. A. (1980). Effectiveness of student-rating feedback for improving college instruction: A meta-analysis of findings, *Research in Higher Education 13*, 321–341.

Cohen, P. A. (1981). Student ratings of instruction and student achievement: A meta-analysis of multisection validity studies, *Review of Educational Research 51*, 281–309.

Cook, T. D., & Campbell, D. T. (1979). *Quasi-experimentation: Design and analysis issues for field settings.* Boston: Houghton Mifflin Co.

Hersen, M., & Barlow, D. H. (1976). *Single case experimental designs: Strategies for studying behavior change in the individual.* New York: Pergamon Press.

Kratochwill, T. R. (1978). *Single subject research: Strategies for evaluating change.* New York: Academic Press.

Kulik, J. A., & Kulik, C. C. (1974). Student ratings of instruction, *Teaching of Psychology 1*, 51–57.

Kulik, J. A., & McKeachie, W. J. (1975). The evaluation of teachers in higher education, *Review of Research in Education 3*, 210-240.

Levinson-Rose, J., & Menges, R. J. (1981). Improving college teaching: A critical review of research, *Review of Educational Research 51*, 403–434.

Marsh, H. W. (1980). Research on students' evaluations of teaching effectiveness: A reply to Vecchio, *Instructional Evaluation 4*, 5–13.

McKeachie, W. J. (1979). Student ratings of faculty: A reprise, *Academe 65*, 384–397.

Millman, J. (Ed.) (1981). *Handbook of Teacher Evaluation.* Beverly Hills, California: Sage Publications.

Overall, J. V., & Marsh, H. W. (1979). Midterm feedback from students: Its relationship to instructional improvement and students' cognitive and affective outcomes, *Journal of Educational Psychology 71*, 856–865.

Rosenthal, R., & Gaito, J. (1963). The interpretation of levels of significance by psychological researchers, *The Journal of Psychology 55*, 33–38.

Rotem, A., & Glasman, N. S. (1979). On the effectiveness of students' evaluative feedback to university instructors, *Review of Educational Research 49*, 497–511.

Stevens, J. P. (1980). Power of the multivariate analysis of variance tests. *Psychological Bulletin 88*, 728–737.

Weisberg, H. I. (1979). Statistical adjustments and uncontrolled studies, *Psychological Bulletin 86*, 1149–1164.

Chapter References*

Mental Measurements Yearbook, James V. Mitchell (Ed.) Buros Institute of Mental Measurements, University of Nebraska, Lincoln: Nebraska, 1985.

Tests in Print, James V. Mitchell (Ed.) Buros Institute of Mental Measurements, University of Nebraska, Lincoln: Nebraska, 1983.

* Portions of this chapter appeared earlier in the following two publications and were used by permission.

Abrami, P. C., & Murphy, V. (1980). *A Catalogue of Systems for Student Ratings of Instruction*, Centre for Teaching and Learning, McGill University, Montreal.

Stevens, J. J., & Aleamoni, L. M. (1985). The use of evaluative feedback for instructional improvement: A longitudinal perspective, *Instructional Sciences, 13,* 285–304.

16

Student Rating Form Selection and Development Kit Part III: Techniques for Designing a Course/Instructor Evaluation Form

The design and development of a valid, reliable form intended to measure the teaching performance of an instructor and/or the perceived effectiveness of a course is a technical task requiring professional expertise in statistics and psychological measurement. It is a common fallacy among educators that all that is required to develop a questionnaire is to sit down and write a set of questions. It should be noted that what is being constructed is a measurement instrument. The fact that the measurement instrument is being designed to measure psychological phenomena (i.e., perceptions, opinions, reactions, etc.) does not excuse it from being held to the same standards as any other measurement tool or instrument. To assume that all one has to do to construct a psychometric instrument is to write a set of questions is analogous to assuming that all one has to do to construct a thermometer is to get a glass tube and put some mercury in it. Both tasks are easier said than done. And both tasks require not only precision and skill, if we wish to construct a valid and reliable measuring instrument, but an understanding of the underlying principles and science involved.

DESIGNING A STUDENT RATING FORM

As was noted earlier, student rating instruments are frequently developed by faculty, students, administrators, and/or committees who lack questionnaire design and scaling expertise. Such instruments typically are not subjected to reliability and validity studies and, therefore, are easily influenced by extraneous variables in the classroom such as time of day, class size, and instructor's personality.

In order for student evaluation ratings to be considered an integral part of a comprehensive instructional evaluation system, they must be both reliable and valid. As a practical matter, certain steps must be followed when designing and/or selecting a student rating instrument.

Determine Purpose of the Form
The first step is to determine the purpose for which the instrument is to be used. One primary purpose is to provide formative evaluation information for the faculty member to use in improving his/her instruction. Another is to provide summative evaluation information to colleagues, administrators, and students for use in promotion, tenure, merit pay, and course selection decisions. Or, alternatively, a third purpose is to provide both formative and summative evaluation information.

Specify Evaluative Elements
The second step is to specify the elements to be addressed in the instrument. If the *course* is to be judged, then there must be questions or statements addressing organization, structure, objectives, difficulty, pace, relevance, content, usefulness, etc. If, on the other hand, the *instruction* is to be judged, then there must be questions or statements addressing method of presentation, student interaction, pacing, level of difficulty, etc. If the *instructor* is to be judged, then there must be questions or statements addressing personal characteristics, skill, rapport, preparation, interest, commitment, etc. If the *learning* is to be judged, then there must be questions or statements addressing level of student satisfaction, student perceived competency, student desire to continue study in the field, etc.

Determine the Types of Items
The third step in constructing a student rating form is to determine the types of items the instrument should contain. The accuracy of the students responses and the

meaningfulness of the ratings to the instructor depend upon the appropriateness of the item and response formats.

Low Inference—High Inference Items. If the purpose of gathering student ratings is to produce measures that require considerable inference from what is seen or heard in the classroom to the labeling of the behavior, then higher inference measures are needed. These measures are obtained as ratings of the instructor on scales such as partial-fair, autocratic-democratic, or dull-stimulating. Such measures are appropriate when making summative (final and global) decisions about the instructor and/or the instruction. If, on the other hand, the purpose is to produce measures that require the student to classify teaching behaviors according to relatively objective categories, then low-inference measures are needed. These measures are obtained as frequency ratings of the instructor on scales such as gesturing, variation in voice, asking questions, or praise and encouragement. Such measures are appropriate when making formative decisions about the instructor and instruction, because it is easier to translate them into specific behaviors that can be used in instructional improvement programs.

Open-Ended and Closed-Ended Items. Open-ended (free-response) items usually produce a colorful array of responses in the student's own words but provide very little representative (consensus) information for the instructor to use in formative evaluation. However, instructors like such responses because they enjoy reading comments to which they can attach their own interpretations. The use of closed-ended (limited response) items, on the other hand, can provide accurate counts on the types of responses to each item. The most acceptable and frequently used approach, to both instructors and students, is to use a combination of closed-ended and open-ended items.

The type of closed-ended responses one should use is largely determined by the type of question or statement being asked or made. When care is not taken to match the appropriate responses to each question or statement, incongruous and unreliable responses will result. For example, an item stated as, "Was the instructor's grading fair?" dictates a Yes or No response; if it is stated as, "The instructor's grading was fair," a response along an Agree Strongly to Disagree Strongly continuum is dictated. Neutral or Don't Know responses should be used only when they represent necessary options; otherwise they will be used by those students who do have an opinion but are somewhat reluctant to indicate it.

If a continuum response format is used with only the end points anchored (e.g., Excellent 1 2 3 4 5 6 Horrible), it tends to produce unreliable responses. It is necessary that each response point along the continuum be identified and, furthermore, that the numbers be replaced with acronyms or abbreviations so that the students will know what they are responding to. In general, the Agree Strongly to Disagree Strongly continuum is appropriate whenever an item is stated either positively or negatively. Another type of closed-ended response scale that can be used is one that requires elaborate behavioral descriptions along the continuum. Such scales are called behaviorally anchored rating scales (Aleamoni, 1981).

Prepare or Select Items
The fourth step is to prepare or select the items. If one is preparing the items then it is important to prepare the appropriate item types along the lines indicated in the third step, above, and have the items independently edited and reviewed by other competent colleagues. If, on the other hand, one is selecting items or instruments in their entirety, then a careful content analysis of the instrument and items must occur to see if the issues described in the first three steps, above, have been satisfied.

Organize the Items. The fifth and final step in the design of a student rating form or in the selection of items is the organization of the items within the instrument. One has to decide how the items are to be grouped and labeled, how they should be organized for easy reading and answering, and how and where the responses should be recorded. If there is a logical or chronological flow to the items, then their organization on the form should reflect that. If there are only a few negative items, then one or two should appear very early in the instrument to avoid positive response set mistakes. It is advisable to have negatively stated items in the instrument, but only if they can be stated negatively in a logical manner.

Most questionnaire items can be grouped into subscales. If the original grouping was done on a logical basis, then an empirical analysis using a statistical technique such as factor analysis should be used to ensure that the grouped items do, in fact, represent a common scale.

Determine Form Reliability and Validity
Once an instrument has been constructed, it is important to determine its reliability and validity through experimental administration. Reliability may be defined in two ways. The first describes the instrument's capability of producing stable student responses from one time to another in a given course. The second describes the consistency (or degree of agreement) among the responders. Because most student rating instruments ask students to respond to different aspects of the instructional setting (e.g., instructor, instruction, textbook, homework), the reliability of the items and the subscales should be the major concern. If one cannot demonstrate that the items and subscales of a particular instrument can yield stable student responses, then the data and resulting evaluations may be meaningless.

If the instrument contains highly reliable items and subscales (e.g., .70 and higher), then one needs to determine

Developing a Comprehensive Faculty Evaluation System

how accurate the student responses are. Once the reliability problem has been resolved, attention should be focused on the validity of student ratings. Logical validation is concerned with the question, "What does the instrument measure?" and empirical validation is concerned with the question, "To what extent does the instrument measure what it is intended to measure?" A logical validation requires judgment on the content validity of the instrument. This is usually accomplished by carefully constructing the instrument so that it contains items and subscales that will yield measures in the areas that are considered appropriate by an individual or group of experts in the field under consideration. Empirical validation procedures require the use of criterion measures against which student ratings may be compared. Validity studies normally report the magnitude of the correlation between criterion measures and student ratings. The rule of thumb here is, the higher the correlation, the better the validity.

The following is an example of the kind of study often carried out in the development of a student rating form and was previously published as "Differential Relationships of Student, Instructor, and Course Characteristics to General and Specific Items on a Course Evaluation Questionnaire " by L. M. Aleamoni and G. S. Thomas. It is presented here, by permission, as a reference and guide. In addition Chapter 17 lists a collection of more than 500 items, based in part on the original CIEQ Optional Items Catalog, which may be used as a resource in constructing a student rating form.

REFERENCE ARTICLE ON THE DEVELOPMENT OF A STUDENT RATING FORM

The results of student evaluations of college instructors and courses can be used for several purposes. Among these are feedback to the instructors about strengths and weaknesses in their courses and methods of instruction and as input in promotion, tenure and salary decisions. Student responses to a series of questionnaire items assessing specific components of courses and methods of instruction are typically used to assist faculty in improving instruction. On the other hand, it is not uncommon for student responses to more global items assessing general aspects of courses and instruction to be used in salary and promotion decisions.

If these general items are to be useful in promotion and salary decisions, it is important that they are not influenced by student and course characteristics that are beyond the control of the instructor. It is also desirable that the general items measure the same aspects of instruction as the specific items. If this situation exists, instructional improvements measured by specific items should also be reflected in student responses to general items on course evaluations.

Although it has been reported that variables such as class size, instructor rank, required versus elective courses, student gender, standard versus pass-fail grading, major versus minor courses, and expected grade may correlate with student responses on various course evaluation items, the majority of studies report no relationship (see reviews by Aleamoni & Hexner, 1980; Costin, Greenough & Menges, 1971; Kulik & Kulik, 1974; Kulik & McKeachie, 1975; and McKeachie, 1979).

The current study is designed to determine if (1) course and student characteristics are more highly correlated with general items than with specific items on the Illinois Course Evaluation (CEQ), (2) student responses on general items are good predictors of their responses on specific items, and (3) specific items are better predictors of instructor ratings of student ability and attitude than are general items.

Method

The CEQ, an instrument used to assess teaching effectiveness with student ratings, was designed through the use of logical grouping of items and factor analysis. In the student information section, students are asked to respond to questions concerning their status, whether they are taking the course as pass/fail vs. standard grading, whether they are taking the course as a required or elective, their gender, their expected grade, and whether the course is within their major or minor. In the course information section the students are asked to rate three general items on a 6-point scale from very poor to excellent: (1) Course Content, (2) Major Instructor, and (3) Course in General.

The standard item section contains 23 items which form six subscales: General Course Attitude (four items), Method of Instruction (four items), Course Content (four items), Interest-Attention (four items), Instructor General (two items) and Instructor Specific (five items). An overall mean consisting of all 23 items was also calculated to form a Total Subscale. To each item, students indicate their degree of agreement or disagreement on a 4-point scale of strongly agree (SA), agree (A), disagree (D), and strongly disagree (SD). Because items are phrased both positively and negatively, a weight of four is assigned to the most favorable response down to a weight of one for the least favorable response. The item reliabilities range from .81 to .94, and the subscale reliabilities range from .88 to .98. See Aleamoni and Spencer (1973) and Brandenburg and Aleamoni (1976) for detailed discussions of the reliability and validity studies conducted with the CEQ.

The units of study were 7242 graduate and undergraduate courses at the University of Illinois. These units represented approximately 145,000 students rating their instructors and courses in class using the CEQ. Course evaluation questionnaires were completed by students in the following number of courses (C): Fall 1972 (C = 1187). Spring 1973 (C = 1002); Fall 1973 (C = 1940); Spring 1974 (C = 1443), and Fall 1974 (C = 1670). All instructors rated their classes on attitude and ability using a 6-point scale ranging from excellent to very poor.

Intercorrelations were calculated for all the following variables: (1) descriptive variables: class size, instructor rank, required versus elective course, student gender, student status, pass/fail versus standard grading, major versus minor course, and expected grade; (2) general ratings: course content, major instructor, and course in general; (3) subscale means on the CEQ: General Course Attitude, Method of Instruction, Course Content, Interest-Attention, Instructor General, Instructor Specific, and Total (overall mean rating); and (4) instructor rating of students (as a class) on ability and attitude.

Hotelling t-tests were used to identify significant differences between (1) correlations among descriptive variables and the three general items and among descriptive variables and the CEQ subscale means, and (2) correlations among general items and instructor ratings of student attitude and ability and among subscale means and the instructor ratings. These t-tests compared general ratings of course content correlations to correlations involving Course Content subscale means: Major Instructor correlations to Instructor General and Instructor Specific subscale means correlations; and Course in General ratings correlations to correlations on General Course Attitude, Method of Instruction, and Interest-Attention subscale means.

Descriptive variables consisted of the following items:

1. Class size consists of the actual class size responding to the questionnaire.

2. Instructor rank consists of five levels: teaching assistant, instructor, assistant professor, associate professor, and full professor (weighted 1, 2, 3, 4, 5, respectively).

3. Required/elective consists of the course average calculated from the students' responses to the two levels: required and elective courses (weighted 1, 2, respectively).

4. Student gender consists of the course average calculated from the students' responses to the two levels: male and female (weighted 1, 2, respectively).

5. Student status consists of the course average calculated from the students' responses to the five levels: freshman, sophomore, junior, senior, and graduate (weighted 1, 2, 3, 4, 5, respectively).

6. Pass/fail consists of the course average calculated from the students' responses to the two levels: pass/fail and standard grading (weighted 1, 2, respectively).

7. Major/minor consists of the course average calculated from the students' responses to the two levels: major and minor course requirement (weighted 1, 2, respectively).

8. Expected grade consists of the course average calculated from the students' responses the five levels: A, B, C, D, and E (weighted 5, 4, 3, 2, 1, respectively).

Results

The correlations (Table 6) indicate the relationships of student responses to the general and specific items to the eight descriptive variables. Partially due to the large sample size, 68 of 80 correlations were found to be statistically significant beyond the .001 level; however, the differences in magnitude of some of these correlations were revealing.

For example, the correlations between the three general items of the CEQ and the descriptive variables were significantly greater (P<.001) than those between the subscale means and six of eight of the descriptive variables. Only the comparisons of general items to subscale means on class size and instructor rank did not result in significant differences across all comparisons. None of the 56 correlations between the CEQ subscale means and the eight descriptive variables exceeded $r = .19$ (range = .013 to .183); whereas 14 to 24 correlations between general item means and descriptive variables were grater than $r = .19$ (range = .052 to .375). Table 6 also indicates which correlations between general item means and subscale means with the descriptive variables were significantly different. Significant differences between correlations of instructor ratings to general items and instructor ratings to specific items are also indicated.

Correlations relating instructors' perception of students' (as a class) ability and attitude to items on the CEQ tended to be higher for the subscale means than for general items. The instructors' rating of students (as a class) correlated from $r = .116$ to $r = .189$ with the subscale means, whereas these instructors' responses correlated with students' (as a class) responses on the three general items in the range of $r = .068$ to $r = .134$. As indicated by the table, all t-test comparisons were significant (P <.001). Although not represented in Table 6, it is of interest to note that the correlations between the two sets of student rated items, as represented by general items and subscale means, ranged between $r = .29$ and $r = .49$.

Discussion

Some previous research has indicated that such variables as student gender, status, and expected grade, and whether courses are major or minor, and required or elective may be correlated with student responses to course evaluation items. If student evaluations of instruction are to be used as a component in promotion and salary decisions, it is important that these evaluations not be influenced by student and course characteristics that are beyond the control of the instructor.

The current data suggest that the degree of relationship between such variables and students responses to instructional evaluation items may be in part a result of the items themselves. The fact that correlations between descriptive variables and general items on the CEQ were greater than comparable correlations with subscale means supports this contention. Therefore, it appears from these data that summative decisions including student evaluations of instruction as a component should be based on subscale means rather than general items on the CEQ, because the highest correlations between subscale means and descriptive variables accounted for only 34% of the variance in subscale ratings.

The relatively low relationships between ratings on general items and ratings on specific items, as reflected by the subscale means, suggests that these items are not measuring the same aspects of courses and instructors. This assertion is further supported by the fact that instructor ratings of students are more closely related to the subscale means than to the general item ratings.

Although the correlations between student ratings on specific items and instructor ratings of students on somewhat general items are relatively low, these relationships provide some insight for further research. It is possible that a more detailed list of instructor-rated items could be used to further specify the degree of relationship between students perception of instruction and instructor perception of students' abilities, attitudes, and progress in courses.

References

Aleamoni, L. M., & Hexner, P. Z. (1980). A review of the research on student evaluation and a report on the effect of different sets of instructions on student, course, and instructor evaluation. *Instructional Science, 9*, 67–84.

Aleamoni, L. M., & Spencer, R. E. (1973). The Illinois course evaluation questionnaire: A description of its development and a report of some of its results. *Educational and Psychological Measurement, 33*, 669–684.

Brandenburg, D. C., & Aleamoni, L. M. (1976). *Illinois course evaluation questionnaire. Results interpretation manual form 73.* University of Illinois-Urbana, Measurement and Research Division, Office of Instructional Resources.

Costin, F., Greenough, W. T., & Menges, R. J. (1971). Student ratings of college teaching: Reliability, validity, and usefulness. *Review of Educational Research, 41*, 511–535.

Kulik, J. A., & Kulik, C. C. (1974). Student ratings of instruction. *Teaching of Psychology, 1*, 51–57.

Table 6 Correlations between Descriptive Variables and Student Instructor Ratings

Ratings	Descriptive Variables									
	Class Size	Inst. Rank	Req. Elect	Sex	Status	Pass Fail	Major Minor	Expec. Grade	Stud. Abil.	Stud. Attit.
General Items										
Rated Content	-.054	.117	.375*	.255*	.256*	.251*	.082*	.311*	.068†	.119†
Rated Instructor	-.056	.052	.284*	.224*	.180*	.239*	.164*	.296*	.076†	.119†
Rated Course	-.069	.095	.363*	.246*	.235*	.233*	.098*	.321*	.086†	.134†
Subscale Means										
General Course Attitude	-.071	.088	.163	.036	.154	-.028	-.109	.084	.142	.177
Method of Instruction	-.077	.021	.117	.026	.056	-.030	-.024	.064	.133	.183
Course Content	-.067	.090	.158	.060	.158	-.027	-.099	.078	.125	.163
Interest-Attention	-.094	.071	.183	.043	.153	-.045	-.076	.070	.140	.189
Instructor General	-.071	.032	.098	.013	.097	-.033	-.037	.067	.140	.180
Instructor Specific	-.091	.057	.073	.057	.102	-.032	-.051	.055	.116	.162
Total	-.076	.061	.137	.042	.127	-.031	-.072	.073	.138	.181

* Correlations that were significantly greater for general items than for subscale means (P<.001)
† Correlations that were significantly smaller for general items than for subscale means (P<.001)

zArreola, R.A. (1995). *Developing a Comprehensive Faculty Evaluation System.* Bolton, MA: Anker Publishing Co., Inc.

Kulik, J. A., & McKeachie, W. J. (1975). "The evaluation of teachers in higher education" in F. N. Kerlinger (Ed.). *Review of Research in Education 3*. Itasca IL: F. E. Peacock.

McKeachie, W. J. (1979). Student ratings of faculty: A reprise. *Academe, 65*, 384–397.

CHAPTER REFERENCES*

Aleamoni, L. M. (1981). Student ratings of instruction. In J. Millman (Ed.), *Handbook of Teacher Evaluation*. Beverly Hills, California: Sage Publications, Inc.

* Portions of this chapter were published earlier as "Differential Relationships of Student, Instructor, and Course Characteristics to General and Specific Items on a Course Evaluation Questionnaire" by L. M. Aleamoni and G. S. Thomas, in *Teaching of Psychology, 7*, (4), 1980, 233–235. Used by permission.

17

Student Rating Form
Selection and Development Kit Part IV:
Catalog of Student Rating Form Items

This chapter contains a lengthy, but by no means exhaustive, collection of possible course and instructor rating items. Instructors may choose a relevant subset for use in their own classes, either as optional items with a professionally developed student rating form such as the CIEQ or to develop a customized rating form. These items have been divided into 24 categories on the basis of their *apparent* content. The category names should not be thought of as definitive identifiers, because they were chosen primarily as an aid in finding items that appear to be related. *No inference should be drawn that the items presented here have sufficient statistical support (i.e., factor loadings) to define the category in which they are listed.*

All items are written so as to be responded to in either one of the two *agree strongly* to *disagree strongly* formats shown below:

    5-point scale
- AS Agree Strongly
- A Agree
- N Neither Agree nor Disagree
- D Disagree
- DS Disagree Strongly

    4-point scale
- AS Agree Strongly
- A Agree
- D Disagree
- DS Disagree Strongly

Other similar response scales may be used, but the items are written in such a way as to make best use of either one of the scales shown above. Also note that some of the items are stated in a *negative* fashion. It is a good idea to include a few negative items which measure the same dimension or category as a check on whether students have fallen into a response set (i.e., marking all the choices down the middle or one side of the rating scale.) When using negatively stated items care must be taken to ensure that the computer analysis program correctly weights the responses to reflect the reversed scale.

In categories A, B, E, F, G, H, I, J, L, M, N, O, P, Q, R, S, T, and U, the subject (*italicized*) in each sentence can be changed depending upon how the instructor wants to state the item. If this catalog is used to develop a customized student rating form, it will be necessary to conduct a factor analysis of the final set of items in order to determine if the items cluster in appropriate categories. At least four items should be picked as a measure of each category to be represented in the final form of the questionnaire.

Item	Categories	Page

A. Contributions by the Instructor and Teaching Assistants (in the lecture, laboratory, discussion)

1. The *instructor* used case studies (or illustrations) to clarify concepts.

2. The *instructor's* lectures broadened my knowledge of the area beyond the information presented in the readings.

3. The *instructor* demonstrated how the course was related to practical situations.

4. The *instructor* demonstrated that the course material was worthwhile.

5. The *instructor* related the course material to my previous learning experiences.

6. The *instructor* incorporated current material into the course.

7. The *instructor* made me aware of the current problems in this field.

8. The *instructor's* use of examples helped to get points across in class.

9. The *instructor's* use of personal experiences helped to get points across in class.

10. The *instructor* clarified complex sections of the text.

11. The *instructor* adapted the course to a reasonable level of comprehension.

12. The *instructor* exposed students to diverse approaches to problem solutions.

13. The *instructor* accepted other viewpoints that could possibly be valid.

14. The *instructor* provided information that supplemented assigned material.

15. The *instructor* provided essential material that was not in the text.

16. The *instructor* used his/her knowledge of other fields to help my understanding of the field being studied.

17. The *instructor's* explanations were clear.

18. The *instructor* encouraged independent thought.

19. The *instructor's* methods of evaluating me were fair.

20. The *instructor* guided the preparation of student reports.

21. The *instructor* stressed important points in lectures.

22. The *instructor* taught near the class level.

23. The *instructor* provided opportunities for self-directed learning.

24. The *instructor* did NOT appear receptive to new ideas.

25. The *instructor* did NOT provide a sufficient variety of topics.

26. The *instructor* required that students employ concepts to demonstrate comprehension.

27. The *instructor* provided discussion material that supplemented lecture content.

28. The *instructor* did NOT provide for students' self-evaluation of their learning.

29. The *instructor* was an excellent resource person.

30. The *instructor's* evaluation of students' performances was constructive.

31. The *instructor* did NOT invite questions.

32. The *instructor* presented contrasting points of view.

33. The *instructor* related topics to other areas of knowledge.

34. The *instructor* did NOT combine theory and practical application.

35. The *instructor* did NOT encourage discussion of a topic.

36. The *instructor* answered all questions to the best of his/her ability.

37. The *instructor* carefully answered questions raised by students.

38. The *instructor* stimulated class discussion.

39. The *instructor* did NOT cover the reading assignments in sufficient depth in class.

40. The *instructor* was too involved with lecturing to be aware of the class.

41. The *instructor* provided very helpful critiques of student papers.

42. The *instructor* adequately prepared me for the material covered in his/her section.

43. The *instructor* clarified lecture material.

44. The *instructor* provided adequate individual remedial attention.

45. The *instructor* stressed important points in discussion.

46. The *instructor* overemphasized minor points.

47. The *instructor* showed mastery of the subject matter.

48. The *instructor* gave me a great deal which I would not get by independent study.

49. The *instructor's* lack of facility with the English language was a hindrance to the communication of ideas.

50. The *instructor* seems to keep current with developments in the field.

51. The *instructor's* teaching methods are effective.

52. The *instructor* uses novel teaching methods to help students learn.

53. The *instructor* uses teaching methods to help students learn.

54. The *instructor* allows students to proceed at their own pace.

55. The *instructor* provides extra discussion sessions for interested students.

56. The *instructor* adequately helped me prepare for exams.

57. The *instructor* is careful and precise when answering questions.

58. The *instructor* is available during office hours.

59. The *instructor's* quizzes stress important points.

60. The *instructor* helps me apply theory for solving homework problems.

61. The *instructor* demonstrated formal knowledge of the topic.

62. The *instructor* accepts suggestions from students.

63. The *instructor* shows enthusiasm when teaching.

64. The *instructor* offers specific suggestions for improving my weaknesses.

65. The *instructor* returns assignments quickly enough to benefit me.

B. Instructor Attitude Toward Students

66. The *instructor* was receptive to the expression of student views.

67. The *instructor* was concerned with whether or not the students learned the material.

68. The *instructor* intimidated the students.

69. The *instructor* embarrassed the students.

70. The *instructor* developed a good rapport with me.

71. A warm atmosphere was maintained in this class.

72. The *instructor* recognized individual differences in students' abilities.

73. The *instructor* seemed to dislike students.

74. The *instructor* often made me feel as if I were wasting his/her time.

75. The *instructor* treated students as inferiors.

76. The *instructor* seemed genuinely interested in me as a person.

77. The *instructor* maintained an atmosphere of good feeling in the class.

78. The *instructor* treated students with respect.

79. Students in this course were free to disagree.

80. The *instructor* could be relied upon for support in stressful situations.

81. The *instructor* criticized students in the presence of others.

82. The *instructor* promoted a feeling of self-worth in students.

83. Students were encouraged to express their own opinions.

84. The *instructor* helped students to feel free to ask questions.

85. The *instructor* was skillful in observing student reactions.

86. The *instructor* was permissive.

87. The *instructor* was friendly.

88. The *instructor* gave individual attention to students in this course.

89. The *instructor* demonstrated sensitivity to students' needs.

90. The *instructor* was aloof rather than sociable.

91. The *instructor* was flexible in dealing with students.

92. The *instructor* encourages students to talk about their problems.

93. The *instructor* meets informally with students out of class.

94. The *instructor* stimulates my thinking.

95. The *instructor* deals fairly and impartially with students.

96. The *instructor* makes me feel I am an important member of this class.

97. The *instructor* relates to students as individuals.

98. The *instructor* tells students when they have done particularly well.

99. The *instructor* motivates me to do my best work.

100. The *instructor* provided me with an effective range of challenges.

101. The *instructor* stimulates intellectual curiosity.

102. The *instructor* offers specific suggestions for improving my weaknesses.

103. The *instructor* helps me realize my full ability.

104. The *instructor* provides me with incentives for learning.

105. The *instructor* rewards success.

C. Student Outcomes

106. I now feel able to communicate course material to others.

107. This course has increased my capacity for analytic thinking.

108. This course was helpful in developing new skills.

109. I learned more in this course than in similar courses.

110. I understood the material presented in this course.

111. This course challenged me intellectually.

112. I have become more competent in this area because of this course.

113. My opinions about some of the course topics changed because of taking this course.

114. I learned more in this course than I expected to learn.

115. Some of the ideas discussed really made me think.

116. I am a better person because of taking this course.

117. The course helped me to become a more critical thinker.

118. The course helped me become a more creative thinker.

119. The course was intellectually exciting.

120. I learned a great deal of factual material in this course.

121. I developed the ability to communicate clearly about the subject.

122. I developed creative ability in this field.

123. I developed the ability to solve real problems in this field.

124. I learned how to identify formal characteristics of works of art.

125. I learned how to identify main points and central issues in this field.

126. I developed the ability to carry out original research in this field.

127. I developed an ability to evaluate new work in this field.

128. I was stimulated to discuss related topics outside of class.

129. I participated actively in class discussion.

130. I developed leadership skills in this class.

131. I developed greater awareness of societal problems.

132. I became interested in community projects related to the course.

133. I learned to value new viewpoints.

134. I gained a better understanding of myself through this course.

135. I gained an understanding of some of my personal problems.

136. I developed a greater sense of personal responsibility.

137. I increased my awareness of my own interests.

138. I increased my awareness of my own talents.

139. I feel that I performed up to my potential.

140. I read independently beyond the required readings in this course.

141. The course significantly changed my outlook on personal issues.

142. I felt free to ask for extra help from the instructor.

D. Relevance of Course

143. This course material will be useful in future courses.

144. The course provided me with a general background in the area.

145. The course material was of personal interest to me aside from its professional application.

146. I have learned the basic concepts from this course which I will be able to relate to other situations.

147. This course has stimulated me to take additional courses in this field.

148. The material covered in this course will be directly relevant to my future occupation.

149. The course gave me skills that will be directly applicable to my career.

150. The concepts in this course were pertinent to my major field.

151. The course was valuable only to majors in this field.

152. This course should be required for a major in this area.

153. The course was related to my personal goals.

154. The course did NOT prepare me to reach my personal goals.

155. The course had NO relevance outside of a grade and credit hours.

156. I was interested in the subject before I took this course.

157. The course stimulated me to read further in the area.

158. The course content was valuable.

159. I gained an excellent understanding of concepts in this field.

160. I learned to apply principles from this course to other situations.

161. I deepened my interest in the subject matter of this course.

162. I developed enthusiasm about the course material.

163. I developed skills needed by professionals in this field.

164. I learned about career opportunities.

165. I developed a clearer sense of professional identity.

166. I would take this course if it were not required.

167. This course has changed my behavior (instructor should specify a behavior here).

168. The class demonstrations were effective in helping me learn.

169. The course content was up-to-date.

170. The catalog description of this course gave an accurate description of its content.

171. The course content included information from related fields.

E. Use of Class Time

172. The *instructor* should do more to restrain students who monopolize class time.

173. I participated more in class discussions in this course than in similar courses.

174. The *instructor* should spend less time in class discussions.

175. The *instructor* should encourage students to participate more actively in class discussions.

176. The class discussions broadened by knowledge of the area beyond what I learned from the readings.

177. More opportunity should be allowed for answering questions in class.

178. Students had an opportunity to ask questions.

179. The amount of time allotted for this class should be reduced.

180. The *instructor* used student questions as a source of discovering points of confusion.

181. The *instructor* overemphasized minor points.

182. The *instructor* was NOT willing to deviate from his/her course plans to meet the needs of the students.

183. Regular class attendance was necessary for understanding course material.

184. The *instructor* used class time well.

185. The *instructor* provided time for discussion.

186. The *instructor* encourages students to ask questions.

187. The *instructor* encourages class participation.

188. The *instructor* encourages contributions concerning the conduct of this class.

189. The *instructor* makes me feel free to ask questions.

F. Organization and Preparation

190. The *instructor* followed his/her stated course outline.

191. The *instructor's* class presentations were designed for easy note-taking.

192. The *instructor* presented material in a clear manner.

193. The course was well organized.

194. The course material appeared to be presented in logical content units.

195. There was continuity from one class to the next.

196. The *instructor* presented a systematic approach to the course material.

197. *Instructor* presentations were well organized.

198. Course concepts were related in a systematic manner.

199. The *instructor* was well prepared for each class.

200. The *instructor* was well prepared for lectures.

201. The *instructor* frequently digressed too far from the subject matter of the course.

202. The *instructor* rarely digressed from a given topic to the detriment of the course.

203. Lectures often seemed disjointed and fragmented.

204. Class discussions were well organized.

205. The *instructor* was prepared for topics brought up during impromptu class discussions.

206. The *instructor* provided a good mixture of lecture and discussion.

207. The *instructor* wrote legibly on the blackboard, papers, etc.

G. Clarity of Presentation

208. The *instructor's* voice was audible.

209. The *instructor's* voice was understandable.

210. The *instructor's* vocabulary made understanding of the material difficult.

211. At times it was difficult to hear what the *instructor* was saying.

212. The *instructor* expressed ideas clearly.

213. The *instructor* could communicate his/her subject matter to the students.

214. The *instructor* should define the words he/she uses.

215. The *instructor's* tendency to stammer or stutter was annoying.

216. The *instructor* often mumbled.

217. The *instructor* often talked with his/her back to the students.

218. The *instructor* recognizes when some students fail to comprehend course material.

219. The *instructor* emphasizes conceptual understanding of course material.

220. The *instructor* lectures at a pace suitable for students' comprehension.

H. Instructor Characteristics

221. The *instructor* should improve his/her personal appearance.

222. The *instructor* flustered easily.

223. The *instructor* seemed to be interested in teaching.

224. The *instructor* was enthusiastic when presenting course material.

225. The *instructor* was relaxed in front of class.

226. At times, the *instructor* displayed only a shallow knowledge of course materials.

227. The *instructor* seemed genuinely interested in what he/she was teaching.

228. At times the *instructor* seemed tense.

229. The *instructor* exhibited self-confidence.

230. The *instructor* displayed a know-it-all attitude.

231. The *instructor* was too cynical or sarcastic.

232. The *instructor* often appeared arrogant.

233. The *instructor* was very entertaining.

234. The *instructor's* jokes sometimes interfered with learning.

235. The *instructor* demonstrated role model qualities that were of use to me.

236. The *instructor* demonstrated an appropriate sense of humor.

237. The *instructor* seemed to enjoy teaching.

238. The *instructor* was confused by unexpected questions.

239. The *instructor* encouraged constructive criticism.

240. The *instructor* has an interesting style of presentation.

241. When lecturing, the *instructor* holds the attention of class.

242. The *instructor* senses when students are bored.

243. The *instructor* is a dynamic and energetic person.

244. The *instructor* seems to have a well rounded education.

245. The *instructor* appears to grasp quickly what a student is saying.

246. The *instructor* knows about developments in other fields.

247. The *instructor* shows enthusiasm when teaching.

248. The *instructor* exhibited distracting mannerisms.

249. The *instructor's* accent prevented me from understanding what was being said.

I. Interest of Presentation

250. The *instructor* should reduce the monotony of his/her speech.

251. The *instructor* made the subject matter interesting.

252. The *instructor* was boring.

253. The *instructor's* presentations were thought-provoking.

254. The *instructor's* classroom sessions stimulated my interest in the subject.

255. It was easy to remain attentive in class.

256. The *instructor* was quite lifeless.

257. Remaining attentive in class was often quite difficult.

258. The course was quite interesting.

259. The *instructor* was an effective speaker.

260. The class presentations were too formal.

J. Expectations and Objectives

261. The course assignments were clearly specified.

262. I was informed of the direction the course was to take.

263. The objectives of the course were well explained.

264. The objectives of this course should be modified.

265. The content of this course was appropriate to the aims and objectives of the course.

266. Student responsibilities in this course were defined.

267. The *instructor* should rewrite the description of the course in the catalog.

268. It was not clear why I was being taught some things.

269. The *instructor's* expectations were NOT clearly defined.

270. The *instructor* informed students of their progress.

271. The *instructor* defined realistic objectives for the students.

272. I have made careful preparations for this course.

273. I really had to think about some of the ideas discussed.

274. Objectives were stated for each unit in the course.

275. The course objectives were clear.

276. I understood what was expected of me in this course.

277. The course objectives allowed me to know when I was making progress.

278. In general, too little work was required in this class.

279. In general, too much work was required in this class.

280. I have made careful preparations for this course.

281. I really had to think about some of the ideas discussed.

K. Behavioral Indications of Student Attitude Toward Course

282. The time spent in this course was worthwhile.

283. My attendance in this course was better than for most other courses.

284. I usually delayed studying for this course as long as possible.

285. I spent more time than usual complaining about this course to others.

286. I would take this course again even if it were not required.

287. I would recommend this course to a fellow student.

288. I looked forward to this class.

289. I cut this class more frequently than I cut other classes.

290. This was a good course.

291. Students frequently volunteered their own opinions.

292. One real strength of this course was the classroom discussion.

293. I had a strong desire to take this course.

294. I enjoyed going to class.

295. In this course I used my study time effectively.

296. I spent more time studying for this course than for other courses with the same amount of credit.

L. General Student Attitude Toward Instructor

297. I would rather NOT take another course from this *instructor*.

298. In comparison to all the other *instructors* I have had, he/she was one of the best.

299. I would recommend this *instructor* to a fellow student.

300. I would avoid courses taught by this *instructor*.

301. The *instructor* was excellent.

302. The *instructor* was inadequate.

M. Speed and Depth of Coverage

303. Too much material was covered in this course.

304. Prerequisites in addition to those stated in the catalog are necessary for understanding the material in this course.

305. Within the time limitations, the *instructor* covered the course content in sufficient depth.

306. For the time allotted, topic coverage was exhaustive enough.

307. The course material was presented at a satisfactory level of difficulty.

308. The *instructor* attempted to cover too much material.

309. The *instructor* presented the material too rapidly.

31(. The *instructor* should present the material more slowly.

311. The *instructor* moved to new topics before students understood the previous topic.

312. The course seemed to drag at times.

313. The course was too easy for me.

314. The course was too difficult for me.

315. The amount of material covered in the course was reasonable.

316. The *instructor* used appropriate amounts of information to teach new concepts.

N. Instructor Availability Outside of Class

317. Assistance from the *instructor* outside of class was readily available.

318. Talking to the *instructor* in his/her office was helpful.

319. I was able to get personal help in this course if I needed it.

320. The office hours were scheduled at times that were convenient for me to attend.

321. The *instructor* was readily available for consultation with students.

322. The *instructor* encouraged out-of-class consultations.

323. The *instructor* made it clear that he/she did not want to be bothered by students at times other than when the class met.

O. Examinations

324. The types of test questions used were good.

325. The *instructor* should give more examinations.

326. Emphasis on memorizing for examinations should be reduced.

327. The *instructor* should cover the course material more adequately in the examinations.

328. The exams were worded clearly.

329. Examinations were given often enough to give the *instructor* a comprehensive picture of my understanding of the course material.

330. The exams covered the reading assignments well.

331. The exams concentrated on factual material.

332. The exams concentrated on reasoning ability.

333. The exams concentrated on important aspects of the course.

334. The exams and quizzes were given too frequently.

335. The exams were fair.

336. The *instructor* took reasonable precautions to prevent cheating.

337. Course objectives were reflected in the exams.

338. Exams adequately covered the text material.

339. Exams were mainly comprised of material presented in class.

340. The answers to exam questions were adequately explained after the exam was given.

341. Enough time was provided to complete the examinations.

342. Too much emphasis was placed on the final exam.

343. Examinations were not too difficult.

344. The exams did not challenge me enough.

345. The *instructor* should use essay examinations rather than multiple-choice.

346. The *instructor* should use multiple-choice examinations rather than essay.

347. Examinations should contain a better mixture of multiple-choice and essay questions.

348. The exams covered the lecture material well.

349. The exams were creative.

350. The exams required original thought.

351. The exams were too long.

352. The exams were returned promptly.

353. The exams were graded carefully.

354. The exams were graded fairly.

355. The exams were used to improve instruction as well as to assign grades.

356. The exams were used to help students find their strengths and weaknesses.

357. The exams were of instructional value.

358. The exams stressed the important points of the lectures.

359. The exams required conceptual understanding of the material in order to be able to get a high score.

360. Feedback on the exams indicated my relative standing within the class.

361. Exams emphasized understanding rather than memorization.

P. Visual Aids

362. The *instructor* should use more audiovisual aids (charts, movies, models, etc.)

363. The audiovisual aids were a valuable part of this course.

364. The audiovisual aids confused me more than they aided my learning.

365. Some of the audiovisual aids did not seem relevant.

366. Audiovisual aids were used too much in this class.

367. Audiovisual aids used in this course were stimulating.

368. The audiovisual aids generally contained material different from the *instructor's* material.

369. The *instructor* generally used the audiovisual aids effectively.

370. The audiovisual aids presented material or situations which could not normally be seen in real life.

371. The audiovisual aids were generally effective.

372. Certain ideas were presented effectively through the use of audiovisual aids than otherwise could have been presented.

373. The audiovisual aids (charts, movies, slides, etc.) used were effective in helping me learn.

Q. Grading

374. Relative to other courses, the grading in this course was harder.

375. I expected to get a higher grade in this course than I received.

376. My field work was given appropriate weight in the formulation of the final grade.

377. My grades accurately reflected my performance in the course.

378. I knew my relative standing in the course.

379. The *instructor* adequately explained the grading system.

380. The *instructor* adequately assessed how well students mastered the material.

381. The procedure for grading was fair.

382. I do not feel that my grades reflected how much I have learned.

383. The method of assigning grades seemed very arbitrary.

384. It was easy to get a good grade in this class.

385. The *instructor* had a realistic definition of good performance.

386. My papers had adequate comments on them.

387. The grades reflected an accurate assessment of my knowledge.

388. The exam accurately reflected my performance on the tests.

R. Assignments (homework, reading, written, textbook, laboratory, etc.)

389. The assignments were challenging.

390. The nontext assignments were helpful in acquiring a better understanding of course materials.

391. I found the coverage of topics in the assigned readings too difficult.

392. The course required a reasonable amount of outside reading.

393. The *instructor* should have required more outside reading.

394. The text used in this course was helpful.

395. The *instructor* helped the students avoid duplication of content in selecting topics.

396. The *instructor* supplemented student summaries with additional material when necessary.

397. The amount of work was appropriate for the credit received.

398. The textbook was easy to understand.

399. The textbook presented various sides of issues.

400. The _____ assignments were relevant to what was presented in class.

401. The _____ assignments provided background for the lectures.

402. The _____ assignments were too time consuming relative to their contribution to my understanding of the course material.

403. The _____ assignments were interesting.

404. The _____ assignments appeared to be chosen carefully.

405. The _____ assignments were stimulating.

406. The _____ assignments made students think.

407. More _____ should have been assigned.

408. There was too much _____ required for this course.

409. Directions for _____ assignments were clear.

410. Directions for _____ assignments were specific.

411. _____ assignments were helpful in understanding the course.

412. _____ assignments covered both sides of issues.

413. _____ assignments required a reasonable amount of effort.

414. _____ assignments were graded fairly.

415. _____ assignments were returned promptly.

416. The *instructor* did not cover reading assignments in sufficient depth in class.

417. The *instructor* should have given additional sources where supplementary information might be found.

418. The course assignments required too much time.

419. The assignments were related to the goals of the course.

420. The assignments were of definite instructional value.

421. Homework assignments were given too frequently.

422. The assigned readings were well integrated into the course.

S. Laboratory and Discussion

423. I found the laboratory/discussion section interesting.

424. The laboratory/discussion *instructor* adequately prepared me for the material covered in his/her section.

425. The laboratory/discussion *instructor* clarified lecture material.

426. The laboratory/discussion *instructor* carried on meaningful dialogue with the students.

427. The laboratory/discussion *instructor* provided adequate individual remedial attention.

428. The laboratory/discussion *instructor* knew my name.

429. The laboratory/discussion *instructor* discovered my trouble areas.

430. The laboratory/discussion *instructor* helped me find supplemental references.

431. The laboratory/discussion *instructor* was available during office hours.

432. The questions on the laboratory/discussion quizzes were a good sample of what I was expected to know.

433. The laboratory increased my competence in manipulating laboratory materials.

434. The laboratory equipment was, on most occasions, effectively set up.

435. The laboratory/discussion *instructor* presented materials supplemental to the lecture material.

436. The laboratory/discussion *instructor* has the potential for being a competent teacher.

437. The laboratory/discussion *instructor* graded my papers (exams, homework, etc.) fairly.

438. The laboratory/discussion *instructor* extended the coverage of topics presented in lecture.

439. The laboratory/discussion section appeared well integrated with the lecture.

440. My laboratory/discussion work was beneficial in terms of the goals of this course.

441. My laboratory/discussion work was beneficial in terms of my personal goals.

442. My laboratory/discussion work was given appropriate weight in the formulation of final grades.

443. The use of laboratory equipment was satisfactorily explained.

444. The laboratory/discussion section was a valuable part of this course.

445. The laboratory/discussion section was a great help in learning.

446. There was ample opportunity to ask questions in the laboratory/discussion section.

447. The laboratory/discussion section clarified lecture material.

448. Students received individual attention in the laboratory/discussion section.

449. The *instructor* gave every student a chance to practice.

450. The laboratories covered too much material to be absorbed in only one period.

451. The material in the laboratories was too easy.

452. I generally found the laboratory (recitations, clinical) sessions valuable.

453. The laboratory (recitations, clinical) *instructor* related lecture material to real life situations.

454. The laboratory/discussion *instructor* explained experiments and/or assignments.

455. The laboratory/discussion *instructor* adequately helps me prepare for examinations.

456. The laboratory/discussion *instructor* is precise when answering questions.

457. The laboratory/discussion *instructor* deals fairly with students.

458. The laboratory/discussion *instructor* is available through the lab/discussion period.

459. The laboratory/discussion *instructor's* quizzes stress important points.

460. The laboratory/discussion *instructor* helps me apply theory for solving problems.

461. The laboratory/discussion *instructor* demonstrates formal knowledge of the topic.

462. The laboratory/discussion *instructor* makes me feel I am an important member of the class.

463. The laboratory/discussion *instructor* accepts criticism from students well.

464. The laboratory/discussion *instructor* accepts suggestions from students well.

465. The laboratory/discussion *instructor* shows enthusiasm when teaching.

466. The laboratory/discussion *instructor* offers specific suggestions for improving my weaknesses.

467. The laboratory/discussion *instructor* evaluates my work quickly enough to benefit me.

468. The laboratory/discussion *instructor* plans the lab/discussion time effectively.

469. The laboratory/discussion *instructor* thoroughly understands the experiments and assignments.

470. The course would be improved by adding a laboratory/discussion section.

471. The lab had adequate facilities.

472. There was opportunity to do imaginative work in the labs.

473. Generally, the equipment used in the lab was adequate and reliable.

474. Most of the lab work was simply routine.

475. The course should require more time in the lab.

T. Clinical

476. The teaching done in clinical settings increased my learning.

477. The *instructor* provided relevant clinical experiences.

478. The *instructor* was NOT helpful when students had questions concerning patient care.

479. The *instructor's* questions in clinical discussions were thought-provoking.

480. The *instructor* observed students' techniques of interviewing.

481. The *instructor* observed students' techniques of physical examination.

U. Student-Instructor Interaction

482. Questions were answered satisfactorily by the *instructor*.

483. The *instructor* had a tight rein on the conduct of the class.

484. I participated *more* in class discussion in this course than in similar courses.

485. I had an opportunity to participate in discussions with the *instructor*.

486. I was hesitant to ask questions in this course.

487. The *instructor* knew the names of the students.

V. Seminars

488. The seminar approach was effectively implemented in the course.

489. The seminar method met my needs.

490. The seminar provided me with diverse insights into the course materials.

491. The *seminar leader* effectively included everyone's views into the discussion.

492. The seminar allowed me to learn from other students.

W. Team Teaching

493. The team teaching method provided me with a valuable learning experience.

494. Instruction was well coordinated among the team members.

495. The team teaching approach was effectively implemented in this course.

496. The team teaching approach met my needs.

497. Team teaching provided me with diverse insights into course materials.

498. Team teaching provided insights that a single instructor could not.

X. Field Trips

499. The field trips were of instructional value.

500. The field trips were well planned.

501. The course should include a field trip.

502. The field trips fit in with the course objectives.

503. The timing of the field trips was well planned relative to the progress of the course.

504. The field trips offered insights that the lectures and/or readings could not provide.

CHAPTER REFERENCE

Aleamoni, L. M., & Carynnk, D. B. (1977). *Optional Item Catalog (Revised)*. (Information Memorandum No. 6) Tucson, Arizona: University of Arizona, Office of Instructional Research and Development.

Appendix

Sample Faculty Evaluation Manual

The following is an example of an actual faculty evaluation manual which was constructed using the principles outlined in this handbook. The manual presents one expression of the concepts of defining the faculty role model, identifying sources, defining roles, and weighting role and source impact, in designing a comprehensive faculty evaluation system. The manual is not presented as an idealized model but simply one college's interpretation of how to design and develop a faculty evaluation system that works for them. The manual your institution develops may differ considerably. However, the manual shown in this section contains various forms and procedures that may be of interest as you develop your own faculty evaluation system. Portions of the manual refer to portfolio A, B, etc. In an actual manual, these portfolios are special vertical file folders inserted in the three-ring manual binder and are designed to hold inserted documents, such as syllabi, tests, etc. Abbreviated versions of these portfolios are shown at the end of the manual.

INTRODUCTION

Faculty members should carefully read the preface and procedures for evaluation. The preface explains the rationale and method for the evaluation process. The procedures discuss the objectives of faculty evaluation and identify the goals of the comprehensive system. Also included are a chart graphically displaying the percentages associated with each evaluation area and a definitive description of the faculty roles in each of the four areas to be evaluated. The rating system is based on a 4-point scale ranging from exceptional to unacceptable with specific explanations for the assignment of each rating. Finally, a calendar pinpointing important deadlines for the components of the evaluation process is presented.

PREFACE

This is a comprehensive, individualized approach to reviewing and evaluating a number of activities associated with the more important roles performed by faculty members. The process allows faculty members the opportunity to define their own professional image.

While it is not possible or desirable to identify and review all the roles of a faculty member for evaluation purposes, those selected for our institution and incorporated within this system include those identified as being most important as a result of a survey of all faculty and those it was determined could be reviewed efficiently and effectively. The evaluation system encompasses four major faculty roles:

1. Teaching and Instruction

2. College Service

3. Professional Growth

4. Community Service

An institutional minimum and maximum value (weight) for each role relative to the total system has been established. These values reflect the philosophy and general value system of the institution as to the importance of each role within the faculty member's total set of professional responsibilities.

Data gathered for review and evaluation are obtained from students, self, a committee of peers, and the faculty member's department head. A value is preestablished for the degree of impact data from each source have on the evaluation of each role.

Each faculty member will enter into an evaluation agreement with the department head prior to the evaluation cycle. A preliminary agreement for the next evaluation period should be written during the final conference between the department head and the faculty member at the end of the current evaluation period. A final agreement must be written at the beginning of the academic year in which the faculty member is to be evaluated. This agreement provides faculty members with an opportunity to relate and individualize their evaluation within predetermined ranges for those roles in which they will be most heavily involved during any particular evaluation cycle.

PURPOSES AND OBJECTIVES OF THE FACUTLY EVALUATION SYSTEM

In an effort to promote understanding among the faculty of the relationship among faculty evaluation, professional growth, and the betterment of the entire educational process at our institution, the following objectives have been developed:

1. To develop a framework within which the instructional process can be effectively assessed to promote student achievement.

2. To establish an evaluative process which assesses the strengths and weaknesses of faculty for the purposes of improving instruction and encouraging professional growth through a meaningful faculty development program.

3. To create a means for assessing performances of non-tenured faculty for the purposes of promotion, retention, and/or awarding of tenure.

4. To create a means of assessing performance of part-time faculty for the purpose of retention.

FACULTY ROLE MODEL

The minimum and maximum weights allowed in the evaluation system for teaching, professional growth, college service, and community service are as follows:

Minimum		*Maximum*
60%	Teaching and Instruction	80%
10%	College Service	20%
10%	Professional Growth	30%
0%	Community Service	10%

ROLE DEFINITIONS

I. *Teaching and Instruction*
Teaching and instruction are defined as those activities associated with the design and delivery of instructional events to the students. For purposes of evaluation, the instructional role will include

  A. Classroom performance

  B. Materials preparation and material relevancy

  C. Record keeping and instructional management

II. *College Service*
College service is defined as service rendered by a faculty member in support of the subdivision, division, department, or college. For purposes of evaluation, service to the college does not include any functions defined and included elsewhere, such as professional growth or community service.

III. *Professional Growth*
Professional growth is defined as improving the competence of faculty members to better fulfill the role and responsibilities of their position within the institution, professional achievement or contribution to the teaching/learning process, or educational profession in the faculty member's area of expertise.

IV. *Community Service*
Community service is defined as the application of a faculty member's recognized area of expertise, in the community, without pay. The acceptance of pay constitutes consulting and, as such, is considered under professional growth.

RATINGS AND LEVEL DEFINITIONS

Ratings for each component of the evaluation are based on a four-point scale defined as follows:

4 *Exceptional*
Exceptional performance is demonstrated by performance levels that are recognized as superior as compared to other professional faculty within the college.

3 *Satisfactory*
Satisfactory performance is demonstrated by performance levels that are recognized as meeting all reasonable and acceptable standards compared to other professional faculty within the college.

2 *Needs Improvement*
Performance that needs improvement is demonstrated by performance levels that are recognized as deficient in one or more criteria, but evidence suggests that satisfactory performance is possible with

appropriate professional development and assistance. Achievements are not well documented or always evident.

1 *Unacceptable*
Unacceptable performance is demonstrated by performance levels that are clearly recognized as not meeting reasonable and minimal standards compared to other professional faculty within the college, or

documentation is not provided by faculty when requested or prescribed in the evaluation process.

For many items, an institutional standard has been established. The stated standard is that which is necessary to achieve a rating of 3. Ratings above or below a 3 are to be based on the degree to which the faculty member exceeded or failed to meet the institutional standard.

CALENDAR FOR EVALUATING FACULTY PERFORMANCE

Mid-September	Orientation to faculty evaluation system.
Mid-October	Evaluation agreement between department head and faculty member.
First Week November–First Week December	Administer student rating form (CIEQ) to students and complete self-rating using the CIEQ instrument.
First Week February	Student rating (CIEQ) summary reports returned to faculty member.
Mid-March	Self-assessment and report completed and materials prepared for peer review.
Mid-April	Peer evaluation and assessment complete.
	Department head evaluation of faculty member complete.
	Materials returned to central source and appointment for final conferences set.
First Week May	Conference and evaluation procedure completed.
	Preliminary evaluation agreement complete.

SUMMARY MATRIX OF FACULTY EVALUATION SYSTEM ROLES, SOURCES, WEIGHTS, AND INDICATORS OF PERFORMANCE

	STUDENT	SELF	PEER	DEPARTMENT HEAD
I. TEACHING AND INSTRUCTION (60%–80%)	STUDENT (40%)	SELF (10%)	PEER (30%)	DEPARTMENT HEAD (20%)
A. Classroom Performance	CIEQ	1. Explanatory comments 2. Portfolio submitted		
B. Materials Preparation / Materials Relevancy		1. Self-rating 2. Portfolio submitted	1. Peer team composite rating 2. Portfolio review	1. Department head rating 2. Portfolio review 3. CIEQ review
C. Record Keeping/Instructional Management		1. Self-rating 2. Portfolio submitted		1. Department head rating 2. Portfolio review 3. CIEQ review
II. COLLEGE SERVICE (10%–20%)	STUDENT (0%)	SELF (40%)	PEER (20%)	DEPARTMENT HEAD (40%)
Items selected		1. Self-rating 2. Portfolio submitted	1. Peer team composite rating 2. Portfolio review	1. Department head rating 2. Portfolio review
III. PROFESSIONAL GROWTH (10%–30%)	STUDENT (0%)	SELF (45%)	PEER (25%)	DEPARTMENT HEAD (30%)
Items selected		1. Self-rating 2. Portfolio submitted a. Transcripts b. Letters c. Publications d. Conference programs e. Etc.	1. Peer team composite rating 2. Portfolio review	1. Department head rating 2. Portfolio review
IV. COMMUNITY SERVICE (0–10%)	STUDENT (0%)	SELF (35%)	PEER (20%)	DEPARTMENT HEAD (45%)
Items selected		1. Self-rating 2. Portfolio submitted	1. Peer team composite rating 2. Portfolio review	1. Department head rating 2. Portfolio review

Arreola, R.A. (1995). *Developing a Comprehensive Faculty Evaluation System.* Bolton, MA: Anker Publishing Co., Inc.

Developing a Comprehensive Faculty Evaluation System

FACULTY MEMBER—DEPARTMENT HEAD

FINAL EVALUATION AGREEMENT

Faculty member's name: _____

Department or Division: _____

For each role, indicate the agreed value to be assigned based on the assigned teaching and instructional duties as well as the expected and planned activities in each role.

   I. Teaching and Instruction (60%–80%)   _____%

  II. College Service (10%–20%)   _____%
      (List planned activities)

        A. _____

        B. _____

        C. _____

        D. _____

 III. Professional Growth (10%–30%)   _____%
      (List planned activities)

        A. _____

        B. _____

        C. _____

        D. _____

 IV. Community Service (0%–10%)   _____%
      (List planned activities)

        A. _____

        B. _____

        C. _____

        D. _____

                                                __100__ %

Faculty member's signature: _____ Date: _____

Department head's signature: _____ Date: _____

SELF-REPORT AND ASSESSMENT

I. TEACHING AND INSTRUCTION

    A. *Classroom Performance—Student Ratings:* Record CIEQ total mean score for each class taught during the evaluation cycle. Compare these scores with those you recorded for yourself on the CIEQ questions and note any significant discrepancies.

	Course Prefix & Number	*Year*	*Total Mean*
1.	_____	_____	_____
2.	_____	_____	_____
3.	_____	_____	_____
4.	_____	_____	_____
5.	_____	_____	_____
6.	_____	_____	_____
7.	_____	_____	_____
8.	_____	_____	_____
9.	_____	_____	_____

    Student CIEQ Rating: Average Total Score   (T-I) [_____]
    (Record this value on the Self-Report and Assessment Summary)

NOTE: The faculty member is requested to provide any information regarding strengths or weaknesses of classroom performance that may or may not be reflected in the student observations and to react to answers to open-ended questions. Record comments below and on reverse side.

B. *Materials Preparation/Materials Relevancy*

    1. *Has current and relevant syllabi.* (Provide copies of two different current syllabi; insert in Portfolio A.)

    Institutional Standard (3): Contains all required components of a syllabus. Evidence that course material is presented as prescribed.

    Paragraph 522.0 of the Board Policy Manual states that a syllabus shall include the following:

        • purposes and objectives of the course

        • a sequential outline of the course content

        • methods of evaluating student achievement

        • a listing of primary and supplementary texts or other resource material

    Syllabi submitted:

	Course Number	Rating
1.	_____	_____ (R1)
2.	_____	_____ (R2)

    Compute and record Average Rating B1:

    Average Rating B1 = (R1 + R2)/2   Average Rating B1: [_____]

    Comments:

    2. *Revisions and/or updates of course materials.*

    (Either indicate areas of revision of syllabi submitted or provide three examples of course material that reflect significant revision since last evaluation; insert in Portfolio A.)

    Institutional Standard (3): Evidence that course goals, objectives, and learning materials have been modified, deleted, added, or revised.

    Comments:

Rating B2: [_____]

3. *Uses evaluation methods that are related to and appropriate for course content.* (Provide examples of at least two or more tests, graded assignments or procedures used to evaluate students; insert in Portfolio A.)

Institutional Standard (3): The tests, graded assignments, evaluation procedures are clearly related to the content and objectives of the course that have been chosen for review.

Comments:

Rating B3: [____]

4 *Informs students of the objectives of the course.* (Provide evidence that course objectives are communicated to students by handouts or CIEQ open-ended responses; insert in Portfolio A.)

Institutional Standard (3): Evidence that course objectives have been communicated to students and that they are aware of the course objectives.

Comments:

Rating B4: [____]

5. *Uses supplemental resources in addition to textbook or other minimal course materials.* (If not reflected in course syllabi, provide evidence of technique or materials used; Insert in Portfolio A.)

Institutional Standard (3): Supplemental resources are fully integrated into course.

Comments:

Rating B5: [____]

Compute and record average category B rating:

Average category B rating = (B1 + B2 + B3 + B4 + B5)/5   [____]*
* Record also on Self-Report and Assessment Summary.

C. *Record Keeping and Instructional Management—Self-Rating*

1. *Keeps scheduled office hours.*

    Institutional Standard (3): Evidence that office hours are posted and maintained.

    Comments:

    Rating C1: [____]

2. *Meets classes as scheduled for prescribed time and uses class time well.*

    Institutional Standard (3): Classes are met as scheduled and instructor uses time productively.

    Comments

    Rating C2: [____]

3. *Submits required reports and documents, i.e., book requests, attendance verification, and grades, as directed.*

    Institutional Standard (3): Required material submitted as directed.

    Comments:

    Rating C3: [____]

4. *Attends required departmental/divisional meetings.*

    Institutional Standard (3): Meetings are attended or proper verification for absence was made.

    Comments:

    Rating C4: [____]

Average category C self-rating = (C1 + C2 + C3 + C4)/4   [____]*
* Record also on Self-Report and Assessment Summary.

(Refer to supplementary questions on the CIEQ student rating instrument; record data from current year CIEQ only.)

5. *CIEQ Question 22:* Instructor encouraged out-of-class consultation.

	Class #1	Class #2	Class #3
Student Ratings	_____	_____	_____

Avg C5: [_____]

6. *CIEQ Question 23:* Instructor was available for consultation with students during scheduled office hours.

	Class #1	Class #2	Class #3
Student Ratings	_____	_____	_____

Avg C6: [_____]

7. *CIEQ Question 24:* The instructor used class time well

	Class #1	Class #2	Class #3
Student Ratings	_____	_____	_____

Avg C6: [_____]

Average student rating—Category C = (C5 + C6 + C7)/3   [_____]*
* Record also on Self-Report and Assessment Summary.

COLLEGE SERVICE, PROFESSIONAL GROWTH, AND COMMUNITY SERVICE

The minimum and maximum weights allowed in the evaluation system for professional growth, college service, and community service are as follows:

Minimum		Maximum
10%	Professional Growth	30%
10%	College Service	20%
0%	Community Service	10%

Activities in each of these areas can vary widely in terms of complexity and effort required. Therefore, when identifying those areas for which the faculty member wishes to have included in the individualized evaluation process, both the faculty member and department head must consider the relationship of the nature of the activities selected in terms of complexity and the effort required with the weight the activities will have in the total evaluation process.

Because the institutional minimum for both professional growth and college service is 10%, each faculty member must become involved in activities in these areas to the extent that the weight of 10% on these activities in the overall evaluation of the faculty member's performance is justified. No minimum for community service has been established; therefore, there is no institutional requirement for involvement or performance in this area.

The items listed in each of the three categories are illustrations of typical activities only. Upon agreement with the department head, the faculty member may select relevant items other than those suggested.

Faculty members are responsible for submitting the appropriate documentation to reflect and support their efforts for the items selected. This may include memos from committee chairpersons regarding committee membership, copies of convention programs, copies of articles, research reports, explanatory comments, etc.

II. COLLEGE SERVICE (restricted to institutional activities)

Suggested activities:

1. Serve on committee(s)

2. Develop or revise course(s) and/or instructional programs

3. Plan, conduct, participate in workshops

4. Participate in approved orientation activities

5. Participate in student recruitment

6. Sponsor a student organization or activity

7. Prepare proposal(s) for external grants

8. Serve as guest lecturer or presenter

9. Other

Activities Selected	Documentation Included (check) (Insert in Portfolio B)
_____	_____
_____	_____
_____	_____
_____	_____
_____	_____
_____	_____

College Service Self-Rating   [_____]*
* Record also on Self-Report and Assessment Summary

Comments: (Add any supportive or explanatory comments, including reason for lack of supporting documentation.)

III. PROFESSIONAL GROWTH (directed toward external activities)

Suggested activities:

1. Attend or participate in workshops or conferences related to one's field.

2. Participate in external visitations to improve professional competency.

3. Pursue additional course work (limited to academic credit from accredited institutions).

4. Publish an article, reviews, or write a book.

5. Involved in research related to one's field.

6. Serve as a consultant.

7. Other

Activities Selected	*Documentation Included (check) (Insert in Portfolio C)*
_____	_____
_____	_____
_____	_____
_____	_____
_____	_____
_____	_____

Professional Growth Self-Rating   [_____]*
* Record also on Self-Report and Assessment Summary

Comments: Add any supportive or explanatory comments.

IV. COMMUNITY SERVICE (limited to application of faculty member's recognized area of expertise in the community without pay)

Brief Description of Activities Selected	*Documentation Included (check) (Insert in Portfolio D)*
_____	_____
_____	_____
_____	_____
_____	_____
_____	_____
_____	_____

Community Service Self-Rating   [_____]*

* Record also on Self-Report and Assessment Summary

Comments: Add any supportive or explanatory comments.

Developing a Comprehensive Faculty Evaluation System

SELF-REPORT AND ASSESSMENT

I. Teaching and Instruction

    A. Classroom Performance

        Student Rating: CIEQ average *total* score   (T-I)   [_____]*

    B. Materials Preparation/Materials Relevancy

        Self-rating: Average *subscore,* category B   [_____]

    C. Record Keeping and Instructional Management

        Self-rating: Average *Self-subscore,* category C   [_____]

        Student rating: Average *Student-subscore,* category C   [_____]

    Average *total self-rating* for teaching and instruction =
        (Average Self-Subscore B + Average Self-Subscore C)/2   (S-I)   [_____]*
        (Do not include student rating subscore, category C)

II. College Services

    Self-rating   (S-II)   [_____]*

III. Professional Growth

    Self-rating   (S-III)   [_____]*

IV. Community Service

    Self-rating   (S-IV)   [_____]*

* To be recorded by department head on Faculty Evaluation Summary Sheet.

PEER EVALUATION OF FACULTY MEMBER

I. TEACHING AND INSTRUCTION

    A. *Classroom Performance*

    Source: Student and Self Only

    B. *Materials Preparation/Materials Relevancy*

       1. *Has current and relevant syllabi.* (Provide copies of two current syllabi.)

         Institutional Standard (3): Contains all required components of a syllabus. Evidence that course material is presented as prescribed. Refer to Portfolio A.

         Paragraph 522.0 of the Board Policy Manual states that a syllabus shall include the following:

          • purposes and objectives of the course

          • a sequential outline of the course content

          • methods of evaluating student achievement

          • a listing of primary and supplementary texts or other resource material

         Syllabi submitted:

Course Number	Rating
1. _____	_____ (R1)
2. _____	_____ (R2)

Compute and record average rating B1:

Average rating $B1 = (R1 + R2)/2$ Average Rating B1: [____]

Comments:

       2. *Reviews and/or updates of course materials.* (Either indicate areas of revision of syllabi submitted or provide three examples of course material that reflect significant revision since last evaluation; refer to Portfolio A.)

         Institutional Standard (3): Evidence that course goals, objectives, and learning materials have been modified, deleted, added, or revised.

         Comments:

Rating B2: [____]

3. *Uses evaluation methods that are related to and appropriate for course content.* (Provide examples of at least two or more tests, graded assignments or procedures used in the evaluation of students; refer to Portfolio A.)

Institutional Standard (3): The tests, graded assignments, evaluation procedures are clearly related to the content and objectives of the course that have been chosen for review.

Comments:

Rating B3: [_____]

4. *Informs students of the objectives of the course.* (Provide evidence that course objectives are communicated to students by handouts or CIEQ open-ended responses; refer to Portfolio A.)

Institutional Standard (3): Evidence that course objectives have been communicated to students and that they are aware of the course objectives.

Comments:

Rating B4: [_____]

5. *Uses supplemental resources in addition to textbook or other minimal course materials.* (If not reflected in course syllabi, provide evidence of technique or materials used; refer to Portfolio A.)

Institutional Standard (3): Supplemental resources are fully integrated into course.

Comments:

Rating B5: [_____]

Compute and record average category B peer rating:

Average category B peer rating = (B1 + B2 + B3 + B4 + B5)/5   [_____]‡
‡ Record also on Peer Team Evaluation Summary.

II. COLLEGE SERVICE

Activities

                                    Documentation Included (check) (See Portfolio B)

1. _____   _____

2. _____   _____

3. _____   _____

College Service Peer Rating   [____]‡

Comments:

III. PROFESSIONAL GROWTH

Activities

                                    Documentation Included (check) (See Portfolio C)

1. _____   _____

2. _____   _____

3. _____   _____

Professional Growth Peer Rating   [____]‡

Comments:

IV. COMMUNITY SERVICE

Activities

                                    Documentation Included (check) (See Portfolio D)

1. _____   _____

2. _____   _____

3. _____   _____

Professional Growth Peer Rating   [____]‡

Comments:

‡ Record also on Peer Team Evaluation Summary

PEER EVALUATION OF FACULTY MEMBER

SUMMARY

  I. Teaching and Instruction

       A. Classroom Performance

          Source: Student and Self Only

       B. Materials Preparation/Materials Relevancy

          Peer Rating: (P-I) [____]*

       C. Record Keeping and Instructional Management

          Source: Student, Self, Department Head Only

  II. College Services

      Peer Rating   (P-II) [____]*

III. Professional Growth

      Peer Rating   (P-III) [____]*

 IV. Community Service

      Peer Rating   (P-IV) [____]*

   * NOTE: The peer ratings record should be the composite rating (average rating) of the team, not individual peer ratings. The ratings recorded should be determined by the peer review committee after a review of the material in the portfolio. Peer ratings are to be recorded by department head on Peer Team Summary Sheet.

PEER TEAM EVALUATION OF FACULTY

SUMMARY

(To be completed by department head)

	Peer 1	Peer 2	Peer 3	Total	*Average
I. Teaching and Instruction (Materials Preparation)					
II. College Service					
III Professional Growth					
IV. Community Service					

_____

Department Head Signature

_____

Date

DEPARTMENT HEAD EVALUATION OF FACULTY MEMBER

I. TEACHING AND INSTRUCTION

    A. *Classroom Performance*

    Source: Student and Self Only

    B. *Materials Preparation/Materials Relevancy*

        1. *Has current and relevant syllabi.* (Provide copies of two current syllabi.)

        Institutional Standard (3): Contains all required components of a syllabus. Evidence that course material is presented as prescribed. Refer to Portfolio A.

        Paragraph 522.0 of the Board Policy Manual states that a syllabus shall include the following:

        • purposes and objectives of the course

        • a sequential outline of the course content

        • methods of evaluating student achievement

        • a listing of primary and supplementary texts or other resource material

        Syllabi submitted:

Course Number	Rating
1. _____	_____ (R1)
2. _____	_____ (R2)

        Compute and record average rating B1:

        Average rating B1 = (R1 + R2)/2   Average Rating B1: [____]

        Comments:

        2. *Reviews and/or updates of course materials.* (Either indicate areas of revision of syllabi submitted or provide three examples of course material that reflect significant revision since last evaluation; refer to Portfolio A.)

        Institutional Standard (3): Evidence that course goals, objectives, and learning materials have been modified, deleted, added, or revised.

        Comments:

                                                      Rating B2: [____]

3. *Uses evaluation methods that are related to and appropriate for course content.* (Provide examples of at least two or more tests, graded assignments, or procedures used in the evaluation of students; refer to Portfolio A.)

Institutional Standard (3): The tests, graded assignments, evaluation procedures are clearly related to the content and objectives of the course that have been chosen for review.

Comments:

Rating B3: [____]

4 *Informs students of the objectives of the course.* (Provide evidence that course objectives are communicated to student by handouts or CIEQ open-ended responses; refer to Portfolio A.)

Institutional Standard (3): Evidence that course objectives have been communicated to students and that they are aware of the course objectives.

Comments:

Rating B4: [____]

5. *Uses supplemental resources in addition to textbook or other minimal course materials.* (If not reflected in course syllabi, provide evidence of technique or materials used; refer to Portfolio A.)

Institutional Standard (3): Supplemental resources are fully integrated into course.

Comments:

Rating B5: [____]

Compute and record average category B department head rating:

Average category B department head rating =

    (B1 + B2 + B3 + B4 + B5)/5   [____]*

* Record also on Department Head Summary Form.

C. *Record Keeping and Instructional Management—Self-Rating*

1. *Keeps scheduled office hours.*

   Institutional Standard (3): Evidence that office hours are posted and maintained.

   Comments:

   Rating C1: [_____]

2. *Meets classes as scheduled for prescribed time and uses class time well.*

   Institutional Standard (3): Classes are met as scheduled and instructor uses time productively.

   Comments

   Rating C2: [_____]

3. *Submits required reports and documents, i.e., book requests, attendance verification, and grades as directed.*

   Institutional Standard (3): Required material submitted as directed.

   Comments:

   Rating C3: [_____]

4. *Attends required departmental/division meetings.*

   Institutional Standard (3): Meetings are attended or proper verification for absence was made.

   Comments:

   Rating C4: [_____]

   Average category C department head rating =

   (C1 + C2 + C3 + C4)/4   [_____]*

   * Record also on Department Head Summary Form.

II. COLLEGE SERVICE

Activities

*Documentation
Included (check)
(See Portfolio B)*

1. _____   _____

2. _____   _____

3. _____   _____

College Service Dept. Head Rating   [_____]*

Comments:

III. PROFESSIONAL GROWTH

Activities

*Documentation
Included (check)
(See Portfolio C)*

1. _____   _____

2. _____   _____

3. _____   _____

Professional Growth Dept. Head Rating   [_____]*

Comments:

IV. COMMUNITY SERVICE

Activities

*Documentation
Included (check)
(See Portfolio D)*

1. _____   _____

2. _____   _____

3. _____   _____

Professional Growth Dept. Head Rating   [_____]*

Comments:

* Record also on Department Head Summary Form.

DEPARTMENT HEAD EVALUATION OF FACULTY MEMBER

SUMMARY

I. Teaching and Instruction

    A. Classroom Performance

       Source: Student and Self Only

    B. Materials Preparation/Materials Relevancy

       Department Head Rating (average subscore Category B):   [_____]

    C. Record Keeping and Instructional Management

       Department Head Rating (average subscore Category C):   [_____]

       Department Head Rating = (B+C)/2   (D-I) [_____]*

II. College Services

    Department Head Rating   (D-II) [_____]*

III. Professional Growth

    Department Head Rating   (D-III) [_____]*

IV. Community Service

    Department Head Rating   (D-IV) [_____]*

* To be recorded by department head on Faculty Evaluation Summary Sheet.

FACULTY EVALUATION SUMMARY SHEET

(To be completed by the department head)

I. Teaching and Instruction

Student	(T-I)	_____	x	40%	=	_____	
Self	(S-I)	_____	x	10%	=	_____	
Peer	(P-I)	_____	x	30%	=	_____	
Dept. Head	(D-I)	_____	x	20%	=	_____	
				Total	=	_____	

Weight (60%–80%)   _____   x   Total _____ = [_____]

II. College Service

Self	(S-II)	_____	x	40%	=	_____
Peer	(P-II)	_____	x	20%	=	_____
Dept. Head	(D-II)	_____	x	40%	=	_____
				Total	=	_____

Weight (10%–20%)   _____   x   Total _____ = [_____]

III. Professional Growth

Self	(S-III)	_____	x	45%	=	_____
Peer	(P-III)	_____	x	25%	=	_____
Dept. Head	(D-III)	_____	x	30%	=	_____
				Total	=	_____

Weight (10%–30%)   _____   x   Total _____ = [_____]

IV. Community Service

Self	(S-IV)	_____	x	35%	=	_____
Peer	(P-IV)	_____	x	20%	=	_____
Dept. Head	(D-IV)	_____	x	45%	=	_____
				Total	=	_____

Weight (0%–10%)   _____   x   Total _____ = [_____]

GRAND TOTAL   [_____]

FINAL CONFERENCE FORM

Based on information obtained from this evaluation process, describe two strengths and two weaknesses you have discovered about your role as a faculty member.

Strengths:

   1.

   2.

Weaknesses:

   1.

   2.

Identify three goals to be pursued during the next evaluation cycle for personal and/or professional development. (Use these goals as a basis for the preliminary contract.)

   1.

   2.

   3.

FACULTY MEMBER—DEPARTMENT HEAD

PRELIMINARY EVALUATION AGREEMENT

Faculty member's name: _____

Department or Division: _____

For each role, indicate the agreed value to be assigned based on the assigned teaching and instructional duties as well as the expected and planned activities in each role.

   I. Teaching and Instruction (60%–80%)   _____%

  II. College Service (10%–20%)   _____%
       (List planned activities)

        A. _____

        B. _____

        C. _____

        D. _____

 III. Professional Growth (10%–30%)   _____%
       (List planned activities)

        A. _____

        B. _____

        C. _____

        D. _____

 IV. Community Service (0%–10%)   _____%
       (List planned activities)

        A. _____

        B. _____

        C. _____

        D. _____

                                                   ___100___%

Faculty member's signature: _____ Date: _____

Department head's signature: _____ Date: _____

PORTFOLIO A: TEACHING AND INSTRUCTION

In this portfolio folder place the following:
- Two current syllabi
- Three examples of revision in course materials or syllabi
- Two examples of evaluation methods, e.g., tests, graded assignments
- Evidence of the use of supplemental resources

PORTFOLIO B: COLLEGE SERVICE (restricted to institutional activities)

Examples of evidence include descriptions of service on committees, evidence of planning for, conducting, or participating in workshops.

PLEASE ARRANGE ITEMS IN THIS PORTFOLIO CORRESPONDING TO THE NUMERICAL LIST BELOW.

1. _____
2. _____
3. _____
4. _____
5. _____
6. _____
7. _____
8. _____
9. _____
10. _____

PORTFOLIO C: PROFESSIONAL GROWTH (directed toward external activities)

Examples of evidence include evidence of attending or participating in conferences related to one's field, and additional course work (limited to academic credit from accredited institutions).

PLEASE ARRANGE ITEMS IN THIS PORTFOLIO CORRESPONDING TO THE NUMERICAL LIST BELOW.

1. _____
2. _____
3. _____
4. _____
5. _____
6. _____
7. _____
8. _____
9. _____
10. _____

PORTFOLIO D: COMMUNITY SERVICE

Limited to application of faculty member's recognized area of expertise in the community without pay.

PLEASE ARRANGE ITEMS IN THIS PORTFOLIO CORRESPONDING TO THE NUMERICAL LIST BELOW.

1. _____

2. _____

3. _____

4. _____

5. _____

6. _____

7. _____

8. _____

9. _____

10. _____

19

Bibliography

These selected resources represent several aspects of the field of faculty evaluation. Many of these resources have been cited as references for various sections of this handbook. This listing is intended to serve only as an entry resource for those wishing to pursue a review of the literature as they develop their own comprehensive faculty evaluation system. It is not intended to represent an exhaustive listing of all references in the field of faculty evaluation.

Abbott, R. D., Wulff, D. H., Nyquist, J. D., Ropp, V. A., & Hess, C. W. (1990). Satisfaction with processes of collecting student opinions about instruction: The student perspective. *Journal of Educational Psychology, 82*(2), 201-206.

Abpianalp, P. H., & Baldwin, W. R. (1983). Good teaching—a rewardable feat. *Journal of Optometric Education, 8*(3), 19-22.

Abrami, P. C. (1980). Using student rating norm groups for summative evaluations. *Proceedings, 6,* 124 -32. (Sixth International Conference on Improving University Teaching).

Abrami, P. C. (1985). Dimensions of effective college instruction. *Review of Higher Education, 8,* 211-28.

Abrami, P. C. (1989). How should we use student ratings to evaluate teaching. *Research in Higher Education, 30*(2), 221-227.

Abrami, P. C., & d'Apollonia, S. (1991). Multidimensional students' evaluations of teaching effectiveness—generalizability of "N = 1" research: Comment on Marsh (1991). *Journal of Educational Psychology, 83*(3), 411-415.

Abrami, P. C., d'Apollonia, S., & Cohen, P. A. (1990). Validity of student ratings of instruction: What we know and what we do not know. *Journal of Educational Psychology, 82*(2), 219-231.

Abrami, P. C., Cohen, P. A., & d'Apollonia, S. (1988). Implementation problems in meta-analysis. *Review of Educational Research, 58*(2), 151-179.

Abrami, P. C., Dickens, W. J., Perry, R. P., & Leventhal, L. (1980). Do teacher standards for assigning grades affect student evaluations of instruction? *Journal of Educational Psychology, 72,* 107-118.

Abrami, P. C., Leventhal, L., & Perry, R. P. (1982). Educational seduction. *Review of Educational Research, 52,* 446-64.

Abrami, P. C., & Mizener, D. A. (1982). Student/instructor attitude similarity, course ratings and student achievement. Paper presented at the annual meeting of the American Psychological Association, Washington, DC, (ERIC ED 233 144).

Abrami, P. C., & Mizener, D. A. (1983). Does the attitude similarity of college professors and their students produce 'bias' in course evaluations? *American Educational Research Journal, 20*(1), 123-36.

Abrami, P. C., & Mizener, D. A. (1985). Student/instructor attitude similarity, student ratings, and course performance. *Journal of Educational Psychology, 77,* 693-702.

Abrami, P. C., & Murphy, V. (1980). *A catalogue of systems for student evaluation of instruction.* Montreal, Canada: McGill University Centre for Teaching and Learning.

Aiken, Lewis R. (1983). Number of response categories and statistics on a teacher rating scale. *Educational and Psychological Measurement, 43*(2), 397-401.

Aleamoni, L. M. (1972). A review of recent reliability and validity studies on the Illinois Course Evaluation Questionnaire (CEQ), *Research Memorandum No. 127.* University of Illinois: Measurement and Research Division.

Aleamoni, L. M. (1972). Response to Professor W. Edwards Deming's "memorandum on teaching." *The American Statistician, 26*(4), 54.

Aleamoni, L. M. (1973). Course evaluation questionnaire at the University of Illinois. *Evaluation, 1*(2), 73-74.

Aleamoni, L. M. (1973). Teaching—its place in the college or university reward system. In *Midwest Association for Physical Education of College Women Annual Report and Conference Proceedings.* Ypsilanti, Michigan: University Printing, Eastern Michigan University. Pp. 26-32.

Aleamoni, L. M. (1973). The usefulness of student evaluations in improving college teaching. In A. L. Sockloff (Ed.), *Proceedings: The First Invitational Conference on Faculty Effectiveness as Evaluated by Students.* Philadelphia, Pennsylvania: Measurement and Research Center, Temple University. Pp. 42-58.

Aleamoni, L. M. (1976). Evaluation of instruction via student ratings. *Note to the Faculty, No. 3,* Tucson, AZ: University of Arizona, Office of Instructional Research and Development.

Aleamoni, L. M. (1976). On the invalidity of student ratings for administrative personnel decisions. *Journal of Higher Education, 47*(5), 607-610.

Aleamoni, L. M. (1976). Proposed system for rewarding and improving instructional effectiveness. *College University, 51*(3), 330-338.

Aleamoni, L. M. (1976). Typical faculty concerns about student evaluation of instruction. *National Association of Colleges and Teachers of Agriculture Journal, 20*(1), 16-21.

Aleamoni, L. M. (1977). Concepts and principles in the evaluation of instruction (courses and instructors). In the *1977 North Central Regional Symposium on the Improvement of Instruction Proceedings: Quality of Instruction in Agriculture and the Renewable Resources.* Madison, Wisconsin: University of Wisconsin. Pp. 32-36.

Aleamoni, L. M. (1977). How can an institution improve and reward instructional effectiveness? *Faculty Development and Evaluation in Higher Education, 3*(4), 4-9.

Aleamoni, L. M. (1977). Indicators of the quality of instruction. In the 1977 North Central Regional Symposium on the Improvement of Instruction Proceedings: *Quality of Instruction in Agriculture and the Renewable Resources.* Madison, Wisconsin: University of Wisconsin. Pp. 16-18.

Aleamoni, L. M. (1977). Student evaluations of instruction proven useful and reliable. *Evaluation, 4,* 58.

Aleamoni, L. M. (1978). Development and factorial validation of Arizona Course/Instructor Evaluation Questionnaire. *Educational and Psychological Measurement, 38,* 1063-1067.

Aleamoni, L. M. (1978). The usefulness of student evaluations in improving college teaching. *Instructional Science, 7,* 95-105.

Aleamoni, L. M. (1979). *Arizona Course/Instructor Evaluation Questionnaire.* Tucson, AZ: Office of Instructional Research and Development, University of Arizona.

Aleamoni, L. M. (1979). Improvement of instruction should be the primary focus of instructional evaluation. *Note to the Faculty, No.8.* Tucson, AZ: University of Arizona, Office of Instructional Research and Development.

Aleamoni, L. M. (1980). Are there differences in perceived teaching effectiveness between males and females in anthropology? *Resources in Education,* (ERIC ED 176 706).

Aleamoni, L. M. (1980). Evaluation as an integral part of instructional and faculty development. In L. P. Grayson & J. M. Biedenbach (Eds.), *Proceedings: 1980 College Industry Education Conference.* Columbia, South Carolina: American Society for Engineering Education. Pp. 120-123.

Aleamoni, L. M. (1980). Students can evaluate teaching effectiveness. *National Forum, 60*(4), 41.

Aleamoni, L. M. (1980). The use of student evaluations in the improvement of instruction. *National Association of Colleges and Teachers of Agriculture, 24*(3), 18-21.

Aleamoni, L. M. (1981) Student ratings of instructor and instruction. In J. Milman (Ed.), *Handbook on teacher evaluation.* Beverly Hills, CA: Sage Publication, Inc.

Aleamoni, L. M. (1981). Systematizing student ratings of instruction. In T. L. Sherman & M. Hassett (Eds.), *Evaluation of introductory college mathematics programs.* Tempe, Arizona: Rocky Mountain Mathematics Consortium.

Aleamoni, L. M. (1982). Components of the instructional setting. *Instructional Evaluation, 7*(1), 11-16.

Aleamoni, L. M. (1982). Instructional improvement in the college classroom. In G. W. Bell (Ed.), *Professional preparation in athletic training.* Champaign, Illinois: Human Kinetics Publishers, Inc.

Aleamoni, L. M. (1984). Developing a comprehensive system to improve and reward instructional effectiveness. *Resources in Education,* (ERIC ED 245 765).

Aleamoni, L. M. (1984). The dynamics of faculty evaluation. In P. Seldin (Ed.), *Changing practices in faculty evaluation.* San Francisco, CA: Jossey-Bass, Inc.

Aleamoni, L. M. (1987). Evaluating instructional effectiveness can be a rewarding experience. *Journal of Plant Disease, 71*(4), 377-379.

Aleamoni, L. M. (1987). Some practical approaches for faculty and administrators. In L. M. Aleamoni (Ed.), *Techniques for instructional improvement and evaluation.* San Francisco, CA: Jossey-Bass, Inc.

Aleamoni, L. M. (1987). Student rating myths versus research facts. *Journal of Personnel Evaluation in Education, 1,* 111-119.

Aleamoni, L. M. (1987). Typical faculty concerns about student evaluation of teaching. In L. M. Aleamoni (Ed.), *Techniques for instructional improvement and evaluation.* San Francisco, CA: Jossey-Bass, Inc.

Aleamoni, L. M. (1988). Evaluation as reflection. In L. M. Aleamoni & D. Kishore (Eds.), *Evaluation and testing in instructional systems.* Hyderabad, India: National Academy of Agricultural Research Management. P. 258.

Aleamoni, L. M. (1988). Instructional process. In L. M. Aleamoni & D. Kishore (Eds.), *Evaluation and testing in instructional systems.* Hyderabad, India: National Academy of Agricultural Research Management. P. 4.

Aleamoni, L. M. (1990). Faculty development research in colleges, universities, and professional schools: The challenge. *Journal of Personnel Evaluation in Education, 3,* 193-195.

Aleamoni, L. M., & Everly, J. C. (1971). Illinois course evaluation questionnaire useful in collecting student opinion. *National Association of Colleges and Teachers of Agriculture Journal, 15*(4), 99-100.

Aleamoni, L. M., & Graham, M. H. (1974). The relationship between CEQ ratings and instructor's rank, class size, and course level. *Journal of Educational Measurement, 11,* 189-202.

Aleamoni, L. M., & Hexner, P. Z. (1980). A review of the research on student evaluation and report on the effect of different sets on instructions on student course and instructor evaluation. *Instructional Science, 9,* 67-84.

Aleamoni, L. M., & Spencer, R. E. (1973). The Illinois Course Evaluation Questionnaire: A description of its development and a report of some of its results. *Educational and Psychological Measurement, 33,* 669-684.

Aleamoni, L. M., & Stevens, J. J. (1984). Peer evaluation. *Note to the Faculty No. 15.* Tucson, Arizona: University of Arizona.

Aleamoni, L. M., & Stevens, J. (1984). The effectiveness of consultation in support of student evaluation feedback: A ten year follow-up. *The Pen, 7.*

Aleamoni, L. M., & Thomas, G. S. (1980). Differential relationships of student, instruction, and course characteristics to general and specific items on course evaluation questionnaire. *Teaching of Psychology, 7* (4), 233-235.

Aleamoni, L. M., & Yimer, M. (1973). An investigation of the relationship between colleague rating, student rating, research productivity, and academic rank in rating instructional effectiveness. *Journal of Educational Psychology, 64*(3), 274-277.

Aleamoni, L. M., & Yimer, M. (1974). *Graduating Senior Ratings Relationship to Colleague Rating, Student Rating, Research Productivity, and Academic Rank in Rating Instructional Effectiveness (Research Report No. 352).* Urbana: University of Illinois, Office of Instructional Resources, Measurement and Research Division.

Aleamoni, L. M., Yimer, M., & Mahan, J. M. (1972). Teacher folklore and sensitivity of a course evaluation questionnaire. *Psychological Reports, 31,* 607-614.

Amin, Martin E. (1993). Correlates of course evaluation at the faculty of letters and social sciences of the University of Yaounde. *Assessment and Evaluation in Higher Education, 18*(2), 135-141.

Andreson, L. W., and others. (1987). Competent teaching and its appraisal. *Assessment and Evaluation in Higher Education, 12*(1), 66-72.

Andrews, H. A. (1985). *Evaluating for excellence.* Stillwater, OK., New Forums Press, Inc.

Anikeef, A. M. (1953). Factors affecting student evaluation of college faculty members. *Journal of Applied Psychology, 37,* 458-460.

Arreola, R. A. (1979). Strategy for developing a comprehensive faculty evaluation system. *Engineering Education,* (December) 239-44.

Arreola, R. A. (1983). Establishing successful faculty evaluation and development programs. In A. Smith (Ed.), *Evaluating Faculty and Staff,* New Directions for Community Colleges, No. 41, Jossey-Bass, San Francisco, pp. 83-93.

Arreola, R. A. (1983). Students can distinguish between personality and content/organization in rating teachers. *Phi Delta Kappan, 65*(3), 222-223.

Arreola, R. A. (1983). What do student ratings measure? *The Articulating Paper, 4* (5), July. The College of Dentistry, The University of Tennessee, Memphis

Arreola, R. A. (1984). Evaluation of faculty performance: Key issues, in P. Seldin (Ed.), *Changing practices in faculty evaluation,* Jossey-Bass, San Francisco, pp. 79-85

Arreola, R. A. (1986). Evaluating the dimensions of teaching, *Instructional Evaluation, 8*(2), 4-14.

Arreola, R. A. (1987). A faculty evaluation model for community and junior colleges. In L. Aleamoni (Ed.) *New directions for teaching and learning,* Jossey-Bass, San Francisco, August/September, pp. 65-74.

Arreola, R. A. (1987). The role of student government in faculty evaluation. In L. Aleamoni (Ed.), *New Directions for Teaching and Learning,* Jossey-Bass, San Francisco, August/September, pp. 39-46.

Arreola, R. A. (1989). Defining and evaluating the elements of teaching. In W. Cashin (Ed.) *Proceedings of the Sixth Annual Academic Chairperson's Conference,* Center for Faculty Evaluation and Development, Kansas State University, Spring, 31, pp. 3-12.

Arreola, R. A., & Aleamoni, L. M. (1990). Practical issues in designing and operating a faculty evaluation system. In M. Theall & J. Franklin, (Eds.), *Student Ratings of Instruction: Issues for Improving Practice New Directions for Teaching and Learning, No. 43*, Fall, Jossey-Bass, San Francisco, pp. 37-55.

Arubayi, Eric. (1986). Students' evaluation of instruction in higher education: A review. *Assessment and Evaluation in Higher Education, 11*(1), 1-10.

Avi-Itzhak, T., & Kremer, L. (1983). The effects of organizational factors on student ratings and perceived instructions. *Higher Education, 12*(4), 411-418.

Avi-Itzhak, T., & Kremer, L. (1985). An investigation into the relationship between university faculty attitudes toward student rating and organizational and background factors. *Educational Research Quarterly, 10*(2), 31-38.

Baird, John S., Jr. (1987). Perceived learning in relation to student evaluation of university instruction. *Journal of Educational Psychology, 79*(1), 90-91.

Baker, Ahmad M. (1986). Validity of Palestinian University students' responses in evaluating their instructors. *Assessment and Evaluation in Higher Education, 11*(1), 70-75.

Ballard, M. J., Reardon, J., & Nelson, L. (1976). Student and peer rating of faculty. *Teaching of Psychology, 3*, 115-119.

Bannister, Brendan D., Kinicki, A. J., & Denisi, A. J. (1987). A new method for the statistical control of rating error in performance ratings. *Educational and Psychological Measurement, 47*(3), 583-596.

Banz, M. L., & Rodgers, J. L. (1985). Dimensions underlying student ratings of instruction: A multidimensional scaling analysis. *American Educational Research Journal, 22*(2), 267-72.

Barke, C. R., Tollefson, N., & Tracy, D.B. (1983). Relationship between course entry attitudes and end-of-course ratings. *Journal of Educational Psychology, 75*(1), 75-85.

Barnes, Laura L. B., & Barnes, Michael W. (1993). Academic discipline and generalizability of student evaluations of instruction. *Research in Higher Education. 34*(2) 135-149.

Basow, S. A., & Distenfeld, M. S. (1985). Teacher expressiveness: More important for male teachers than female teachers? *Journal of Educational Psychology, 77*, 45-52.

Basow, Susan A., & Silberg, Nancy T. (1987). Student evaluations of college professors: Are female and male professors rated differently? *Journal of Educational Psychology, 79*(3), 308-314.

Batista, E. E. (1976). The place of colleague evaluation in the appraisal of college teaching: A review of the literature. *Research in Higher Education, 4*(3), 257-271.

Bednash, Geraldine. (1991). Tenure review: Process and outcomes. *Review of Higher Education, 15*(1), 47-63.

Behrendt, R. L., & Parsons, M. H. (1983). Evaluation of part-time faculty. *New Directions for Community Colleges, 11*(1), 33-43.

Bejar, I. I. (1975). A survey of selected administrative practices supporting student evaluation of instructional programs. *Research in Higher Education, 3*, 77-86.

Bell, M. E., (1977). Peer evaluation as a method of faculty development. *Journal of the College and University Personnel Association, 28*(4), 15-17.

Bendig, A. W. (1952). A preliminary study of the effect of academic level, sex, and course variables on student rating of psychology instructors. *Journal of Psychology, 34*, 21-26.

Bendig, A. W. (1953). Relation of level of course achievement of students, instructor, and course ratings in introductory psychology. *Educational and Psychological Measurement, 13*, 437-488.

Bennet, J. B. (1985). Periodic evaluation of tenured faculty performance. *New Directions for Higher Education, 13*(1), 65-73.

Bennett, S. K. (1982). Student perceptions of and expectations for male and female instructors: Evidence relating to the question of gender bias in teaching. *Journal of Educational Psychology, 74*, 170-179.

Benton, S. E. (1982). Rating college teaching: Criterion validity studies of student evaluation-of-instruction instruments. *AAHE-Eric/Higher Education Report No. 1.* Washington, DC: American Association for Higher Education. (ERIC ED 221 147).

Bergman, J. (1980). Peer evaluation of university faculty: A monograph. *College Student Journal, 14*(3, Pt. 2), 1-21.

Bingham, R. D., and others. (1982). The personal assessment feedback program for prospective teachers. *Action in Teacher Education, 4*(4), 55-57.

Blackburn, R. T., & Clark, M. J. (1975). An assessment of faculty performance: Some correlates between administrators, colleague, student and self-ratings. *Sociology of Education, 48*, 242-256.

Blai, B. J. (1982). *Faculty perceptions of "effective" teachers: A parallel-perceptions inquiry.* (ERIC ED 219 029).

Bogue, E. G. (1967). Student appraisal of teaching effectiveness in higher education: Summary of the literature. *Education Quest, 11*, 6-10.

Boice, R. (1984). Reexamination of traditional emphases in faculty development. *Research in Higher Education, 21*(2), 195-209.

Bonge, D. (1982). Using TA ratings to validate student evaluations: A reply to Lamberth and Kosteski. *Teaching of Psychology, 9*(2), 102.

Borgatta, E. F. (1970). Student ratings of faculty. *American Association of University Professors Bulletin, 56,* 6-7.

Brandenburg, D. C., & Aleamoni, L. M. (1976). *Illinois Course Evaluation Questionnaire: Results Interpretation Manual, Form 73.* Urbana, Illinois: University of Illinois, Measurement and Research Division, Office of Instructional Resources.

Brandwein, A. C., & DiVittis, A. (1985). The evaluation of peer tutoring program: A quantitative approach. *Educational and Psychological Measurement, 45*(1), 15-27.

Braskamp, L. A. (1982). Evaluation systems are more than information systems. *New Directions for Higher Education, 10*(1), 55-66.

Braskamp, L. A., Brandenburg, D. C., & Ory, J. C. (1984). *Evaluating teaching effectiveness: A practical guide.* Beverly Hills, CA: Sage Publications, Inc.

Braskamp, L. A., Ory, J. C., & Pieper, D. M. (1980) Written student comments: Dimensions of instructional quality. *Journal of Educational Psychology, 73,* 65-70.

Braskamp, L. A., and others. (1982). Faculty uses of evaluative information. (ERIC ED 218 308).

Braunstein, D. N., Klein, G. A., & Pachla, M. (1973). Feedback, expectancy, and shifts in student ratings of college faculty. *Journal of Applied Psychology, 58,* 254-258.

Braxton, John M., Bayer, A. F., & Finkelstein, M. J. (1992). Teaching performance norms in academia. *Research in Higher Education, 33*(5), 533-569.

Brown, D. L. (1976). Faculty ratings and student grades: A university-wide multiple regression analysis. *Journal of Educational Psychology, 68,* 573-578.

Bruton, B. T., & Crull, S. R. (1981). Causes and consequences of student evaluation of instruction. *Research in Higher Education, 17*(3), 195-206.

Bryant, J., Comisky, P. W., Crane, J. S., & Zillman, D. (1980). Relationship between college teachers' use of humor in the classroom and students' evaluations of their teachers. *Journal of Educational Psychology, 72,* 511-519.

Burdsal, C. A., & Bardo, J. W. (1986). Measuring students' perceptions of teaching: Dimensions of evaluation. *Educational and Psychological Measurement, 46,* 63-79.

Cadwell, J., & Jenkins, J. (1985). Effects of the semantic similarity of items on student ratings of instructors. *Journal of Educational Psychology, 77,* 383-393.

Cahn, D. D. (1983). Relative importance of perceived understanding in initial interaction and development of interpersonal relationships. *Psychological Reports, 52,* 923-929.

Cahn, D. D. (1983). Relative importance of perceived understanding in students' evaluation of teachers. *Perceptual and Motor Skills, 59,* 610.

Camp, Robert C., Gibbs, Jr., M.C., & Masters II, R. J. (1988). The finite increment faculty merit pay allocation model. *Journal of Higher Education, 59*(6), 652-667.

Cashin, W. E. (1983). Concerns about using student ratings in community colleges. *New Directions for Community Colleges, 11*(1), 57-65.

Cashin, W. E., & Bruce, B. M. (1983). Do college teachers who voluntarily have their courses evaluated receive higher student ratings. *Journal of Educational Psychology, 75*(4), 595-602.

Cashin, William E., & Downey, Ronald G. (1992). Using global student rating items for summative evaluation. *Journal of Educational Psychology, 84*(4), 563-572.

Centra, J. A. (1973). Effectiveness of student feedback in modifying college instruction. *Journal of Educational Psychology, 65,* 395-401.

Centra, J. A. (1973). The student as godfather? The impact of student ratings on academia. In A. L. Sockloff (Ed.), *Proceedings of the First Invitational Conference on Faculty Effectiveness as Evaluated by Students.* Philadelphia: Temple University, Measurement and Research Center.

Centra, J. A. (1975). Colleagues as raters of classroom instruction. *Journal of Higher Education, 46,* 327-338.

Centra, J. A. (1981). *Determining faculty effectiveness.* San Francisco, CA: Jossey-Bass, Inc.

Centra, J. A. (1981). Research productivity and teaching effectiveness. *Educational Testing Service Research Reports* (81-11). Princeton, NJ: Educational Testing Service.

Centra, J. A. (1983). Research productivity and teaching effectiveness. *Research in Higher Education, 18*(4), 379-389.

Centra, J.A., & Bonesteel, P. (1990). College teaching: An art or a science? In M. Theall & J. Franklin, (Eds.), *Student Ratings of Instruction: Issues for Improving Practice.* New Directions for Teaching and Learning, No. 43, Fall 1990, 37-55, Jossey-Bass, San Francisco.

Champion, C. H., Green, S. B., & Sauser, W. I. (1988). Development and evaluation of shortcut-derived behaviorally anchored rating scales. *Educational and Psychological Measurement, 48*(1), 29-41.

Charkins, R. J., O'Toole, D. M., & Wetzel, J. N. (1985). Linking teacher and student learning styles with student achievement and attitudes. *Journal of Economic Education, 16*(2), 111-120.

Chiu, Chi-Kwan, & Alliger, George M. (1990). A proposed method to combine ranking and graphic rating in performance appraisal: The quantitative ranking scale. *Educational and Psychological Measurement, 50*(3), 493-503.

Ciscell, R. E. (1987). Student ratings of instruction: Change the timetable to improve instruction. *Community College Review, 15*(1), 34-38.

Clark, B. L. (1984). Responding to students: Ughs, awks, and ahas. *Improving College and University Teaching, 32*(4), 169-172.

Clark, K. E., & Keller, R. J. (1954). Student ratings of college teaching. In R. A. Eckert (Ed.), *A university looks at its program.* Minneapolis: University of Minnesota Press.

Clift, John, and others. (1989). Establishing the validity of a set of summative teaching performance scales. *Assessment and Evaluation in Higher Education, 14*(3), 193-206.

Cohen, P. A. (1980). *A Meta-Analysis of the Relationship between Student Ratings of Instruction and Student Achievement.* The Univ. of Michigan. (Doctoral Disst.)

Cohen, P. A. (1980). Effectiveness of student-rating feedback for improving college instruction: A meta-analysis of findings. *Research in Higher Education, 13,* 321-341.

Cohen, P. A. (1981). Student ratings of instruction and student achievement: A meta-analysis of multi-section validity studies. *Review of Educational Research, 51,* 281-309.

Cohen, P. A. (1982). Validity of student ratings in psychology courses: A research synthesis. *Teaching of Psychology, 9*(2) 78-82.

Cohen, P.A. (1990). Bringing research into practice, in M. Theall & J. Franklin, (Eds.), *Student Ratings of Instruction: Issues for Improving Practice.* New Directions for Teaching and Learning, No. 43, Fall 1990, 37-55, Jossey-Bass, San Francisco.

Cohen, P. A., & Herr, G. A. (1979). A procedure for diagnostic instructional feedback: The Formative Assessment of College Teaching (FACT). *Educational Technology, 19,* 18-23.

Cohen, P., & McKeachie, W. J. (1980). The role of colleagues in the evaluation of college teaching. *Improving College and University Teaching, 28*(4), 147-154.

Coleman, J., & McKeachie, W. J. (1980). Effects of instructor/course evaluations on student course selections. *Journal of Educational Psychology, 73,* 224-226.

Comer, J. C. (1980). The influence of mood on student evaluations of teaching. *Journal of Educational Research, 73,* 229-232.

Conway, Robert, and others (1993). Peer assessment of an individual's contribution to a group project. *Assessment and Evaluation in Higher Education, 18*(1), 45-56.

Cook, Stuart S. (1989). Improving the quality of student ratings of instruction: A look at two strategies. *Research in Higher Education, 30*(1), 31-45.

Cooper, C. R. (1982). Getting inside the instructional process: A collaborative diagnostic process for improving college teaching. *Journal of Instructional development, 3,* 2-10.

Cooper, P. J., Stewart, L. P., & Gudykunst, W.B. (1982). Relationship with instructor and other variables influencing student evaluations of instruction. *Communication Quarterly, 30*(4), 308-315.

Costin, F., Greenough, W.T., & Menges, R. J. (1971). Student ratings of college teaching: Reliability, validity, and usefulness. *Review of Educational Research, 41,* 511-535.

Cowen, D. L. (1976). Peer review in medical education. *Journal of Medical Education, 51*(2), 130-131.

Cranton, P. A., & Smith, R. A. (1986). A new look at the effect of course characteristics on student ratings of instruction. *American Educational Research Journal, 23,* 117-128.

Cranton, Patricia, & Smith, Ronald A. (1990). Reconsidering the unit of analysis: A model of student ratings of instruction. *Journal of Educational Psychology, 82*(2), 207-212. Special section with title "Instruction in Higher Education."

Crook, J., et al. (1982). A question of timing: When is the best time to survey graduates to obtain feedback about an educational program. *Assessment and Evaluation in Higher Education, 7*(2), 152-158.

Cundy, D. T. (1982). Teacher effectiveness and course popularity: Patterns in student evaluations. *Teaching Political Science, 9*(4), 164-173.

Darling-Hammond, L., Wise, A. E., & Pease, S. R. (1983). Teacher evaluation in the organizational context: A review of the literature. *Review of Educational Research, 53*(3), 285-328.

DeCette, J., & Kenney, J. (1982). Do grading standards affect student evaluations of teaching? Some new evidence on an old question. *Journal of Educational Psychology, 74,* 308-314.

DeJung, J. E. (1964). Effects of rater frames of reference on peer ratings. *Journal of Experimental Education, 33*(2), 121-131.

Deming, W. E. (1972). Memorandum on teaching. *The American Statistician, 26,* 47.

DeNeve, H. M. F., & Janssen, P. J. (1982). Validity of student evaluation of instruction. *Higher Education, 11*(5), 543-552.

Dick, R. C. (1983). Paper giving, play directing, and paid consulting: A position paper on faculty evaluation. *Association for Communication Administration Bulletin, 44,* 5-8.

Dick, W. (1982). Evaluation in diverse educational settings. *Viewpoints in Teaching and Learning, 58*(3), 84-89.

Dienst, E. R. (1981). Evaluation of colleagues. Paper presented at the 65th annual meeting of the American Educational Research Association, April 13-17, Los Angeles (ERIC ED 209 341).

Donald, J. G. (1982). A critical appraisal of the state of evaluation in higher education in Canada. *Assessment and Evaluation in Higher Education, 7*(2), 108-126.

Donald, J. G. (1984). Quality indices for faculty evaluation. *Assessment and Evaluation in Higher Education, 9*(1), 41-52.

Donald, J. G. (1985). The state of research on university teaching effectiveness. *New Directions for Teaching and Learning (Using Research to Improve Teaching), 23,* 7-20.

Dowell, D. A., & Neal, J. A. (1982). A selective review of the validity of student ratings of teaching. *Journal of Higher Education, 53*(1), 51-62.

Downie, N. W. (1952). Student evaluation of faculty. *Journal of Higher Education, 23,* 495-496, 503.

Doyle, K. O. (1975). *Student evaluation of instruction.* Lexington, MA: Lexington Books, Inc.

Doyle, K. O. (1983). *Evaluating teaching.* Lexington, MA: Lexington Books, Inc.

Doyle, K. O., & Crichton, L. I. (1978). Student, peer, and self evaluations of college instructors. *Journal of Educational Psychology, 70*(5), 815-826.

Doyle, K. O., & Whitely, S. E. (1974). Student ratings as criteria for effective teaching. *American Educational Research Journal, 11,* 259-274.

Dressel, P. L. (1982). Values (virtues and vices) in decision making. *New Directions for Higher Education, 10*(1), 31-43.

Drucker, A. J., & Remers, H. H. (1951). Do alumni and students differ in their attitudes toward instructors? *Journal of Educational Psychology, 42,* 129-143.

Earl, Shirley E. (1986). Staff and peer assessment—measuring an individual's contribution to group performance. *Assessment and Evaluation in Higher Education, 11*(1), 60-69.

Easton, J. Q. (1985). National study of effective community college teachers. *Community & Junior College Quarterly of Research and Practice, 9*(2), 153-163.

Eble, K. E. (1972). *Professors as teachers.* San Francisco, CA: Jossey-Bass, Inc.

Elton, L. (1984). Evaluating teaching and assessing teachers in universities. *Assessment and Evaluation in Higher Education, 9*(2), 97-115.

Erdle, S., & Murray, H. G. (1986). Interfaculty differences in classroom teaching behaviors and their relationship to student instructional ratings. *Research in Higher Education, 24,* 115-127.

Erdle, S., Murray, H. G., & Rushton, J. P. (1985). Personality, classroom behavior, and student ratings of college teaching effectiveness: A path analysis. *Journal of Educational Psychology, 77*(4), 394-407.

Everly, J. C., & Aleamoni, L. M. (1972). The rise and fall of the advisor ... Students attempt to evaluate their instructors. *Journal of the National Association of Colleges and Teachers of Agriculture, 16*(2), 43-45.

Feldman, K. A. (1976). Grades and college students' evaluations of their courses and teachers. *Research in Higher Education, 4,* 69-111.

Feldman, K. A. (1978). Course characteristics and college students' rating of their teachers: What we know and what we don't. *Research in Higher Education, 9,* 199-242.

Feldman, K. A. (1983). Seniority and instructional experience of college teachers as related to evaluations they receive from their students. *Research in Higher Education, 18*(1), 3-124.

Feldman, Kenneth A. (1984). Class size and college students' evaluations of teachers and courses: A closer look. *Research in Higher Education, 21*(1), 45-116.

Feldman, K. A. (1986). The perceived instructional effectiveness of college teachers as related to their personality and attitudinal characteristics: A review and synthesis. *Research in Higher Education, 24,* 139-213.

Feldman, Kenneth A. (1988). Effective college teaching from the students' and faculty's view: Matched or mismatched priorities? *Research in Higher Education, 28*(4), 291-344.

Feldman, Kenneth A. (1989). Instructional effectiveness of college teachers as judged by teachers themselves, current and former students, colleagues, administrators, and external (neutral) observers. *Research in Higher Education, 30*(2), 137-194.

Feldman, Kenneth A. (1990). An Afterword for "The Association between Student Ratings of Specific Instructional Dimensions and Student Achievement: Refining and Extending the Synthesis of Data from Multisection Validity Studies." *Research in Higher Education, 31*(4), 315-318.

Feldman, Kenneth A. (1993). College students' views of male and female college teachers: Part II—Evidence from students' evaluations of their classroom teachers. *Research in Higher Education, 34*(2), 151-211.

Feldman, R. S., Saletsky, R. D, & Sullivan, J. (1983). Student locus of control and response to expectations about self and teacher. *Journal of Educational Psychology, 75*(1), 27-32.

Feldman, R. S., Saletsky, R. D., Sullivan, J., & Theiss, A. (1983). Student locus of control and response to expectations about self and teacher. *Journal of Educational Psychology, 75*(1), 27-32.

Fink, L. D. (1984). The situational factors affecting teaching. *New Directions for Teaching and Learning (The First Year of College Teaching), 17,* 37-60.

Fitzgerald, M. J., & Grafton, C. L. (1981). Comparisons and implications of peer and student evaluation for a community college faculty. *Community & Junior College Research Quarterly, 5*(4), 331-337.

Frankhouser, Willis M., Jr. (1984). The effects of different oral directions as to disposition of results on student ratings of college instruction. *Research in Higher Education, 20*(3), 367-374.

Freilich, M. B. (1983). A student evaluation of teaching techniques. *Journal of Chemical Education, 60*(3), 218-221.

French-Lazovik, Grace, (Ed.). (1982). *Practices that Improve Teaching Evaluation,* New Directions for Teaching and Learning, No. 11: San Francisco, CA: Jossey-Bass, Inc.

Frey, P. W. (1973). Student ratings of teaching: Validity of several rating factors. *Science, 182,* 83-85.

Frey, P. W. (1976). Validity of student instructional ratings: Does timing matter? *Journal of Higher Education, 47,* 327-336.

Frey, P. W. (1978). A two-dimensional analysis of student ratings of instruction. *Research in Higher Education, 9,* 69-91.

Frey, P. W., Leonard, D. W., & Beatty, W. W. (1975). Student ratings of instruction: Validation research. *American Educational Research Journal, 12,* 435-447.

Fry, Stuart A. (1990). Implementation and evaluation of peer marking in higher education. *Assessment and Evaluation in Higher Education, 15*(3), 177-189.

Gage, N. L. (1961). The appraisal of college teaching. *Journal of Higher Education, 32,* 17-22.

Gessner, P. K. (1973). Evaluation of instruction. *Science, 180,* 566-569.

Gibbs, G., Habeshaw, S., & Habeshaw, T. (1984). *53 interesting things to do in your lectures.* Bristol, England: Technical and Educational Services, Ltd.

Gibbs, Graham, et al. (1985). Son of teaching tips, or 106 interesting ways to teach. *Journal of Geography in Higher Education, 9*(1), 55-68.

Gibson, K. (1992). Communicating with faculty using a diagnostic performance appraisal process. *Resources in Education,* (ERIC ED 354 053).

Gigliotti, Richard J. (1987). Expectations, observations, and violations: Comparing their effects on course ratings. *Research in Higher Education, 26*(4), 401-415.

Gigliotti, Richard J., & Buchtel, Foster S. (1990). Attributional bias and course evaluations. *Journal of Educational Psychology, 82*(2), 341-351, June.

Gillmore, G. M. (1973). *Estimates of Reliability Coefficients for Items and Subscales of the Illinois Course Evaluation Questionnaire* (Research Report No. 341). Urbana: University of Illinois, Office of Instructional Resources, Measurement and Research Division.

Gillmore, G. M. (1984). Student ratings as a factor in faculty employment decisions and periodic review. *Journal of College and University Law, 10*(4), 557-576.

Gillmore, G. M., & Brandenburg, D. C. (1974). *Would the Proportion of Students Taking a Class as a Requirement Affect the Student Rating of the Course?* (Research Report No. 347). Urbana: University of Illinois, Office of Instructional Resources, Measurement and Research Division.

Gillmore, G. M., Kane, M. T., & Smith, P. L. (1983). The dependability of student evaluations of teaching effectiveness: Matching the conclusions to the design. *Educational and Psychological Measurement, 43*(4), 1015-1018.

Goldfinch, Judy, & Raeside, Robert (1990). Development of a peer assessment technique for obtaining individual marks on a group project. *Assessment and Evaluation in Higher Education, 15*(3), 210-231.

Goodhartz, A. S. (1948). Student attitudes and opinions relating to teaching at Brooklyn College. *School and Society, 68,* 345-349.

Goodman, Madeleine J. (1990). The review of tenured faculty: A collegial model. *Journal of Higher Education, 61*(4), 408-424.

Goodwin, Laura D., & Stevens, Ellen A. (1993). The influence of gender on university faculty members' perceptions of "good" teaching. *Journal of Higher Education. 64*(2) 166-185.

Grasha, Anthony F., (1977). *Assessing and developing faculty performance,* Cincinnati, Ohio: Communication and Education Associates.

Gray, D. M., & Brandenburg, D. C. (1985). Following student ratings over time with a catalog-based system. *Research in Higher Education, 22*(2), 155-168.

Greene, M. M. (1982). The use of microcomputers in educational evaluation. *The Computer: Extension of the Human Mind.* Eugene, OR. (Proceedings of the 3rd Annual Summer Conference). Eugene, OR: College of Education, University of Oregon. (ERIC ED 219 870).

Greenwood, G. E., & Ramagli, H. J. (1980). Alternatives to student ratings of college teaching. *Journal of Higher Education, 51*(6), 673-684.

Grush, J. E., & Costin, F. (1975). The student as consumer of the teaching process. *American Educational Research Journal, 12,* 55-66.

Gutherie, E. R. (1949). The evaluation of teaching. *Educational Record, 30,* 109-115.

Hammons, J. (1983). Faculty development: A necessary corollary to faculty evaluation. *New Directions for Community Colleges, 11*(1), 75-82.

Hanna, Gerald S., Hoyt, D. P., & Aubrecht, J. D. (1983). Identifying and adjusting for biases in student evaluations of instruction: Implications for validity. *Educational and Psychological Measurement, 43*(4), 1175-1185.

Developing a Comprehensive Faculty Evaluation System

Harris, E. L. (1982). Student ratings of faculty performance: Should departmental committees construct the instruments? *Journal of Educational Research, 76*(2), 100-106.

Hativa, Nira, & Raviv, Alona. (1993). Using a single score for summative evaluation by students. *Research in Higher Education, 34*(5), 625-646.

Haugen, R. E. (1984). Educationists and academics: Ratings of community college instructors. *Community & Junior College Quarterly of Research and Practice, 8*(1-4), 103-113.

Hausknecht, M. (1982). Bromides and ideology. *Academe, 68*(6), 24-28.

Hayes, J. R. (1971). Research, teaching, and faculty fate. *Science, 172,* 227-230.

Hebron, Chris de Winter (1984). An aid for evaluating teaching in higher education. *Assessment and Evaluation in Higher Education, 9*(2), 145-163.

Heilman, J. D., & Armentrout, W. D. (1936). The rating of college teachers on ten traits by their students. *Journal of Educational Psychology, 27,* 197-216.

Helmstadter, G. C., & Krus, D. J. (1982). The factorial validity of student ratings in faculty promotions. *Educational and Psychological Measurement, 42*(4), 1135-1139.

Hildebrand, M., Wilson, R. C., & Dienst, E. R. (1971). *Evaluating University Teaching.* Berkeley: University of California, Center for Research and Development in Higher Education.

Hogan, T. P. (1973). Similarity of student ratings across instructors, courses, and time. *Research in Higher Education, 1,* 149-154.

Hollander, E. P. (1956). The friendship factor in peer nomination. *Personnel Psychology,* (9), 435-447.

Howard, G. S., Conway, C. G., & Maxwell, S. E. (1985). Construct validity of measures of college teaching effectiveness. *Journal of Educational Psychology, 77*(2), 187-196.

Howard, G. S., & Maxwell, S. E. (1980). Correlation between student satisfaction and grades: A case of mistaken causation? *Journal of Educational Psychology, 72,* 810-820.

Hunnicutt, G. G., Lesher-Taylor, R. L., & Keeffe, M. J. (1991). An exploratory examination of faculty evaluation and merit compensation systems in Texas colleges and universities. *CUPA Journal, 42*(1), 13-21.

Husbands, Christopher T., & Fosh, Patricia. (1993). Students' evaluation of teaching in higher education: Experiences from four European countries and some implications of the practice. *Assessment and Evaluation in Higher Education. 18*(2) 95-114.

Hutton, J. (1979). *Evaludent: A manual of course and instructor evaluation.* Morgantown, West Virginia: School of Dentistry, West Virginia.

Isaacs, Geoff. (1989). Changes in ratings for staff who evaluated their teaching more than once. *Assessment and Evaluation in Higher Education, 14*(1), 1-10.

Isaacson, R. L., McKeachie, W. J., Milholland, J. E., Lin, Y. G., Hofeller, M., Baerwaldt, J. W., & Zinn, K. L. (1964). Dimensions of student evaluations of teaching. *Journal of Educational Psychology, 55,* 344-351.

Iyaser, Marla. M. (1984). Responding to colleagues: Setting standards in multiple-section courses. *Improving College and University Teaching, 32*(4), 173-179.

Jacobson, C. R. (1983). Outstanding teachers: How do UND students describe them. *Instructional Development Report.* Grand Forks, ND: University of North Dakota, Office of Instructional Development, Box 8161, University Station. (ERIC ED 224 427).

Jensen, M. D. (1987, April). "Ethics, grades, and grade inflation: Student evaluations as a factor in multi-sectioned courses." Paper presented at the Joint Meeting of the Central States Speech Association and the Southern Speech Communication Association, St. Louis, MO. (ERIC ED 281 259).

Jolly, Brian, & Macdonald, Morag M. (1987). More effective evaluation of clinical teaching. *Assessment and Evaluation in Higher Education, 12*(3), 175-190.

Kagan, Dona M. (1990). Ways of evaluating teacher cognition: Inferences concerning the Goldilocks principle. *Review of Educational Research, 60*(3), 419-469.

Kane, M. T., Gillmore, G. M., & Crooks, T. J. (1976). Student evaluations of teaching: The generalizability of class means. *Journal of Educational Measurement, 13,* 171-184.

Kappelman, M. M. (1983). The impact of external examinations on medical education programs and students. *Journal of Medical Education, 58*(4), 300-308.

Kierstead, D., D'Agostino, P. & Dill, H. (1988). Sex role stereotyping of college professors: Bias in students' ratings of instructors. *Journal of Educational Psychology, 80*(3), 342-344.

Kimlicka, T. M. (1982). Student evaluation of course content, teaching effectiveness and personal growth in an experimental course. *College Student Journal, 16*(2), 198-200.

Kingsbury, M. (1982). How library schools evaluate faculty performance. *Journal of Education for Librarianship, 22*(4), 219-238.

Kinney, Daniel P., & Smith, Sharon P. (1992). Age and teaching performance. *Journal of Higher Education, 63*(3), 282-302.

Kirkpatrick, J. S., & Aleamoni, L. M. (1983). *Experimental research in counseling,* Springfield, IL: Charles C. Thomas.

Kloeden, P. E., & McDonald, R. J. (1981). Student feedback in teaching and improving an external mathematics course. *Distance Education, 2*(1), 54-63.

Koehler, W. F. (1986). From evaluations to an equitable selection of merit-pay recipients and increments. *Research in Higher Education, 25*(3), 253-263.

Kohlan, R. G. (1973). A comparison of faculty evaluations early and late in the course. *Journal of Higher Education, 44,* 587-595.

Kratochwill, T. R. (1978). *Single subject research: Strategies for evaluating change.* New York: Academic Press.

Kremer, John F. (1990). Construct validity of multiple measures in teaching, research, and service and reliability of peer ratings. *Journal of Educational Psychology, 82*(2), 213-218. Special section with title "Instruction in Higher Education."

Kremer, John (1991). Identifying faculty types using peer ratings of teaching, research, and service. *Research in Higher Education, 32*(4), 351-361.

Kulik, J. A., & Kulik, C.-L. C. (1974). Student ratings of instruction. *Teaching of Psychology, 1,* 51-57.

Kulik, J. A., & McKeachie, W. J. (1975). The evaluation of teachers in higher education. *Review of Research in Education, 3,* 210-240.

Kurz, R. S., Meuller, J. J., Gibbons, J. L., & DiCataldo, F. (1989). Faculty performance: Suggestions for the refinement of the concept and its measurement. *Journal of Higher Education, 60*(1), 43-58.

Lacefield, Warren E. (1986). Faculty enrichment and the assessment of teaching. *Review of Higher Education, 9*(4), 361-379.

Land, M. L., & Smith, L. R. (1980). Student perception of teacher clarity in mathematics. *Journal for Research in Mathematics Education, 11,* 137-146.

Land, M. L., & Smith, L. R. (1980). Student ratings and teacher behavior: An experimental study. *Research Report:* Missouri Southern State College.

Larson, R. (1984). Teacher performance evaluation—what are the key elements? *NASSP Bulletin, 68*(469), 13-18.

Lee, B. A. (1983). Balancing confidentiality and disclosure in faculty peer review. Impact of Title VII legislation. *Journal of College and University Law, 9*(3), 279-314.

Lee, Barbara A. (1985). Federal court involvement in academic personnel decisions: Impact on peer review. *Journal of Higher Education, 56*(1), 38-54.

Lester, D. (1982). Students' evaluation of teaching and course performance. *Psychological Reports, 50,* 1126.

Leventhal, L., Turcotte, S. J. C., Abrami, P. C., & Perry, R. P. (1983). Primacy/recency effects in student ratings of instruction: A reinterpretation of gain-loss effects. *Journal of Educational Psychology; 75*(5), 692-704.

Levinson-Rose, J., & Menges, R. J. (1981). Improving college teaching: A critical review of research. *Review of Educational Research, 51*(3), 403-434.

L'Hommedieu, R., Menges, R. J., & Brinko, K.T. (1990). Methodological explanations for the modest effects of feedback from student ratings. *Journal of Educational Psychology, 82*(2), 232-241. Special section with title "Instruction in Higher Education."

Licata, C. M. (1985). "An Investigation of the Status of Post-Tenure Faculty Evaluation in Selected Community Colleges." *ASHE 1985 Annual Meeting Paper.* Paper presented at the Annual Meeting of the Association for the Student of Higher Education, Chicago, IL. (ERIC ED 259 635).

Lichty, R. W., & Peterson, J. M. (1979). *Peer Evaluations: A Necessary Part of Evaluating Teaching Effectiveness.* Duluth, MN: University of Minnesota [NSD 52721]. (ERIC ED 175352).

Lin, Y. (1984). The use of student ratings in promotion decision. *Journal of Higher Education, 55*(5), 583-589.

Linsky, A. S., & Straus, M. A. (1973). Student evaluation of teaching. *Teaching Sociology, 1*(1), 103-118.

Linsky, A. S., & Straus, M. A. (1975). Student evaluations, research productivity, and eminence of college faculty. *Journal of Higher Education, 46,* 89-102.

Lovell, G. D., & Haner, C. F. (1955). Forced-choice applied to college faculty rating. *Educational and Psychological Measurement, 15,* 291-304.

Magnusen, Karl O. Faculty evaluation, performance, and pay: Application and issues. *Journal of Higher Education, 58*(5), 516-529.

Mahmoud, Mohamed M. (1991). Descriptive models of student decision behaviour in evaluation of higher education. *Assessment and Evaluation in Higher Education, 16*(2), 133-148.

Marchant, G. J., & Newman, I. (1991). "Faculty Evaluation and Reward Procedures: Views from Education Administrators." Paper presented at the Annual Meeting of the American Educational Research Association, Chicago, IL. (ERIC ED 331 377).

Marlin, James W., Jr. (1987). Student perception of end-of-course evaluations. *Journal of Higher Education, 58*(6), 704-716.

Marques, T. E., Lane, D. M., & Dorfman, P. W. (1979). Toward the development of a system for instructional evaluation: Is there consensus regarding what constitutes effective teaching? *Journal of Educational Psychology, 71,* 840-849.

Marsh, H. W. (1977). The validity of students' evaluations: Classroom evaluations of instructors independently nominated as best and worst teachers by graduating seniors. *American Educational Research Journal, 14,* 441-447.

Marsh, H. W. (1980). Research on students' evaluations of teaching effectiveness: A reply to Vecchio. *Instructional Evaluation, 4,* 5-13.

Marsh, H. W. (1980). The influence of student, course and instructor characteristics on evaluations of university teaching. *American Educational Research Journal, 17,* 219-237.

Marsh, H. W. (1982). Factors affecting students' evaluations of the same course by the same instructor on different occasions. *American Educational Research Journal, 19*(4), 485-497.

Marsh, H. W. (1982). Validity of students' evaluations of college teaching: A multitrait-multimethod analysis. *Journal of Educational Psychology, 74*(2), 264-279.

Marsh, H. W. (1983). Multidimensional ratings of teacher effectiveness by students from different academic settings and their relation to student/course/instructor characteristics. *Journal of Educational Psychology, 75*(1), 150-166.

Marsh, H. W. (1983). Multitrait-multimethod analysis: Distinguishing between items and traits. *Educational and Psychological Measurement, 43*(2), 351-358.

Marsh, H. W. (1984). Students' evaluations of university teaching: Dimensionality, reliability, validity, potential biases, and utility. *Journal of Educational Psychology, 76*, 707-754.

Marsh, H. W. (1986). Applicability paradigm: Students' evaluations of teaching effectiveness in different countries. *Journal of Educational Psychology, 78*(6), 465-473.

Marsh, Herbert W. (1991). A multidimensional perspective on students' evaluations of teaching effectiveness: Reply to Abrami and d'Apollonia (1991). *Journal of Educational Psychology, 83*(3), 416-421, Sep.

Marsh, H. W. (1991). Multidimensional students' evaluations of teaching effectiveness: A test of alternative higher-order structures. *Journal of Educational Psychology, 83*(2), 285-296.

Marsh, H.W. (1993). The use of students' evaluation and an individually structured intervention to enhance university teaching effectiveness. *American Educational Research Journal, 30*(1), 217-251.

Marsh, H. W., & Bailey, M. (1993). Multidimensional students' evaluations of teaching effectiveness. *Journal of Higher Education, 64*(1), 1-18.

Marsh, H. W., & Cooper, T. L. (1981). Prior subject interest, students' evaluations and instructional effectiveness. *Multivariate Behavioral Research, 16*, 81-104.

Marsh, H. W., Fleiner, H., & Thomas, C. S. (1975). Validity and usefulness of student evaluations of instructional quality. *Journal of Educational Psychology, 67*, 833-839.

Marsh, H. W., & Hocevar, D. (1984). The factorial invariance of student evaluations of college teaching. *American Educational Research Journal, 21*(2), 341-366.

Marsh, H. W., & Overall, J. U. (1979). Long-term stability of students' evaluations: A note on Feldman's "Consistency and variability among college students in rating their teachers and courses." *Research in Higher Education, 10*, 139-47.

Marsh, H. W., & Overall, J. U. (1980). Validity of students' evaluations of teaching effectiveness: Cognitive and affective criteria. *Journal of Educational Psychology, 72*, 468-475.

Marsh, H. W., & Overall, J. U. (1981). The relative influence of course level, course type, and instructor on students' evaluations of college teaching. *American Educational Research Journal, 18*, 103-112.

Marsh, H. W., Overall, J. U., & Kesler, S. P. (1979). Class size, students' evaluations, and instructional effectiveness. *American Educational Research Journal, 16*, 57-70.

Marsh, H. W., Overall, J. U., & Kesler, S. P. (1979). Validity of student evaluations of instructional effectiveness: A comparison of faculty self-evaluations and evaluations by their students. *Journal of Educational Psychology, 71*, 149-160.

Marsh, H. W., & Ware, J. E. (1982). Effects of expressiveness, content coverage, and incentive on multidimensional student rating scales: New interpretations of the Dr. Fox effect. *Journal of Educational Psychology, 74*(1), 126-134.

Martin, R. E., et al. (1983). A planned program for evaluation and development of clinical pharmacy faculty. *American Journal of Pharmaceutical Education, 47*(2), 102-107.

Maslow, A. H., & Zimmerman, W. (1956). College teaching ability, scholarly activity, and personality. *Journal of Educational Psychology, 47*, 185-189.

Mathias, H. (1984). The evaluation of university teaching: Context, values and innovation. *Assessment and Evaluation in Higher Education, 9*(2), 79-96.

Mathias, H., & Rutherford, D. (1981). Course evaluation at Birmingham: Some implications for the assessment and improvement of university teaching. *Studies in Educational Evaluation, 7*(3), 263-266.

Mathias, H., & Rutherford, D. (1982). Lecturers as evaluators: The Birmingham experience. *Studies in Higher Education, 7*(1), 47-56.

Matthews, J. R. (1982). Evaluation: A major challenge for the 1980s. *Teaching of Psychology, 9*(1), 49-52.

McBean, E. A., & Al-Nassri, S. (1982). Questionnaire design for student measurement of teaching effectiveness. *Higher Education, 11*(3), 273-288.

McBean, E. A., & Lennox, W. C. (1982). Issues of teaching effectiveness as observed via course critiques. *Higher Education, 11*(6), 645-655.

McBean, E. A., & Lennox, W. C. (1985). Effect of survey size on student ratings of teaching. *Higher Education, 14*(2), 117-25.

McCabe, M. V. (1982). Faculty attitudes toward evaluation at southern universities. *Phi Delta Kappan, 63*(6), 419.

McCallum, L. W. (1984). A meta-analysis of course evaluation data and its use in the tenure decision. *Research in Higher Education, 21*(2), 150-158.

McCarthy, P. R., & Shmeck, R. R. (1982). Effects of teacher self-disclosure on student learning and perceptions of teacher. *College Student Journal, 16*(1), 45-49.

McConnell, David, & Hodgson, Vivien (1985). The development of student constructed lecture feedback questionnaires. *Assessment and Evaluation in Higher Education, 9*(3), 2-27.

McDaniel, E. D., & Feldhusen, J. F. (1970). Relationships between faculty ratings and indexes of service and scholarship. *Proceedings of the 78th Annual Convention of the American Psychological Association, 5*, 619-620.

McGrath, E. J. (1962). Characteristics of outstanding college teachers. *Journal of Higher Education, 33*, 148.

McIntyre, C. J. (1978). "Peer Evaluation of Teaching." Paper presented at the American Educational Research Association convention, Toronto, Canada, August 31 - September 1. (ERIC ED 180295).

McKeachie, W. J. (1979). Student ratings of faculty: A reprise. *Academe, 65*, 384-397.

McKeachie, W. J. (1983). The role of faculty evaluation in enhancing college teaching. *National Forum: Phi Kappa Phi Journal, 63*(2), 37-39.

McKeachie, W. J. (1986). *Teaching tips: A guidebook for the beginning college teacher*. Lexington, Mass.: D. C. Heath and Co.

McKeachie, Wilbert J. (1990). Research on college teaching: The historical background. *Journal of Educational Psychology, 82*(2), 189-200. Special section with title "Instruction in Higher Education."

McKeachie, W. J., & Lin, Y. G. (1979). A note on validity of student ratings of teaching. *Educational Research Quarterly, 4*(3), 45-47.

McKeachie, W. J., Lin, Y. G., Daugherty, M., Moffett, M. M., Neigler, C., Nork, J., Walz, M., & Baldwin, R. (1980). Using student ratings and consultation to improve instruction. *British Journal of Educational Psychology, 50*, 168-174.

McKeachie, W. J., Lin, Y. G., & Mendelson, C. N. (1978). A small study to assess teacher effectiveness: Does learning last? *Contemporary Educational Psychology, 3*, 352-357.

Meier, R. S., & Feldhusen, J. F. (1979). Another look at Dr. Fox: Effect of stated purpose for evaluation, lecturer expressiveness, and density of lecture content on student ratings. *Journal of Educational Psychology, 71*, 339-345.

Menges, R. J. (1973). The new reporters: Students rate instruction. In C. R. Pace (Ed.), *New Directions in Higher Education: Evaluating Learning and Teaching*. San Francisco: Jossey-Bass.

Menges, R. J. (1979). Evaluating teaching effectiveness: What is the proper role for students? *Liberal Education, 65*, 356-370.

Menges, R. J. (1988). Research on teaching and learning: The relevant and the redundant. *Review of Higher Education, 11*(3), 259-268.

Meredith, G. M. (1979). Brief scale for teaching appraisal in engineering courses. *Perceptual and Motor Skills, 45*, 817-818.

Meredith, G. M. (1979). Factored items for appraising classroom effectiveness of teaching assistants. *Psychological Reprints, 45*, 229-230.

Meredith, G. M. (1979). Summative evaluation of teaching effectiveness in legal education. *Perceptual and Motor Skills, 49*, 765-766.

Meredith, G. M. (1980). Brief scale for measuring the impact of a textbook. *Perceptual and Motor Skills, 51*, 370.

Meredith, G. M. (1980). Impact of lecture size on student-based ratings of instruction. *Psychological Reports, 46*, 21-22.

Meredith, G. M. (1980). Marker items for evaluating graduate-level teaching assistants. *Psychological Reprints, 46*.

Meredith, G. M. (1982). Grade-related attitude correlates of instructor/course satisfaction among college students. *Psychological Reports, 50*, 1142.

Meredith, G. M. (1982). Marker items for a single-factor scale for appraisal of teaching in architecture courses. *Perceptual and Motor Skills, 55*(2), 678.

Meredith, G. M. (1983). Factor-specific items for appraisal of laboratory and seminar/discussion group experiences among college students. *Perceptual and Motor Skills, 56*(1), 133-134.

Meridith, G. M., & Ogasawara, T. H. (1981). Lecture size and students' ratings of instructional effectiveness. *Perceptual and Motor Skills, 52*, 353-354.

Mikula, A. R. (1979). "Using Peers in Instructional Development." Paper presented at the conference on Faculty Development and Evaluation in Higher Education, Orlando, Florida (ERIC ED 172 599).

Miller, A.H. (1988). Student assessment of teaching in higher education. *Higher Education, 17*, 3-15.

Miller, M. D. (1982). Factorial validity of a clinical teaching scale. *Educational and Psychological Measurement, 42*(4), 1141-1147.

Miller, M. T. (1971). Instructor attitudes toward, and their use of, student ratings of teachers. *Journal of Educational Psychology, 62*, 235-239.

Miller, R. I., (1972). *Evaluating faculty performance*. San Francisco, CA: Jossey-Bass, Inc.

Miller, R. I., (1987). *Evaluating faculty for promotion and tenure*. San Francisco, CA: Jossey-Bass, Inc.

Miller, S. (1984). Student rating scales for tenure and promotion. *Improving College University Teaching, 32*(2), 87-90.

Developing a Comprehensive Faculty Evaluation System

Milman, J. (Ed.) (1981). *Handbook of teacher evaluation*. Beverly Hills, California: Sage Publications.

Mintzes, J. J. (1982). Relationship between student perceptions of teaching behavior and learning outcomes in college biology. *Journal of Research in Science Teaching, 19*(9), 789-794.

Moore, Don, Schurr, K. T., & Henriksen, I. W. (1991). Correlations of national teacher examination core battery scores and college grade point average with teaching effectiveness of first-year teachers. *Educational and Psychological Measurement, 51*(4), 1023-1028.

Moses, Ingrid. (1986). Self and student evaluation of academic staff. *Assessment and Evaluation in Higher Education, 11*(1), 76-86.

Moses, Ingrid. (1986) Student evaluation of teaching in an Australian University—Staff perceptions and reactions. *Assessment and Evaluation in Higher Education, 11*(2), 117-129.

Moses, Ingrid. (1989). Role and problems of heads of departments in performance appraisal. *Assessment and Evaluation in Higher Education, 14*(2), 95-105.

Murphy, K. R., Balzer, W. K., Kellam, K. L., & Armstrong, J. G. (1984). Effects of the purpose of rating on accuracy in observing teacher behavior and evaluating teacher performance. *Journal of Educational Psychology, 76*, 45-54.

Murray, H. G. (1975). Predicting student ratings of college teaching from peer ratings of personality types. *Teaching of Psychology, 2*(2), 66-69.

Murray, H. G. (1979). Evaluation of university teaching: A selective bibliography. E. Roe (Ed.), *Labyrinth 5: Clearinghouse Bulletin for Higher Education Research and Development Units in Australia and New Zealand*. Brisbane, Australia: Tertiary Education Institute, University of Queensland. (Reprinted in Ontario Universities Program for Instructional Development Newsletter, February/March 1980).

Murray, H. G. (1979). Student evaluation of teaching and its use for decisions regarding tenure and promotion at the University of Western Ontario. *Tertiary Education Institute Newsletter*, University of Queensland, Australia.

Murray, H. G. (1979). Student evaluation of university teaching: Uses and abuses. *Report # 5*. Vancouver: University of British Columbia, Centre for the Improvement of Teaching.

Murray, H. G. (1980). *Evaluating university teaching: A review of research*. Toronto, Canada: Ontario Confederation of University Faculty Associations.

Murray, H. G. (1982). Use of student instructional ratings in administrative personnel decisions at the University of Western Ontario. Paper presented at the annual meeting the American Psychological Association, Washington, D.C. (ERIC ED 223 162)

Murray, H. G. (1983). Low-inference classroom teaching behaviors and student ratings of college teaching effectiveness. *Journal of Educational Psychology, 75*(1), 138-149.

Murray, H. G. (1984). The impact of formative and summative evaluation of teaching in North American universities. *Assessment and Evaluation in Higher Education, 9*(2), 117-132.

Murray, H. G. (1985). Classroom teaching behaviors related to college teaching effectiveness. *New Directions for Teaching and Learning (Using Research to Improve Teaching), 23*, 21-34.

Murray, H. G., & Newby, W. G. (1982). Faculty attitudes toward evaluation of teaching at the University of Western Ontario. *Assessment and Evaluation in Higher Education, 7*(2), 144-151.

Murray, H. G., Rushton, J. P., & Paunonen, S. V. (1990). Teacher personality traits and student instructional ratings in six types of university courses. *Journal of Educational Psychology, 82*(2), 250-261.

Myers, C. J., Rubeck, R. F., & Meredith, K. (1983). An investigation of nonresponse bias in medical student assessment of instruction. *Research in Higher Education, 19*(4), 461-467.

Needham, D. (1982). Improving faculty evaluation and reward systems. *Journal of Economic Education, 13*(1), 6-18.

Nespoli, L. A., & Radcliffe, S. K. (1983). Student evaluation of college services. *Research Report No. 29*: Howard Community College. (ERIC ED 224 541).

Newell, S., & Price, J. H. (1983). Promotion, merit and tenure decisions for college health education faculty. *Health Education, 14*(3), 12-15.

Newstead, S. E., & Arnold, J. (1989). The effect of response format on ratings of teaching. *Educational and Psychological Measurement, 49*(1), 33-43.

Newton, R. R. (1982). Performance evaluation in education. *Journal of the College and University Personnel Association, 33*(2), 39-43.

Nimmer, James G., & Stone, Eugene F. (1991). Effects of grading practices and time of rating on student ratings of faculty performance and student learning. *Research in Higher Education, 32*(2), 195-215.

Null, E. J., & Nicholson, E. W. (1972). Personal variables of students and their perception of university instructors. *College Student Journal, 6*, 6-9.

O'Hanlon, J. O., & Mortensen, L. (1980). Making teacher evaluation work. *Journal of Higher Education, 51*, 664-672.

Ohara, T., & Purcell, D. T. (1981). Factors affecting student reported achievement: Necessary information to determine effective instructional strategies. *Proceedings of the Seventh International Conference on Improving University Teaching*. 658-664.

O'Hear, M. F., & Poherson, V. E. (1982). Computer-generated evaluation in developmental programs. *Journal of Developmental and Remedial Education, 6*(1), 20-23.

Orpen, C. (1980). Student evaluation of lecturers as an indicator of instructional quality: A validity study. *Journal of Educational Research, 74*, 5-7.

Ory, J. C. (1980). Evaluative criteria: How important and to whom? *Center on Evaluation Development and Research Quarterly, 13*, 14-16.

Ory, J. C. (1982). Item placement and wording effects on overall ratings. *Educational and Psychological Measurement, 42*(3), 767-775.

Ory, J. C., & Braskamp, L. A. (1981). Faculty perceptions of the quality and usefulness of three types of evaluative information. *Research in Higher Education, 15*, 271-282.

Ory, J. C., Brandenburg, D. C., & Pieper, D. M. (1980). Selection of course evaluation items by and low rated faculty. *Research in Higher Education, 12*, 245-253.

Ory, J. C., Braskamp, L. A., & Pieper, D. M. (1980). The congruency of student evaluation information collected by three methods. *Journal of Educational Psychology, 72*, 181-185.

Ory, J. C., & Parker, Stephanie A. (1989). Assessment activities at large, research universities. *Research in Higher Education, 30*(4), 375-385.

Overall, J. U., & Marsh, H. W. (1979). Midterm feedback from students: Its relationship to instructional improvement and students' cognitive and affective outcomes. *Journal of Educational Psychology, 71*, 856-865.

Overall, J. U., & Marsh, H. W. (1980). Students' evaluations of instruction: A longitudinal study of their stability. *Journal of Educational Psychology, 72*, 321-325.

Overall, J. U., & Marsh, H. W. (1982). Students' evaluations of teaching: An update. *AAHE Bulletin, 35*(4), 9-13.

Pace, Robert C. (Ed.). (1973). *Evaluating Learning and Teaching*, New Directions for Higher Education. Vol. 1, No. 4., San Francisco, CA: Jossey-Bass, Inc.

Palmer, J. (1983). Sources and information: Faculty and administrator evaluation. *New Directions for Community Colleges, 11*(1), 109-118.

Pasen, R. M. (1977). *The differential effect of grade, sex, and discipline on two global factors: A within-class analysis of student ratings of instruction.* Ph.D. Dissertation, Northwestern University, June.

Pasen, R. M., Frey, P.W., Menges, R. J., & Rath, G. J. (1978). Different administrative directions and student ratings on instruction: Cognitive versus affective states. *Research in Higher Education, 9*, 161-168.

Payne, B. D. (1984). Interrelationships among college supervisor, supervising teacher, and elementary pupil ratings of student teaching. *Educational and Psychological Measurement, 44*(4), 1037-43.

Pearson, P., & Tiefel, V. (1982). Evaluating undergraduate library instruction at the Ohio State University. *Journal of Academic Librarianship, 7*(6), 351-357.

Perkins, D., & Abbott, R. (1982). Validity of student ratings for two affective outcomes of introductory psychology. *Educational and Psychological Measurement, 42*(1), 317-323.

Perry, R. P. (1985). Instructor expressiveness: Implications for improving teaching. *New Directions for Teaching and Learning (Using Research to Improve Teaching), 23*, 35-49.

Perry, R. P., Abrami, P. C., & Leventhal, L. (1979). Educational seduction: The effect of instructor expressiveness and lecture content on students ratings and achievement. *Journal of Educational Psychology, 71*, 107-116.

Peterson, C., & Cooper, S. (1980). Teacher evaluation by graded and ungraded students. *Journal of Educational Psychology, 72*, 682-685.

Peterson, K., Gunne, G. M., Miller, P., & Rivera, O. (1984). Multiple audience rating form strategies for student evaluation of college teaching. *Research in Higher Education, 20*(3), 309-321.

Peterson, M. W., & White, T. H. (1992). Faculty and administrator perceptions of their environments: Different views or different models of organization? *Research in Higher Education, 33*(2), 177-204.

Petrie, H. G. (1982). Program evaluation as an adaptive system. *New Directions for Higher Education, 10*(1), 17-29.

Pfister, F. C., & Chrisman, L. G. (1983). The evaluation of professional training for librarianship. *Catholic Library World, 54*(10), 399-405.

Pinkney, J., & Williams, V. (1982). Taking your programs to court: Evaluating a new evaluation strategy. *Journal of College Student Personnel, 23*(3), 209-216.

Pittman, R. B. (1985). Perceived instructional effectiveness and associated teaching dimensions. *Journal of Experimental Education, 54*(1), 34-39.

Pohlmann, J. T. (1975). A multivariate analysis of selected class characteristics and student ratings of instruction. *Multivariate Behavioral Research, 10*(1), 81-91.

Poole, L. H., & Dellow, D. A. (1983). Evaluation of full-time faculty. *New Directions for Community Colleges, 11*(1), 19-31.

Pugach, M. C., & Rahs, J. D. (1983). Testing teachers: Analysis and recommendations. *Journal of Teacher Education, 34*(1), 37-43.

Quay, R. H. (1982). *On programs and principles in the evaluation of higher education: A bibliography of Paul L. Dressel.* Monticello, IL: Vance Bibliographies. (Public Administration Series Bibliography, P-900).

Rayder, N. F. (1968). College student ratings of instructors. *Journal of Experimental Education, 37*, 76-81.

Razor, J. E. (1979). "The evaluation of administrators and faculty members—or evaluating the 'boss' and each other." Paper presented at the Midwest Association for Health, Physical Education and Recreation, Madison, WI, (ERIC ED 180 355).

Renner, Richard R., & Greenwood, Gordon E. (1985). Professor "X": How experts rated his student ratings. *Assessment and Evaluation in Higher Education, 10*(3), 203-212.

Renner, Richard R., and others. (1986). Responsible behaviour as effective teaching: A new look at student rating of professors. *Assessment and Evaluation in Higher Education, 11*(2), 138-145.

Renz, F.J. (1984). Study examining the issues of faculty evaluation. *Resources in Education*, (ERIC ED 243 559).

Reynolds, Anne. (1992). What is competent beginning teaching? A review of the literature. *Review of Educational Research, 62*(1), 1-35.

Rich, H. E. (1976). Attitudes of college and university faculty toward the use of student evaluation. *Educational Research Quarterly, 1*(3), 17-28.

Riley, J. W., Ryan, B. F., & Lipschitz, M. (1950). *The student looks at his teacher*. New Brunswick, NJ: Rutgers University Press.

Rodin, M. J. (1982). By a faculty member's yard-stick, student evaluations don't measure up. *Teaching Political Science, 9*(4), 174-176.

Rodin, M., Frey, P. W., & Gessner, P. K. (1975). Student evaluation. *Science, 187*, 555-559.

Rodin, M., & Rodin, B. (1972). Student evaluations of teachers. *Science, 177*, 1164-1166.

Rogerts, T. H., & Gamson, Z. F. (1982). Evaluation as a developmental process: The case of liberal education. *Review of Higher Education, 5*(4), 225-238.

Root, Lawrence S. (1987). Faculty evaluation: Reliability of peer assessments of research, teaching, and service. *Research in Higher Education, 26*(1), 71-84.

Roskens, R. W. (1983). Implications of Biglan model research for the process of faculty advancement. *Research in Higher Education, 18*(3), 285-97.

Rotem, A., & Glasman, N. S. (1977). Evaluation of university instructors in the United States: The context. *Higher Education, 6*, 75-92.

Rotem, A., & Glasman, N. S. (1979). On the effectiveness of student evaluation feedback to university instructors. *Review of Educational Research, 49*, 497-511.

Rubin, Donald L. (1992). Nonlanguage factors affecting undergraduates' judgments of nonnative English-speaking teaching assistants. *Research in Higher Education, 33*(4), 511-531.

Rushinek, A., Rushinek, S. F., & Stutz, J. (1981). The effects of computer assisted instruction upon computer facility and instructor ratings. *Journal of Computer-Based Instruction, 8*(2), 43-44.

Rushinek, A., Rushinek, S. F., & Stutz, J. (1982). Improving instructor evaluations by the use of computer-assisted instruction in business data processing. *AEDS Journal, 15*(3), 151-163.

Saaty, T. L., & Ramanujam, V. (1983). An objective approach to faculty promotion and tenure by the analytical hierarchy process. *Research in Higher Education, 18*(3), 311-331.

Sacken, Donald M. (1990). Taking teaching seriously: Institutional and individual dilemmas. *Journal of Higher Education, 61*(5), 548-564.

Sagen, H. B. (1974). Student, faculty, and department chairmen ratings of instructors: Who agrees with whom? *Research in Higher Education, 2*, 265-272.

Salomone, R. E., & Vorhies, A. L. (1985). Just rewards: Ensuring equitable salary reviews. *Educational Record, 66*(3), 44-47.

Salsberg, H. E., & Schiller, B. (1982). A decade of student evaluations. *College Student Journal, 16*(1), 84-88.

Sauter, R. C., & Walker, J. K. (1976). A theoretical model for faculty 'peer' evaluation. *American Journal of Pharmaceutical Education, 40*(2), 165-166.

Schein, M. W. (1985). Student achievement as a measure of teaching effectiveness. *Journal of College Science Teaching, 14*(6), 471-474.

Scheurich, V., Graham, B., & Drolette, M. (1983). Expected grades versus specific evaluations of the teacher as predictors of students' overall evaluation of the teacher. *Research in Higher Education, 19*(2), 159-173.

Schneider, L. S. (1975). Faculty opinion of the spring 1974 peer evaluation. (ERIC ED 104 493).

Scott, O. (1978). Anomalies in the construction and suggested uses of inventories of students' appraisals of college instruction. *Psychological Reports, 43*, 563-566.

Scott, O., & Harrison, P. L. (1978). "A comparison of alternate forms of a global item for appraising teaching effectiveness." Paper presented at the meeting of the Georgia Educational Research Association, West Georgia College, Carrollton, GA.

Scott, O., & Hsu, Y. (1982). Effect of item context on students' global appraisals of instruction. *Perceptual and Motor Skills, 54*(3), Part 2, 1191-1194.

Scott, O., Perrodin, A. F., & Schnittjer, C. (1978). The stability of students' appraisal of college instruction: A further look. *College Student Journal, 12*, 338-342.

Scriven, M. (1980). The evaluation of college teaching. *National Council Prof. Inservice Educ. News, 1*.

Scwier, R. A. (1982). Design and use of student evaluation instruments in instructional development. *Journal of Instructional Development, 5*(4), 28-34.

Seldin, P. (1980). *Successful faculty evaluation programs.* Crugers, NY: Coventry Press.

Seldin, P. (1982). Improving faculty evaluation systems. *Peabody Journal of Education, 59*(2), 93-99.

Seldin, P. (1982). Self-assessment of college teaching. *Improving College and University Teaching, 30*(2), 70-74.

Seldin, P. (1984). *Changing practices in faculty evaluation.* San Francisco, California: Jossey-Bass, Inc.

Seldin, P. (1988). *Evaluating and developing administrative performance.* San Francisco, CA: Jossey-Bass, Inc.

Selmes, Cyril. (1989). Evaluation of Teaching. *Assessment and Evaluation in Higher Education. 14*(3), 167-178.

Shapiro, E. Gary. (1990). Effect of instructor and class characteristics on students' class evaluations. *Research in Higher Education. 31*(2), 135-148.

Sherman, T. M. (1978). The effects of student formative evaluation of instruction on teacher behavior. *Journal of Educational Technology Systems, 6,* 209-217.

Silvernail, David L., & Johnson, Judith L. (1992). The impact of interactive televised instruction on student evaluations of their instructors. *Educational Technology. 32*(6) 47-50.

Singhal, S. (1968). *Illinois Course Evaluation Questionnaire Items by Rank of Instructor, Sex of the Instructor, and Sex of the Student* (Research Report No. 282). Urbana: University of Illinois, Office of Instructional Resources, Measurement and Research Division.

Singhal, S., & Stallings, W. M. (1967). *A Study of the Relationships between Course Evaluations by Students and Severity of Grading by Instructors in Freshman Rhetoric at the University of Illinois* (Research Report No. 252). University of Illinois: Measurement and Research Division.

Skoog, G. (1980). Improving college teaching through peer observation. *Journal of Teacher Education, 31*(2), 23-25.

Small, A. C., Hollenbeck, A. R., & Haley, R. L. (1982). The effect of emotional state on student ratings of instructors. *Teaching of Psychology, 9*(4), 205-208.

Smith, A. (1983). A conceptual framework for staff evaluation. *New Directions for Community Colleges, 11*(1), 3-18.

Smith, A. (1983). Concluding comments. *New Directions for Community Colleges, 11*(1), 105-107.

Smith, L. R. (1982). A review of two low-inference teacher behaviors related to performance of college students. *Review of Higher Education, 5*(3), 159-167.

Smith, M. (1982). Protecting confidentiality of faculty peer review records: Department of Labor vs. the University of California. *Journal of College and University Law, 8*(1), 20-53.

Smith, P. L. (1979). The generalizability of student ratings of courses: Asking the right questions. *Journal of Educational Measurement, 16,* 77-87.

Smith, Ronald A., & Cranton, Patricia A. (1992). Students' perceptions of teaching skills and overall effectiveness across instructional settings. *Research in Higher Education. 33*(6), 747-764.

Smock, H. R. (1982). Planning for an evaluation of network and institutionalization. *New Directions for Higher Education, 10*(1), 67-73.

Sorcinelli, M. D. (1984). An approach to colleague evaluation of classroom instruction. *Journal of Instructional Development, 7*(4), 11-17.

Spencer, R. E. (1965). *Course Evaluation Questionnaire Anonymous vs. Identified Student Responses* (Research Report No. 202). University of Illinois, Measurement and Research Division.

Spencer, R. E., & Aleamoni, L. M. (1970). A student course evaluation questionnaire. *Journal of Educational Measurement, 7*(3), 209-210.

Stallings, W. M., & Singhal, S. (1968). *Some Observations on the Relationships between Productivity and Student Evaluations of Courses and Teaching* (Research Report No. 274). Urbana: University of Illinois, Office of Instructional Resources, Measurement and Research Division.

Stedman, C. H. (1983). The reliability of a teaching effectiveness rating scale for assessing faculty performance. *Tennessee Education, 12*(3), 25-32.

Stevens, J. J., & Aleamoni, L. M. (1984). "A preliminary study of methods for the evaluation of televised instruction." In L. P. Grayson & J. M. Biedenbach (Eds.), *Engineering Education: Preparation for Life,* 92nd Annual ASEE Conference Proceedings. Washington, D. C.: American Society for Engineering Education. 386-394.

Stevens, J. J., & Aleamoni, L. M. (1985). Issues in the development of peer evaluation systems. *Instructional Evaluation, 8* (1), 4-9.

Stevens, J. J., & Aleamoni, L. M. (1985). The use of evaluative feedback for instructional improvement: A longitudinal perspective. *Instructional Science, 13,* 285-304.

Stier W F, J. (1982). *Faculty Evaluation: A Positive Approach.* (ERIC ED 223 119).

Stumpf, S. A. (1979). Assessing academic program and department effectiveness using student evaluation data. *Research in Higher Education, 11,* 353-64.

Stumpf, S. A., & Freedman, R. D. (1979). Expected grade co-variation with student ratings of instruction: Individual versus class effects. *Journal of Educational Psychology, 71*, 293-302.

Stumpf, S. A., Freedman, R. D., & Aguanno, J. A. (1979). A path analysis of extrinsic factors related to student ratings of teaching effectiveness. *Research in Higher Education, 11*, 111-123.

Stumpf, S. A., Freedman, R. D., & Aguanno, J. (1979). Validity of the Course-Faculty Instrument (CFI): Intrinsic and extrinsic variables. *Educational and Psychological Measurement, 39*, 153-158.

Stumpf, S. A., Freedman, R. D., & Krieger, K. M. (1979). Validity extension of the Course Faculty Instrument (CFI). *Research in Higher Education, 11*, 13-22.

Sullivan, A. M. (1985). The role of two types of research on the evaluation and improvement of university teaching. *New Directions for Teaching and Learning (Using Research to Improve Teaching), 23*, 71-82.

Sullivan, A. M., & Skanes, G. R. (1974). Validity of student evaluation of teaching and the characteristics of successful instructors. *Journal of Educational Psychology, 66*, 584-590.

Swanson, R. A., & Sisson, D. J. (1971). The development, evaluation, and utilization of a departmental faculty appraisal system. *Journal of Industrial Teacher Education, 9*(1), 64-79.

Theall, M., & Franklin, J. (1990). Student ratings in the context of complex evaluation systems. In M. Theall & J. Franklin (Eds.), *Student Ratings of Instruction: Issues for Improving Practice, New Directions for Teaching and Learning*, No. 43, 37-55, San Francisco, CA: Jossey-Bass.

Thomas, Angela. (1989). Further education staff appraisal: What teachers think. *Assessment and Evaluation in Higher Education. 14*(3), 149-157.

Thomas, D., et al. (1982). The relationship between psychological identification with instructors and student ratings of college courses. *Instructional Science, 11*(2), 139-154.

Thompson, Gerald E. (1988). Difficulties in interpreting course evaluations: Some Bayesian insights. *Research in Higher Education, 28*(3), 217-222.

Thorman, J. H. (1982). Criterion referenced evaluation and its effect on achievement and attitude. *Performance and Instruction, 21*(10), 15-18.

Tiberius, R. G., Sackin, H. D., Slingerland, J. M., Jubas, K., Bell, M., & Matlow, A. (1989). The influence of student evaluative feedback on the improvement of clinical teaching. *Journal of Higher Education, 60*(6), 665-681.

Todd-Mancillas, W. R., & Essig, T. (1982). Alternative approaches to evaluating communication instruction. *Association for Communication Administration Bulletin, 42*, 56-61.

Tollefson, H., & Hracy, D. B. (1983). Comparison of self-reported teaching behaviors of award-winning and non-award winning university faculty. *Perceptual and Motor Skills, 56*(1), 39-44.

Tollefson, N. (1983). Course ratings as measures of instructional effectiveness. *Instructional Science, 12*(4), 389-395.

Tollefson, N., Chen, J. S., & Kleinsasser, A. (1989). The relationship of students' attitudes about effective teaching to students' ratings of effective teaching. *Educational and Psychological Measurement. 49*(3), 529-536.

Turcotte, S. J. C., & Leventhal, L. (1984). Gain-loss versus reinforcement-affect ordering of student rating of teaching: Effect of rating instructions. *Journal of Educational Psychology, 76*(5), 782-791.

Uguroglu, M. E., & Dwyer, M. M. (1981). Staff review system. *Improving College and University Teaching, 29*(3), 121-24.

Ulricht, K. (1982). Summative evaluation of a course of study in computer science. *Higher Education, 1*(6), 713-724.

Van Allen, G. H. (1982). Students rate community college faculty as slightly above average. *Community College Review, 10*(1), 41-43.

Vasta, R., & Sarmiento, R. F. (1979). Liberal grading improves evaluations but not performance. *Journal of Educational Research, 71*, 207-211.

Voeks, V. W. (1962). Publications and teaching effectiveness. *Journal of Higher Education, 33*, 212.

Walker, C. J. (1982). Study efficiency: Where teaching effectiveness and learning effectiveness meet. *Teaching of Psychology, 9*(2), 92-95.

Walker, J. W. A successful revision of a faculty evaluation procedure. (ERIC ED 220 142).

Ward, Marilyn D., and others. (1981). "The observer effect in classroom visitation." Paper presented at the 65th annual meeting of the American Educational Research Association, Los Angeles, California (ERIC ED 20444384).

Ware, J. E., & Williams, R. G. (1977). Discriminate analysis of student ratings as a means of identifying lecturers who differ in enthusiasm or information giving. *Educational and Psychological Measurement, 37*, 627-639.

Waters, L. K., Reardon, M., & Edwards, J. E. (1983). Multitrait-multimethod analysis of three rating formats. *Perceptual and Motor Skills, 55*(3, Pt. 1), 927-933.

Watkins, David. (1990). Student ratings of tertiary courses for "alternative calendar" purposes. *Assessment and Evaluation in Higher Education. 15*(1) 12-21.

Watkins, David, & Thomas, Babu (1991). Assessing teaching effectiveness: An Indian perspective. *Assessment and Evaluation in Higher Education, 16*(3), 185-198.

Weaver, C. H. (1960). Instructor rating by college students. *Journal of Educational Psychology, 51,* 21-25.

Webb, W. B. (1955). The problem of obtaining negative nominations in peer ratings. *Personnel Psychology, 8,* 61-63.

Weber, L. J., & Frary, R. B. (1982). Profile uniqueness in student ratings of instruction. *Journal of Experimental Education, 51*(1), 42-45.

Webster, David S. (1985). Institutional effectiveness using scholarly peer assessments as major criteria. *Review of Higher Education. 9*(1) 67-82.

Weeks, Kent M. (1990). The peer review process: Confidentiality and disclosure. *Journal of Higher Education. 61*(2), 198-219.

Wherry, R. J., & Fryer, D. H. (1945). Buddy ratings: Popularity contest or leadership criteria? *Personnel Psychology, 2,* 147-159.

Whitley, J. S. (1984). Are student evaluations constructive criticism? *Community and Junior College Journal, 54*(7), 41-42.

Whitely, S. E., & Doyle, K. O. (1979). Validity and generalizability of student ratings from between-classes and within-class data. *Journal of Educational Psychology, 71,*117-124.

Whitman, N., & Weiss, E. (1982). Faculty evaluation: The use of explicit criteria for promotion, retention, and tenure. *AAHE-Eric/Higher Education Research Report No. 2.* Washington, DC: American Association for Higher Education. (ERIC ED 221-148).

Whitmore, J., & Gillespie, P. P. (1983). Resolved: That directing plays and readers theater productions should be evaluated more as a part of teaching than as research and creative work. *Association for Communication Administration Bulletin, 44,* 21-24.

Widmeyer, W. Neil, & Loy, John W. (1988). When you're hot, you're hot: Warm-cold effects in first impressions of persons and teaching effectiveness. *Journal of Educational Psychology. 80*(1), 118-121.

Wigington, H., Tollefson, N., & Rodriquiez, E. (1989). Students' ratings of instructors revisited: Interactions among class and instructor variables. *Research in Higher Education. 30*(3), 331-344.

Williams, E. D. (1982). "Teacher and course evaluations that really discriminate." Paper presented at the annual meeting of the Rocky Mountain Psychological Association, April 28 - May 1, 1982 (ERIC ED 223 135).

Williams, Eira. (1992). Student attitudes towards approaches to learning and assessment. *Assessment and Evaluation in Higher Education. 17*(1) 45-58.

Wilson, R. C. (1986). Improving faculty teaching: Effective use of student evaluations and consultants. *Journal of Higher Education, 57,* 196-211.

Wilson, R. C. (1990). Commentary: The education of a faculty developer. *Journal of Educational Psychology. 82*(2) 272-724. Special section with title "Instruction in Higher Education."

Wilson, T. C. (1988). Student evaluation-of-teaching forms: A critical perspective. *Review of Higher Education. 12*(1), 79-95.

Wilson, T., & Stearns, J. (1985). Improving the working relationship between professor and TA. *New Directions for Teaching and Learning (Strengthening the Teaching Assistant Faculty), 22,* 35-45.

Wood, P. H. (1977). "The description and evaluation of a college department's faculty rating system." Paper presented at the annual meeting of the American Educational Research Association, New York, NY, (ERIC ED 142 128).

Wood, P. H. (1978). "Student and peer ratings of college teaching and peer ratings of research and service: Four years of departmental evaluation." Paper presented at the 62nd annual meeting of the American Educational Research Association, Toronto, Canada, (ERIC ED 155 218).

Wood, K., Linsky, A. S., & Straus, M. A. (1974). Class size and student evaluations of faculty. *Journal of Higher Education, 45,* 524-534.

Wotruba, T. R., & Wright, P. L. (1975). How to develop a teacher-rating instrument: A research approach. *Journal of Higher Education, 46,* 653-663.

Wulff, D. H., et al. (1985). The student perspective on evaluating teaching effectiveness. *ACA Bulletin, 53,* 39-47.

Yongkittikul, C., Gillmore, G. M., & Brandenburg, D. C. (1974). *Does the Time of Course Meeting Affect Course Rating by Students?* (Research Report No. 346). Urbana: University of Illinois, Office of Instructional Resources, Measurement and Research Division.

Young, R. J., & Gwalamubisi, Y. (1986). Perceptions about current and ideal methods and purposes of faculty evaluation. *Community College Review, 13*(4), 27-33.

Index